Managing Macroeconomic Policy
THE JOHNSON PRESIDENCY

An Administrative History of the Johnson Presidency Series

Managing Macroeconomic Policy
THE JOHNSON PRESIDENCY

By *James E. Anderson and Jared E. Hazleton*

University of Texas Press, Austin

First edition, 1986

Requests for permission to reproduce material from
this work should be sent to:
  Permissions
  University of Texas Press
  Box 7819
  Austin, Texas 78713

Library of Congress Cataloging-in-Publication Data
Anderson, James E.
    Managing macroeconomic policy.
    (An Administrative history of the Johnson presidency
series)
    Includes index.
    1. United States—Economic policy—1961–1971.
I. Hazleton, Jared E. II. Title. III. Series: Admin-
istrative history of the Johnson presidency.
HC106.6.A673 1986   338.973   85-15064
ISBN 0-292-75084-6

To Alberta and Elaine

Contents

Figure

Foreword

This is the fourth of a group of publications designed to form the series An Administrative History of the Johnson Presidency. The first study, by Emmette S. Redford and Marlan Blissett, *Organizing the Executive Branch: The Johnson Presidency*, was published in 1981. The second, by Richard L. Schott and Dagmar S. Hamilton, *People, Positions and Power: The Political Appointments of Lyndon Johnson*, was published in 1983. The third, by W. Henry Lambright, *Presidential Management of Science and Technology: The Johnson Presidency*, was published in 1985. Ten to twelve special studies, including the first four and an overall volume, are planned.

Our objective is to provide a comprehensive view of how a president and those who assisted him managed the White House and the executive branch to achieve the objectives of law and presidential policy. Administration is studied as part of the responsibility of a president—in this case, President Lyndon B. Johnson.

The view taken of administration is comprehensive. It includes the inter-relations among policy, administration, and program development. It encompasses administration in its various aspects: development of the infrastructure, including structuring and staffing the executive branch and budgeting for its operations; implementation of policy; and presidential management of the executive branch.

We aim for an authentic and adequate historical record based primarily on the documentary materials in the Lyndon B. Johnson Library and on interviews with many people who assisted President Johnson. We hope the historical record as presented from a social science perspective will amplify knowledge of administrative processes and of the tasks and problems of the presidency.

The study is being financed primarily by a grant from the National Endowment for the Humanities, with additional aid from the Lyndon Baines Johnson Foundation, the Hoblitzelle Foundation, and the

Lyndon B. Johnson School of Public Affairs of the University of Texas at Austin.

The findings and conclusions in publications resulting from this study do not necessarily represent the view of any donor.

EMMETTE S. REDFORD

Project Director

Acknowledgments

This book had its genesis in a policy research project taught by the authors at the Lyndon B. Johnson School of Public Affairs at the University of Texas at Austin. We would like to express appreciation to our students whose enthusiasm for the subject and initial research encouraged us to proceed with the project: Matthew Burns, Jeffrey Clark, Benjamin Cole, Anthony Grigsby, Glenn Martin, Brooks Myers, Virgil Rambo, Barbara Storbeck, Don Watson, and Richard Wiggins.

Claudia Anderson, Linda Hansen, Nancy Smith, and Bob Tissing of the staff of the Lyndon B. Johnson Presidential Library in Austin gave generously of their time and talent in helping us identify and use the archival material under their care. We are especially grateful for the personal interest they took in this project and their patience in responding to the many inquiries of two novices to the game.

Finally, we are indebted to Tom Cronin, Erwin Hargrove, and Michael Reagan, who reviewed the manuscript and offered many helpful suggestions.

Of course, we bear final responsibility for any errors of fact or judgment which remain.

JEA

JEH

Managing Macroeconomic Policy
THE JOHNSON PRESIDENCY

1. The President as Economic Manager

Well into the twentieth century it was assumed that government could do little that was positive to control fluctuations in the business cycle. This cycle was supposedly governed by natural economic laws that made government action unnecessary and unwise. According to the conventional wisdom, the best course of action for a government in a recession was to cut spending, increase taxes, and balance its budget, lest things be made worse by public concern over the government's finances. This point of view was well expressed in 1921 by President Warren Harding in his remarks to a national Conference on Unemployment: "There has been vast unemployment before and there will be again. There will be depression and inflation just as surely as the tides ebb and flow. I would have little enthusiasm for any proposed remedy which seeks palliation or tonic from the Public Treasury."[1] There was no expectation or requirement that the government should act positively to deal with economic decline.

All of this changed as a consequence of such factors as the experience with the Great Depression; the advent of Keynesian economics, which provided a theory and rationale for government intervention; the development of better tools for economic analysis, such as national income accounting; and the fiscal aspects of World War II. The national government is now expected to act to stabilize the economy, and the president is assigned primary responsibility for developing appropriate policies. Presidential administrations are importantly evaluated on how well, or whether, they have succeeded at this task. The Carter administration suffered at the polls in 1980 at least partly because of its economic-policy difficulties, especially its inability to control inflation adequately.[2] The administration was often criticized for indecision and disarray in the development of economic policy.

In this book, our focus is on the presidential management of the development and implementation of macroeconomic policies during the administration of Lyndon B. Johnson. Macroeconomic policies involve courses of government action intended to influence the over-all operation of the economy and to deal with such important public problems as economic growth, inflation, unemployment, and reces-sion. (Because the term *macroeconomic* is a bit cumbersome, we will often refer to such policies simply as economic policies.) The management focus means that we are more concerned with the pro-cess by which policy actions were designed and taken than with the nature or substance of the policy involved. To put it another way, our attention is directed to the president's role as economic manager. This management focus will be presented in more detail at the end of this chapter. We turn now to an examination of the president's role as economic manager and the policy goal of economic stability.

The Development of Presidential Responsibility

In his widely read study of the presidency, Clinton Rossiter alerted his readers to the emergence of a new presidential role:

> The people of this country are no longer content to let economic disaster fall upon them unopposed. They now expect their gov-ernment, under the direct leadership of the President, to prevent a depression or panic and not simply wait until one has devel-oped before putting it to rout. Thus the President has a new func-tion which is still taking shape, that of Manager of Prosperity.[3]

Public expectations strongly contributed to the development of the president's role as (to use a somewhat less lofty and more de-scriptive job title) economic manager. Franklin D. Roosevelt's ac-tions in dealing with the economic problems created by the Great Depression were especially instrumental in this regard. Based partly on particular statutes and partly on the emergency powers of the president, New Deal economic relief and recovery policies, although often inconsistent and limited both in quantity and effect, sought to meet the public's desire for corrective action.[4] Henceforth, presidents would be expected to act, *inter alia*, as economic managers. They have so acted, although their performances and success have varied.

So far as the formal basis for this presidential role is concerned, the Constitution is essentially silent. Two statutes, neither of which was really strongly sought by the chief executive, constitute the pri-mary sources of formal presidential authority. These are the Budget and Accounting Act of 1921 and the Employment Act of 1946.

Until the enactment of the Budget and Accounting Act, the president's involvement in budgeting was quite limited; indeed, it was largely nonexistent. The act changed this by providing for an executive budget system, in which the president was directed to prepare an annual budget and submit it to the Congress for its consideration. Agencies were required to channel their budget requests through the president rather than send them directly to Congress. To assist the president in handling his budget responsibilities, the act established an executive staff agency, the Bureau of the Budget (now the Office of Management and Budget). Other provisions of the act established single appropriations committees in the House and Senate and created the General Accounting Office.

The Employment Act arose out of widespread concern that a recession might follow World War II and determination that the government should be prepared for that eventuality.[5] In its preamble, which reflects a variety of political compromises, the act declares that

it is the continuing policy and responsibility of the federal government to use all practicable means consistent with its needs and obligations and other essential considerations of national policy, with the assistance and cooperation of industry, agriculture, labor, and state and local governments, to coordinate and utilize all of its plans, functions, and resources for the purpose of creating and maintaining, in a manner calculated to foster and promote free competitive enterprise and the general welfare, conditions under which there will be afforded useful employment opportunities, including self-employment, for those able, willing, and seeking to work, and to promote maximum employment, production, and purchasing power.

There seems to be something for everyone in this declaration, but to dismiss it, and the act itself, as merely symbolic would be erroneous: they reflect a substantial amount of political agreement, a general direction for policy, and a commitment to action. Herbert Stein has noted that the act "helped put an end to a futile, tiresome, and largely meaningless debate between extremists, and cleared the way for practical work to evolve a program [of economic stabilization]."[6]

The Employment Act directs the president to present an economic report to Congress at the beginning of each annual session. In it he analyzes current economic trends and conditions, presents a program for carrying out the statute's policy declaration, and makes recommendations for necessary legislation. To consider the economic report and advise the Congress thereon, a congressional Joint Economic Committee was set up; it has become a major source of economic information for Congress and the nation.

A three-member Council of Economic Advisers (CEA) was also created by the act. Its specified responsibilities include:

> (1) to assist and advise the President in the preparation of the Economic Report; (2) to gather timely and authoritative information . . . ; (3) to appraise the various programs and activities of the Federal Government in the light of the policy declared in section 2 [quoted above] . . . ; (4) to develop and recommend to the President national economic policies to foster and promote free competitive enterprises, to avoid economic fluctuations or to diminish the effects thereof, and to maintain employment, production, and purchasing power; (5) to make and furnish studies, reports thereon, and recommendations . . . as the President may request.

Located in the Executive Office of the President, the CEA is assigned only staff responsibilities. Its sole client is the president.[7]

For operating authority on macroeconomic matters beyond these two statutes, the president must depend on either the general provisions of the Constitution or statutes enacted by Congress authorizing presidential action in particular areas, and these sources may not confer much authority. Thus, in August 1966, a Johnson White House search for "Presidential Authorities in the Economy" found that (a) no authority existed for direct wage or price controls, (b) across-the-board consumer credit controls could be imposed by executive order under the 1950 Trading with the Enemy Act, (c) the president had some power to defer or curtail expenditure of appropriated funds, and (d) under his constitutional authority as chief executive the president could enter into voluntary wage-and-price restraint agreements with labor and business.[8] In all, not an overly impressive list.

One concludes that in his role as economic manager the president has more responsibility than authority. The president, however, does not manage alone. He shares fiscal power with Congress, and monetary policy is mostly in the domain of the Federal Reserve Board. In the exercise of their powers, they may or may not be cooperative with the president. There is an adage in public administration that in administrative matters "authority should be commensurate with responsibility." That it is not in this instance means that to be a successful economic manager, the president must be innovative, imaginative, persuasive, and a little lucky.

Two other points should be made concerning the president's role as economic manager and the importance of macroeconomic policy for his administration. First, the state of the economy is an important constraint on the president's capacity to act in other policy areas. Even if the public did not hold the president directly responsible for the health of the economy, an activist president would soon realize that the health of the economy can impinge on his freedom to initiate policies in most other areas. Funding for domestic programs is more likely to be expanded during times of prosperity than in times of recession. Economic growth, by increasing national income, provides government with a growth dividend that is more easily directed into new program areas than existing levels of expenditure are redistributed. A president who wishes, say, to maintain troops in Europe for reasons of foreign policy will find this action much more difficult when the nation faces a balance-of-payments deficit than when the balance of payments is in equilibrium.

Second, the problem of developing and implementing macroeconomic policy is never ending. While there are established schedules for action—for example, the Open Market Committee of the Federal Reserve System meets every three weeks, the president is required to submit an annual report on the state of the economy to Congress each January, and the budget cycle is continuous and rigidly established—the need for a policy response does not always coincide with these established cycles. The state of the economy and its tendencies are continually being revealed by the emergence of new data and information, and are frequently affected by events occurring in areas far removed from the economy. Thus, from the day the president enters the White House to the day of his departure, he must be continually concerned with the conduct of macroeconomic policy and its consequences.

The Goal: Economic Stability

If there is general agreement that the government should act to maintain economic stability, there is less than full agreement about what comprises economic stability. Some have defined it as the absence of sharp fluctuations, periods of boom and bust, in the economy. An economic stabilization policy in which this is the prime focus may be referred to as a countercyclical policy. The Eisenhower administration followed what has been called a "stop-go" stabilization policy: action was focused upon either restraining or encouraging expansion, depending upon the stage of the business cycle. For its part, the Federal Reserve Board mostly attempted to "lean against the wind," expanding the money supply during times of recession and exercising monetary restraint during expansionary periods.

The Kennedy and Johnson administrations followed a somewhat different tack. The "new economists" who dominated the economic advisory process during the 1960s did not accept the 1950s view of the inevitability of business cycles. Rather, they believed that government policy "could and should keep the economy close to a path of steady real growth at a constant target rate of unemployment."[9] In 1969, on the basis of the Johnson administration's experience in managing the economy, Arthur Okun was moved to remark upon "the obsolescence of the business cycle pattern."[10] He observed that while "recessions are now generally considered to be fundamentally preventable . . . it is not clear that we have the wisdom or ability" to so act.[11] Events were soon to prove his pessimism justified and his declaration of business cycle obsolescence premature: a recession began in November 1969.

Our concern, however, is not so much with how different presidential administrations have viewed the task of maintaining economic stability, but with how it was defined by policymakers in the Johnson administration. The Employment Act, as noted above, speaks of the promotion of "maximum employment, production, and purchasing power." Former CEA Chairman Walter Heller, writing in 1966, stated that "through 'judicious interpretation' under four Presidents, this mandate has gradually evolved into the four dimensional mandates of full employment, high growth, price stability, and balance of payments equilibrium. . . ."[12] These were indeed the goals of stabilization policy during the Johnson years. They are not, however, without contradictions. Thus, the attainment of full employment, which may be defined as less than 4 percent unemployment (this was the "interim goal" set in the Kennedy administration and carried over into the Johnson administration), could be achieved only at the cost of some price instability, that is, inflation. Although Johnson officials were certainly concerned about inflation, a strong rate of economic growth and high employment mattered more to them. Some trade-offs were necessary, some balances had to be struck. Developing a definition of economic stability to use in formulating and implementing economic policy is more a political than a technical judgment.

A variety of macroeconomic policy instruments are available to government decisionmakers in their efforts to achieve economic stability. These include fiscal policy, monetary policy, wage and price controls (either mandatory or voluntary), and international economic policies. An innovative and imaginative administration can also perform a variety of microeconomic actions that influence the general level of economic activity. Thus, to combat rising prices, production controls may be loosened to permit increased agricultural production, timber cutting in national forests may be expanded, stockpiles of strategic materials may be sold, job training programs may be focused on labor bottlenecks that are slowing production, and the Defense Department may opt to buy margarine rather than higher-priced butter. All of these illustrations are drawn from the Johnson administration and were usually based on discretionary authority available to the administration.[13]

Concluding Comments

One of the roles the president must handle is that of economic manager. In the day-to-day run of events, this role cannot be neatly separated from his various other roles—chief executive, chief legislator, commander-in-chief: it both overlaps and extends beyond them. But to separate out and focus our attention analytically upon one very important area of public policy, namely, management of the economy to secure economic stability, is in itself intellectually valuable. Beyond that, it enables us to add substance to our generalizations concerning the nature of presidential responsibility and the exercise of presidential capability.

Since the 1950s the president has had the responsibility of acting as economic manager. (Rossiter's phrase "Manager of Prosperity" connotes the expectation that he will do so successfully.) Our discussion in this chapter indicates, first, that the concept of economic stability is not without ambiguity and, second, that the formal or legal authority of the president is not commensurate with his responsibility. To act successfully as economic manager, the president needs the support and cooperation of many others—in Congress, in the departments and agencies, in his own Executive Office, and elsewhere. Powers of persuasion and bargaining are more important than powers of command in the macroeconomic area.

The Focus of This Book

Our primary focus is not upon the president's role as economic manager as such, because this directs one's attention to the substance of policy, to what was actually done and with what consequences in pursuing the goals of economic stability. Others, especially economists, have extensively covered these matters. Rather, our concern is with the presidential management of macroeconomic institutions in the development of executive policies and policy proposals, and in the implementation of policies intended to achieve economic stability.

We are interested in how institutions and people are organized and managed in the process of presidential policy development. Policy development, as we see it, is a management task as well as a substantive concern. Advisors must be selected and their roles defined, advisory structures or arrangements established, and the policy formulation process organized and managed so as to ensure that the president receives needed information and advice in ready fashion to make informed and timely policy decisions. Such things do not just happen: they must be managed. Process, which is shaped by management, is an important influence on the nature of resultant decisions.

We are equally interested in the structures, arrangements, and techniques used to implement policy decisions (including the elaboration of these decisions into more precise policies) at the presidential level. There is, of course, more politics involved in some areas of macroeconomic-policy activity than in others. Implementing a tax increase, once authorized by Congress, is largely technical, a matter of writing the appropriate regulations and directing their application. However, implementing a decision to control prices and wages through voluntary means is quite different because of the broad administrative leeway involved. Decisions must be made concerning the specific goals of the control activity, the standards and guidelines to inform action, the actual administrators, the enforcement techniques to be employed, and so on. In our view, once the policy decision to have voluntary controls has been made, all else becomes administration. Policy, of course, will be further shaped and refined in the course of its administration.

Presidential management of macroeconomic institutions involves the performance of four interrelated tasks. First, the president has to develop and maintain an information and decision-making system to provide necessary information, policy options, and advice on macroeconomic issues. This system may comprise arrangements that are formal or informal, regularized or ad hoc, or some combination of these, in nature. The president needs such assistance to make decisions and perform his other management functions. Second, with the administrative and policy dispersion in the macroeconomic area, there is a need for coordinative processes, such as to harmonize monetary and fiscal policies. Third, the president must seek to influence the other participants and affected parties whose consent and cooperation are required for effective policy development and implementation. Here the president must rely substantially upon persuasion and bargaining techniques.[14] The need for consent is an important constraint on presidential capability in the macroeconomic area. Fourth, the president must supply administrative leadership. Lest the macroeconomic policy process be characterized by conflict and drift, he must direct and guide policy development processes and make needed policy decisions. Presidential leadership may not guarantee successful management of macroeconomic policy, but without it the likelihood of success is greatly reduced. There is no other locus of effective leadership in this policy area.

Presidential macroeconomic management also includes strategic and operational components. Strategic management involves the exercise of leadership in clearly defining macroeconomic-policy objectives and formulating programs to achieve these objectives. Operational management involves such actions as periodic assessment of the performance of the economy, prediction of future economic activity, analysis of alternative policy proposals, and the implementation of programs for the attainment of policy objectives. The strategic and operational categories focus attention on the basic purposes underlying the management tasks enumerated above.

Drawing largely upon the presidential papers of the Johnson administration, other primary source materials, and interviews with administration officials, the basic thrust of this book is to discuss and analyze the actions of Lyndon Johnson and his administration in the management of economic-stability institutions. The broad question we seek to answer is this: How did President Lyndon Johnson and his administration, operating in a volatile society and dispersed governmental system, organize and manage people and executive institutions in trying to achieve economic stability, a task for which the president's responsibility exceeded his authority? The study does not seek to test particular hypotheses relating to administrative behavior and presidential performance, to generate a general theory of presidential managerial behavior (assuming that such a theory is really possible), or to compare extensively the Johnson administration with other presidential administrations.

Viewed from one perspective, this volume is a case study focused on a single policy area during one presidential administration.[15] However, because macroeconomic policy is divided into the four subareas of fiscal, monetary, wage-price, and international economic policies, it can also fairly be viewed as partly comparative in design. The president's management tasks and problems differ among these subareas because of variations in such matters as governmental structure, participation, and affected parties.

This can be illustrated by a glimpse at the president's problems in building consent for his policies. In the monetary field, the central problem faced throughout the Johnson years was that of persuading the Federal Reserve Board to act in accordance with presidential preferences. As will be seen in Chapter 4, this problem was compounded by the structural independence of the Federal Reserve Board and the lack of formal presidential ties to the agency. By contrast, in the area of fiscal policy, once the administration was able to settle on a policy proposal (a problem in itself), the task became one of inducing Congress to take the actions desired by the administration. The focus of such efforts was not only on persuading and bargaining with members of Congress directly—an art at which Johnson was quite skilled—but also on appealing to the public and its groups in order to bring pressure to bear indirectly on Congress. In the area of wage-price controls, the administration, having decided on voluntary rather than mandatory controls, had the burden of seeking compliance without formal sanctions from unions and companies in the private sector. In the international area, a basic task confronting the administration was the need to motivate other nations to accommodate the U.S. balance-of-payments disequilibria. Here management took on aspects of diplomacy. Attentiveness to such similarities and differences provides us with a better, more comprehensive grasp of the management or macroeconomic institutions.

Although by academic training we are a political scientist and an economist, we believe there are useful lessons to be learned from historically based analyses, whether one is concerned with the more practical aspects of presidential management or the more scientific study of politics. Such studies also can generate data and information essential for comparative treatments of presidential performance as well as for testing extant theories and developing theories and propositions for future research.

There is a strong need for more studies of presidential management. Perhaps because of the notion that presidents "are not interested" in management or administration, there is a paucity of literature in this area. In actuality, presidents cannot avoid getting involved in management: it suffuses their position and importantly affects the accomplishment of their purposes. Our study will help fill this gap.

2. The Johnson Administration: Structure and Policy

In this chapter we have two major concerns. First, we will discuss Johnson's style as an economic manager and examine the economic subpresidency that aided him in the discharge of his duties. Second, to set the context for subsequent chapters and to provide the reader with some notion of what Johnson administration officials were involved in substantively, we will briefly survey the major policy actions taken by the administration. In subsequent chapters we will deal in detail with the administration's management of the major areas of macroeconomic policy.

The President's Role and Style

In his role as economic manager, the president can draw upon a substantial number of agencies and officials for information, advice, recommended decisions, and administrative assistance. In one sense the office of president may be a lonely place, but the president does not act alone. Final decisions on economic issues rest with the president, but along the way many persons, committees, and agencies may become involved in the process of making and implementing presidential decisions. What the president does, the choices he makes, will depend also upon his assessment of the economic advice he receives; his appraisal of relevant political forces and conditions; his values, beliefs, and goals; his view of the public interest; and perhaps some hunches or guesswork. All of these blend together to produce a presidential perspective.

Although the power of the president is limited, and indeed sometimes he appears almost powerless, presidential power certainly extends beyond the "power to persuade," as Richard Neustadt has put it.[1] Presidents do seek to persuade, but they can and do accomplish things also by bargaining and by command, which should be differentiated from persuasion. Johnson's decision not to seek an income tax increase in 1966 was clearly an exercise of presidential power, a command that something would not be done. Gardner Ackley, chairman of the Council of Economic Advisers (CEA), accepted this decision although he was not persuaded of its correctness. In 1968 Johnson found that he had to bargain with Wilbur Mills, the chairman of the House Ways and Means Committee, and to agree to an expenditure reduction, in order to obtain congressional action on the income tax surcharge.

Johnson was an activist with populist inclinations who favored the full use of the government's powers to promote economic growth and stability. Any doubts he may have had in this respect seem to have been resolved by the success of the 1964 tax cut and "the triumph of the New Economics." Next to foreign policy, economic-policy matters occupied the largest share of his time as chief executive.

Johnson possessed neither a profound grasp of economic theory nor much interest in the underlying theory of proposed actions. His, in short, was not an intellectual approach to economic issues. However, he knew what he liked (economic growth, low interest rates, high employment), he grasped economic ideas readily, and he absorbed large quantities of economic information. Walter Heller stated that he "expects, gets, and—close president-watchers are agreed—reads no less than 250 memos a year" from the CEA alone.[2] Some memorandums came to him on a regular basis, others as the occasion demanded, still others at his own request. Thus, various CEA memorandums to the president in 1966–67 began with such statements as "you asked for a paper on the state of construction"; "Califano says you wanted to know the impact of the proposed Social Security program on the National Income Accounts budget"; "Joe Califano said you would like a memo laying out the structure of gasoline pricing"; "You asked me [Ackley] what's bugging the labor leaders."

He relied substantially upon economic advice from persons he trusted. Ackley provides an explanation of Johnson's style in this respect:

The impression I increasingly got of the way LBJ was approaching economic problems and economic advice was that his first questions about anyone who proposed to advise him on anything was to ascertain as best he could whether this adviser was giving it to him straight, or whether he had an axe to grind. He particularly wanted to discover whether he was a Kennedy man, or someone who sneered at Johnson's intellectual and social characteristics as he thought all Kennedy people and Kennedy supporters did. But once he was convinced that the adviser was not going to stab him in the back, that he was not going to go out and talk to the press, that he was really devoted to the interests of the enterprise and loyal to him personally, then when complicated questions came up—and particularly if previous advice had turned out well—he developed confidence that, if you told him that the thing that ought to be done was this, he assumed that was correct, and he didn't really want to know all the proof. All the argument. He had confidence in you. Within no more than a year, I think he did have that confidence in us [the CEA].[3]

Such practices obviously reduced his intellectual costs in decision-making.

Advice that was apparently economically sound might not be politically feasible, a matter which was of much concern to Johnson, or substantively sound when viewed from a broader perspective. Given an economic-policy recommendation, he wanted to know whether it was politically feasible, how it could be accomplished, what sorts of "levers" were available to secure its approval or acceptance, whether it was the right thing to do. His decision not to seek a general tax increase in 1966 was essentially a political judgment. He did not so much reject the advice of the CEA and others as decide he could not act on it because of various political considerations, for example, a lack of political support in Congress for a tax increase.

Economic policy is only one of many things competing for and requiring the time of a president. Presidents do not have time for everything; however, they do have quite a bit of control over how they use their time.[4] Johnson chose to devote quite a bit of time to economic policy, partly perhaps because he could not avoid it, given economic conditions and public expectations, but also because he strongly wanted an expanding economy with high employment and rising incomes.

The Economic Subpresidency Concept

Within the Executive Office of the President, the executive branch, and elsewhere, an extensive system of assistance and advice has developed to aid the president in the discharge of his myriad duties and responsibilities. How it is used, the extent to which it is used, and the very composition of it depend upon the president's goals, interests, and style. We shall call this system of advice and assistance as it relates to the development and implementation of economic policy the *economic subpresidency*. It is part of the presidency and under the control of the president. As Redford and Blissett have stated in defining the concept of the subpresidency:

> It does not have—it does not share—responsibility; its function is to assist the president. It assists him at the level at which he operates and in his responsibility to the nation as president. This may include assistance in making, defining, and communicating decisions, and in gaining their acceptance and assuring their execution.[5]

The economic subpresidency consists of all who perform such activities involving economic policy, whether they act personally or as part of an institution. Persons are considered part of the economic subpresidency when, and to the extent that, they are helping the president in the performance of his duties in the economic-policy area. Some will be regularly and deeply involved (e.g., the CEA); others will be involved only on an occasional or ad hoc basis (e.g., a personal friend like Clark Clifford or the secretary of agriculture). What we are talking about is thus more than the "institutionalized presidency" and should not be confused with it. Membership in the economic subpresidency is behavioral rather than formal or institutional.

Persons are viewed as part of the economic subpresidency not only when they interact directly with the president but also when their relationships with one another pertain to the exercise of presidential power. The advisory relationship, say, between the secretary of the treasury and the president is an example of this system, and so is the interaction between the secretary and the chairman of the CEA in developing a policy recommendation for the president. On the other hand, when the secretary of the treasury or any other official is engaged in the performance of legally delegated tasks, such as directing the operation of the Treasury Department, he would not be part of the economic subpresidency.

A final point. There is not a single subpresidency. Tom Cronin states that there are subpresidencies for foreign affairs and national security, aggregate economics (what we call economic policy), and domestic policy. The composition of each of them will vary, although some actors will be involved in more than one. During the Johnson administration, Joseph Califano was an important participant in both the economic and domestic subpresidencies, as was the director of the Bureau of the Budget.

The White House Office

Some 300 to 400 persons were employed in the White House office during the Johnson years. Only a few dozen of them, however, could be accurately described as staff aides to the president; most were secretaries, clerks, and other support personnel. Of the staff aides, only a few were involved in economic policy, and then not always on a regular basis. The organization of the Johnson White House has been described as "rather loose and chaotic," with staff members sometimes being given overlapping assignments.[6] Johnson apparently found that a somewhat loose organizational structure suited his operational style and needs. On the other hand, Arthur Okun indicated that a clearer delegation of authority and jurisdiction would have made it easier to work with the White House. When in doubt as to whom to deal with, the CEA "always turned to Califano and had very close relations with him."[7]

Responsibility for economic policy, and also domestic policy, was first assigned to Bill Moyers and then to Califano, who served as the president's special assistant for domestic affairs from mid-1965 until the end of the administration. Califano never had more than four or five assistants and handled most economic-policy matters himself, although he was not an expert by any means in economic matters. He did get some help on wage-price and other economic matters from first John Robson and then Stanford Ross. Ross, for example, operated without any staff assistance of his own, dealing directly with department and agency officials. It was his view that Johnson wanted to keep the White House operation "lean" and to avoid developing a bureaucracy.[8]

In the fiscal-policy area Califano acted as a stimulator, coordinator, and a seeker of agreement among the president's major advisers. He spent much time arranging meetings, participating in them, advising the president of what was happening, and conveying presidential instructions to other administration officials. He usually was not, however, a major contributor of substantive ideas and information to the decisionmaking process. He has described his role in these terms:

> The most important thing is to get the alternatives clearly laid out, and in such a way that the president can understand the differences between them. Next, I try to get the alternatives narrowed down to two or three real choices. The alternatives that are sent over here by the Council are usually too many and too complicated. Third, I organize a number of meetings and consul-

tations to get agreement on one or two of the alternatives. This is sometimes a fairly time-consuming process. Finally, after the President has made a decision, I write or coordinate the writing of the President's message announcing his policy decision.[9]

All memorandums on economic policy flowed through his office on the way to the president, but he appears to have done little screening of them. Some memorandums, such as from the secretary of the treasury because of their long and tedious style, were summarized for the president. He recounts that if he summarized a five-page memorandum in a paragraph he would call the writer and ask whether it accurately reflected the original memorandum. "And they'd usually say, 'No, not as accurately as my memo does,' and I'd say, 'Well, the President's not going to read your whole memo.'"[10]

Califano was more deeply involved in the implementation of the wage-price guidelines, actively helping to search for levers and devising and implementing strategies to deal with proposed wage and price increases. Given the nature of this operation, political and administrative skills were often more important than economic knowledge. Califano was sometimes more willing to take harsh action than others who were involved. During the 1966 dispute with the steel industry, Califano and Ackley held a press session in which they discussed various sanctions available to the government. "Ackley couldn't bring himself to use the 'word' [profiteering]," Califano reported to the president, "however, I managed to get it in. . . ."[11]

The Johnson administration never had an economist on the White House staff. Califano has stated that he never wanted an economist as such on his staff. "I did use Okun and Schultze [among other economists] as my staff as well as the President's, but basically I put generalists on the staff."[12] A different version of events here comes from the Council of Economic Advisers. Walter Heller had requested early in the Kennedy administration that an economist not be included on the White House staff. The CEA thereafter continued to worry that this might happen, and acted to prevent it by performing a variety of "chores" such as speech-writing for the White House. "One of the things we were interested in was making it unnecessary for Califano to want to have his own economist," Okun has stated. "We would do anything that he needed to be done. He didn't need an economics staff of his own. We managed to convince him several times when that issue came up. 'You really don't need to recruit a young economist. You know, Joe, we've got all the young economists you need around. . . .'"[13] Irrespective of the correctness of the CEA viewpoint, they most likely saw this as a way of protecting or enhancing their access to the White House.

The Council of Economic Advisers

The 1960s were the peak years of influence for the Council of Economic Advisers in the development of presidential economic policies. Under highly capable, activist leadership, and working for the presidents who were receptive to its advice, the council was the dominant actor in the economic subpresidency. Truly, it did seem to be "the age of the economist."[14] Information, advice, and policy recommendations flowed in large quantities from the CEA to President Johnson. Sometimes described as "consulting agency with a single client," the council amply demonstrated that knowledge can be power when the client president wants, needs, and uses its services.

The CEA was a small organization, consisting of the three members, a professional staff of fifteen to eighteen economists, and about two dozen support personnel. The council members and staff were drawn mostly from the ranks of academic economists, with many of the staff members serving on a one-year rotational basis. (See Table 1 for a listing of CEA members.) This could be seen as both an advantage and a problem. On the one hand, it was contended that the council was able to attract to staff positions talented academic economists such as Robert Solow and Kenneth Arrow, who would not have been available to other agencies or on a long-term basis.[15] Moreover, "the infusion of new people and ideas stopped the council from becoming stale and provided it with a healthy enthusiasm."[16] The short-term staff members were also willing to work very long hours. In contrast, David Lusher, a very capable staff member but "a long time bureaucrat" in the view of one CEA member, worked an eight-to-five day. On the other hand, the turnover meant that the council members had to spend a lot of time recruiting new staff members, who then required training and breaking in when they joined the agency and time to establish other agency contacts.

Professional staff members were drawn primarily from the academic community. The raiding of other agencies was avoided. The recruitment process, which was handled by the CEA itself, took the following form:

Candidates for the staff were identified by contacting leaders in the profession and, more importantly, previous Council staff members for suggestions. The list of candidates was then cross-

Table 1. The Council of Economic Advisers during the Johnson Administration

Name	Position	Took Office	Left Office	Institutional Affiliation
Walter W. Heller	Chairman	29 Jan. 1961	15 Nov. 1964	Minnesota
Gardner Ackley	Member	3 Aug. 1962		Michigan
	Chairman	16 Nov. 1964	15 Feb. 1968	
John P. Lewis	Member	17 May 1963	31 Aug. 1964	Indiana
Otto Eckstein	Member	2 Sept. 1964	1 Feb. 1966	Harvard
James S. Duesenberry	Member	2 Feb. 1966	30 June 1968	Harvard
Arthur M. Okun	Member	16 Nov. 1964		Yale
	Chairman	16 Feb. 1968	20 Jan. 1969	
Merton J. Peck	Member	16 Feb. 1968	20 Jan. 1969	Yale
Warren L. Smith	Member	1 July 1968	20 Jan. 1969	Michigan

checked and ranked with leaders in the profession and the most promising candidates were invited to Washington for an interview. Although technical excellence was always paramount in evaluating staff members, important criteria for selection also included adaptability, sensitivity to policy, and a willingness to subordinate personal professional interests in order to give the Council full support in its mission.[17]

This helps explain why the council could be viewed as "the profession's baby"; its linkage to the academic community was indeed strong.

Further, the council was largely responsible for finding persons to fill vacancies on the council itself, thus giving the agency a self-perpetuating quality. Usually two names for a vacancy were submitted to the president, who chose between them. A memorandum from Gardner Ackley to the president in 1967 recommended either Kenneth Arrow (Harvard) or Merton J. Peck (Yale) for an upcoming vacancy. Ackley indicated the council had considered a long list of potential candidates and was agreed upon these two. Criteria included their quality as economists, suitability for CEA work, "commitment to the kind of economic policy you favor," balance of specialization needed on the CEA, and geography.[18] Yet no attempt was made at ticket balancing to represent a range of interests or policy viewpoints. A Department of Commerce official who was critical of the monopoly of university professors on CEA appointments contended that economists from business and labor would have brought a "new and broader dimension" to the council. The professors, he contended, had a tendency "to exaggerate the role of government fiscal policy" and to underestimate the dynamic potential of the private sector.[19]

In operation, the CEA was informal and in style, nonbureaucratic. The chairman served as the spokesman for the council, as its primary communication link with the president and the White House, and as overall director of operations. The other two council members divided responsibility for the various areas of CEA activity. Thus, in 1965, Arthur Okun was responsible for economic forecasting and for fiscal, monetary, and international economic policies. Otto Eckstein took care of wage-price matters, microeconomic (agriculture, labor relations, etc.), and tax reform. Professional staff members who concentrated on particular areas such as prices, productivity, and microeconomics had easy, direct access to the chairman and council members. "We all tried to keep informed on everything that was going on," recalled Ackley. "The Council never met as a Council, we were just in sort of continuous session."[20]

The only formal responsibility the CEA had was preparation of the annual economic report for the president. Beyond that, the council served, in its own words, "as an intelligence unit to the President, providing him with a continuous flow of information about the state of the economy and its problems."[21] (See Table 2 for an illustration of the volume and variety of information the CEA sent to the president.) Other activities included participation in the Troika and Quadriad operations; service on a variety of committees, such as the Cabinet Committee on Balance of Payments; participation in the activities of international economic organizations, for example, the Organization for Economic Cooperation and Development; and assistance in the drafting of presidential speeches and messages. Walter Heller even found time to offer some partisan political help, like when he proposed some television spots for the president's election campaign in 1964 based on the "you never had it so good" theme.[22] Customarily, though, the CEA shied away from partisan politics, if not presidential policy politics. It also generally avoided testifying before congressional committees except on broad economic-policy matters like the probable impact of the president's budget on the economy.

Several factors contributed to the influential role played by the CEA in the Johnson administration's efforts to manage the economy. First was its competence and alacrity in providing advice and information on macroeconomics. Its forecasts of economic activity were generally timely and accurate. It won its spurs from LBJ with the 1964 income tax cut. Its only major error came in 1968 following the adoption of the Revenue and Expenditure Control Act, which levied an income tax surcharge and reduced government spending, when it advocated expansion of the money supply because of a concern about too much restraint on the economy.

Second, the CEA lacked policy biases coming from institutional commitments, program responsibilities, and clientele pressures, while it shared with the president a strong concern for maintaining high employment and stable prices. Heller made the point that

> the President knows that the Council's expertise is fully at his command, undiluted by the commitments to particular programs and particular interest groups that, in the nature of things, tend to build up in the various line agencies of government. So although no law and no hierarchical flow of business force a President to rely on the Council of Economic Advisers—not even the

Employment Act, which places the Council at his disposal but does not require him to use it. . . . it is his most natural ally in economic matters.[23]

Third, the council was very effective in communicating ideas and information to the president. Ackley has stated that Johnson liked short, well-organized memorandums with "lots of dots, dashes, indentations, short sentences, short paragraphs, small words." This style was regarded by the CEA as its "secret weapon"; no other agency learned or adopted it. A typical memorandum from the secretary of the treasury, for instance, was long, single-spaced, and difficult to understand. Ackley recalls that

> LBJ would look at it, obviously at night, read a couple of paragraphs, and throw it aside. And very often these things would come over to the Council the next morning with a little note, "Tell me what this says." And we'd have to rewrite Joe Fowler's damned memorandum for him. . . . And the same way with the Labor Department. . . . he just loved information, just ate it up, but he wanted information that he didn't have to work too hard to get. I don't think this was writing down, I think it was in a sense writing up to him, in the sense of giving him the kind of information he needed, and in a form that he could get it quickly, understand it, and he really read the stuff.[24]

Fourth, the council was willing to become involved in presidential politics and policymaking rather than to act simply as a detached provider of economic information. They did not provide political advice as such—this Johnson would not have welcomed, as he viewed himself as the expert there—but in making recommendations they took into account presidential needs and circumstances. They made political and economic judgments and accepted the need for action and the responsibility, therefore, to meet deadlines. They were professional economists, but they also considered themselves assistants to the president, and hence, political economists. Gardner Ackley saw no reason why he should not exercise his judgment on policy matters. As he explained:

> Those in authority get plenty of advice from others who show no great delicacy in distinguishing technical questions within their competence from questions of values. The President hears from other members of his administration, from businessmen, from labor leaders, from journalists—yes, from economists. If his eco-

Table 2. Memorandums, Council of Economic Advisers to the President, May 1966

Date	Title	Content
2 May	More on Asset Sales	On sale of participation certificates
2 May	Some Examples of Excessive Wage Settlements	Percentage figures on some union wage increases
2 May	Construction and Machinery Orders	Business activities in February and March
2 May	Attitudes of Union Leaders	Issues of concern to them
4 May	Economic News Note	Automobile sales
4 May	Economic News Note	Wholesale price movements
5 May	Economic News Note	Employment figures
5 May	Views of Your Labor-Management Advisory Committee in Texas	Survey of attitudes on a tax increase
7 May	Weekly Balance of Payments Report	Balance-of-payments data and intelligence
7 May	Weekly Price Report	Price increases, decreases, etc.
9 May	Economic News Note	Construction activity
10 May	Economic News Note	Retail sales
10 May	The Case for Higher Taxes	Council argues need for tax increases to fight inflation
11 May	Economic News Note	Data on GNP and corporate profits
12 May	Economic News Note	Data on industrial production and sales
13 May	Survey of Investment Plans	Company investment plans
13 May	Economic News Note	Data on increasing personal incomes
14 May	Weekly Price Report	Price reviews, actions to hold down prices, etc.
14 May	Weekly Balance of Payments Report	Balance-of-payments data and intelligence

Date	Title	Description
16 May	The Economy's Pulse	Business activity and attitudes
17 May	The Savings and Loan Problem	Movement of funds out of savings and loan institutions
18 May	Economic News Note	Housing starts
19 May	Economic News Note	Slower pace in economy
20 May	Economic News Note	Area trends in employment
20 May	Economic News Note	Census Bureau survey of household buying
20 May	International Comparisons of Consumer Prices	Comparison of cost of living in five industrial countries
21 May	Weekly Price Report	Price movements, actions to hold down prices, etc.
21 May	Weekly Balance of Payments Report	Balance-of-payments data and intelligence
23 May	Economic News Note	Machine tool business
24 May	Economic News Note	Exports and imports
24 May	European and United States Price Levels	Comparisons in 1961 and 1965
25 May	Federal Pay and the Guideposts	1966 pay act conforms to guideposts
25 May	Economic News Note	Automobile sales
26 May	Representative Patman's Proposed Rollback of the Ceiling Rate on Time Deposits	CEA expresses opposition thereto
26 May	Economic News Note	Construction activity and retail sales
27 May	Mexican Farm Workers	Concerns admission of more into U.S.
27 May	Projected GNP Growth in Calendar 1966	Troika report on fiscal policy
28 May	Weekly Balance of Payments Report	Balance-of-payments data and intelligence
28 May	Weekly Price Report	Price changes and actions
31 May	Farm and Food Prices	Changes in prices

Source: May 1966, FG 11-3 and C.F. FO 4-1, WHCF, LBJ Library.

nomic adviser refrains from advice on the gut questions of policy, the President should and will get another one.[25]

The activism of the Johnson CEA stands in sharp contrast to the first CEA in the Truman administration, which sought to act as a detached, impartial provider of economic information.

Fifth, under the leadership of Heller and Ackley, the CEA actively sought to expand and protect its influence and position. It not only provided the president with information and advice, it also sought to "educate" him on economic matters. A series of memorandums the CEA sent to the president in 1964 entitled "Background Series on International Problems" are illustrative. The memorandums dealt with the operation of the present monetary system, the problem of international liquidity, and solutions to international monetary problems.[26] The CEA was also represented on a wide variety of interdepartmental committees, and sought additional assignment. All such efforts did not succeed, however. In a 1964 memorandum to White House assistant Jack Valenti, Heller noted that during the Eisenhower administration the CEA chairman had been an adjunct member of the National Security Council (NSC). He then referred to the economic effects of intervention in Vietnam, and queried "whether the CEA Chairman ought to be an adjunct member of the NSC to come in when economic questions may be involved—much as the Budget Director is drawn in when budget matters are involved." This inquiry, when transmitted to Johnson by Valenti, evoked a scrawled response: "No—I'll bring [him] in when I need him."[27]

The CEA also acted to defend its domain against intrusion by other agencies. One such incident involved the Office of Emergency Planning (OEP), which informed the president in January 1966 that it had set up an Economic Surveillance Committee to develop information on price problems, defense bottlenecks, and the general health of the economy.[28] In Ackley's view, this activity, initiated without the participation of the CEA, duplicated "the work of the Troika, whose continuing assignment is to undertake precisely this kind of estimates." He went on to recommend that OEP should be informed that current surveillance of the civilian economy and general economic projections for situations other than "general war" are the responsibility of the Council of Economic Advisers and the Troika, respectively. If OEP needed advice on the current state of the economy, or overall projections of economic developments, they should be secured directly from the Council of Economic Advisers rather than independently from other government agencies and outside sources.[29] High-level negotiations ensued to resolve this conflict. The outcome was recorded in a "memorandum of understanding" written at the request of the White House: OEP would continue to be concerned with contingency planning for emergency conditions, including limited or general war and recovery. CEA would have primary responsibility for economic surveillance and selective "price watching." Efforts would be made to secure more coordination of OEP, CEA, and Troika operations.[30] The OEP, thus repulsed, never played a significant role in the economic policy area.

Sixth, the staffing patterns within the executive branch also contributed to the influential position of the CEA; that is, other agencies lacked the economic support personnel needed to enable them to participate effectively in economic-policy formation. (Nor did Congress then have the services of the Congressional Budget Office.) A former Johnson administration official has explained:

In the 1960's there were a lot of people who would have liked to get into the game but just did not have the staff. They were unsupported and when you weren't supported, you couldn't carry the issue. Nobody had a group of economists to evaluate all these issues for them. The CEA had a monopoly on it along with a few people at the Treasury. What has changed today is that every agency has an economic policy and planning group and it is not easy to tear their arguments apart. CEA cannot blow people out of the water with the depth of its analysis like it could in the 1960's. Few people understood what the term "multiplier" meant in the 1960's much less were able to argue with CEA's arguments about a tax policy to stimulate the economy. When CEA said the effect of a specific tax action on investment was such-and-such there wasn't any other agency doing its own empirical work to argue with it. . . .[31]

The 1960s may have been the "age of the economist," as Walter Heller proclaimed, but the times were especially good for economists located in the CEA. The council has not been as influential in subsequent administrations, partly because other agencies have strengthened their capabilities.

The Bureau of the Budget

The role of the Bureau of the Budget (BOB) in economic-policy formation flowed from its responsibility for preparing the annual budget for the president and from the economic-policy effects of the budget. Because of the importance of the budget as an economic-stabilization instrument, the director of the BOB was an important presidential adviser, particularly on expenditures, but often on other economic matters as well. The bureau also had responsibilities for legislative clearance, organization and management improvement, and legislative program development.

The day after Johnson became president, Kermit Gordon, director of the BOB, wrote to him concerning the status of the 1965 budget. Gordon's memorandum went on to inform him that the bureau was "a staff agency to the President which, by tradition and in fact, has no constituency other than the Presidency and no obligations which complicate its allegiance to the president." One of the areas in which the bureau could "meet your needs" was public expenditures. (Others were proposed legislation and government organization and management.) On such matters, Gordon went on, "we can provide you, in short order, with a statement of the pros and cons of particular courses of action, and our recommendations."[32] Johnson quickly incorporated the bureau into his advisory system.

Directors of the BOB during the Johnson administration tended to view themselves, and to be viewed, as special assistants to the president as well as directors of a staff agency serving the presidency. This was especially true of Charles L. Schultze, who succeeded Gordon as director in May 1965. The fact that Gordon and Schultze were both highly capable economists served to enhance their involvement in economic-policy matters. An internal working paper prepared for a 1967 BOB self-study both acknowledged this and contended that the agency had suffered as a consequence:

> Bureau Directors since [1960] have been program rather than management oriented. They have reflected the predominant inclinations of their bosses. Moreover, the White House style during this period has tended to emphasize the individual rather than the institution. The quality and individual competence of Bureau Directors during this period has been so great that the Bureau's overall stature in the minds of the President and the Congress has probably never been higher. Paradoxically, the institution has suffered internally during this same period because of the lack of attention paid to its day-to-day management.[33]

Traditionally people in the Bureau of the Budget viewed the agency as one that served the presidency. Indeed, as part of the institutionalized presidency in earlier administrations, the BOB had become somewhat separated from the president. This belief in "separation" apparently continued at the lower levels of the agency. The director of the bureau, however, and some other top-level people, such as Associate Director Phillip Hughes, were coopted by President Johnson. Schultze was a regular participant in economic-policy meetings and a major economic adviser to the president, as well as the chief budget officer.

The Treasury Department

The Treasury Department, with its responsibilities of tax collection, debt management, currency control, and customs control, is possessed of much institutional power. It is the best source of information in the government on tax revenues, the tax structure, and financial markets. Moreover, it usually serves as the lead agency in the development of tax legislation and its presentation to Congress. In the area of foreign economic policy, the Treasury Department has a larger role than the CEA. Ackley asserts that the department was able to dominate the Cabinet Committee on Balance of Payments because the staff work for it was done by Treasury officials and reflected Treasury policy positions.[34]

Henry H. Fowler, who served as secretary of the treasury during much of the Johnson administration, enjoyed a good personal relationship with the president and was an active participant in economic-policy meetings. However, he does not appear to have been especially influential on substantive matters; indeed, he opposed the president on suspension of the investment tax credit in 1966, and he also urged the acceptance of large expenditure cuts in 1968 to help secure enactment of the tax surcharge. Johnson nevertheless appeared to value his political judgment and advice. Fowler had a closer relationship with the president than did his predecessor, C. Douglas Dillon.

Because of his institutional position, the secretary of the treasury is likely to be somewhat less activist- and expansionist-oriented than other economic advisers. The soundness of the dollar, balance-of-payments equilibrium, and adequacy of revenues are likely to be important concerns. Other agencies, for example, may expend funds, but the responsibility for their collection rests with the Treasury. Moreover, the Treasury will be an important link between an administration and the financial community.

The Federal Reserve Board

Because of its responsibility for monetary policy, and because it does not act without regard for the positions and interests of the administration, the Federal Reserve Board (FRB) must be included in the subpresidency for economic policy when it provides the president with information and advice on fiscal and other economic-policy issues. Described as "independent in but not of the government," the Federal Reserve Board was also guided by the policy goals of the Employment Act. While not acknowledging that the president could direct its actions, the FRB was not unresponsive to many of the policy preferences of the Johnson administration, as in the expansion of the money supply in 1968. Good working relationships generally existed between the CEA and FRB staffs. Moreover, LBJ did from time to time seek the personal advice of William McChesney Martin, Jr., chairman of the FRB, on economic issues. Thus, in April 1968, following a telephone conversation with the president, Martin sent him a lengthy memorandum analyzing the economic situation and recommending a tax increase to impose more restraint on the economy.[35] The FRB also played a major role in implementing the balance-of-payments and international monetary policies of the administration.

Other Cabinet Departments

The cabinet was not used much by Johnson as a mechanism for the formulation of policy, or as a decisionmaking mechanism. Cabinet meetings were used, however, as an "informational forum" where, for example, the department secretaries were informed of the need to engage in budget reductions or the president solicited their reactions to different tax proposals.

Various individual cabinet members were involved in economic-policy matters, although not, in the case of Willard Wirtz (Department of Labor) and John Connor (Department of Commerce), to the extent they would have preferred. They tended to be consulted after policy proposals had been developed, when their reactions and those of the labor and business communities were sought. One explanation for their limited participation is provided by Gardner Ackley:

> But on fiscal or monetary policy, tax policy, size of the budget, Connor and Wirtz didn't really have much to contribute. Their ideas about these subjects were ill-formed; it wasn't that there weren't people in their agencies who were intelligent in respect to these issues, but that they were further down [in the departmental hierarchy]; the principals spent most of their time at a big administrative job and couldn't really get into the analysis of these issues. They didn't really represent an independent source

of ideas or advice . . . or didn't really have much to contribute, except perhaps prejudices or political notions.[36]

The Departments of Labor and Commerce were also variously viewed as claimant, ambassadorial, or clientele departments whose responses on policy matters would predictably support the interests of the groups they represented. There was a sound basis for this viewpoint, as the following anecdote told by White House aide Harry McPherson illustrates:

We would have meetings on textile policy [tariffs] in the Commerce Department and if I were so foolish as to walk back to the White House on a nice spring day after the meeting, I would have two or three phone calls on my desk from industry representatives who were complaining about what had been decided in the Commerce Department; and the leaks came almost entirely from Commerce. They see themselves essentially as industry's representatives to government and are very intimate with industry representatives.[37]

It should be noted, however, that Alexander Trowbridge, who succeeded Connor as secretary of commerce, did become more actively involved, especially in the implementation of the wage-price guideposts. His explanation for this provides an interesting commentary on bureaucratic behavior:

Jack Connor was frustrated over the exclusion [from economic policy-making]. I felt that exclusion too, but I didn't make as much fuss about it as Jack did. And I think for that reason, and by the contrast of that . . . I got included a little bit more than he did. . . . I think that a lot of meetings were called, and I was asked to join them because I didn't publicly complain about being excluded.[38]

Trowbridge also undoubtedly benefited from his previous experience in the executive branch.

Robert McNamara, the secretary of defense, was very actively involved in economic-policy matters. For one thing, defense expenditures constituted a very substantial portion of the national budget during the 1960s. More important, McNamara was very knowledgeable on economic matters (he had been president of the Ford Motor Company) and Johnson had much respect for his ability and judgment. Strong, talented persons like McNamara will be relied upon by the White House when they are available and can contribute information or advice that will strengthen presidential decisionmaking.

Outside Advisers

Johnson frequently sought advice from a variety of persons outside the government. Clark Clifford, Abe Fortas, and David Ginsburg, lawyers and long-term members of the Washington establishment, were consulted on many important economic matters. They also served on ad hoc committees that made recommendations to the president on fiscal policies. Johnson apparently viewed them as broad-gauged, wise individuals who could give useful judgments on the wisdom and feasibility of economic proposals. Also, Johnson continued to draw upon Walter Heller and Kermit Gordon for advice after they left their positions with the Council of Economic Advisers and the Bureau of the Budget. Other economists were also called upon on occasion. Before he made major economic decisions Johnson often consulted business and labor leaders: "Particularly when measuring the value of divergent proposals, he would present the labor arguments to a Henry Ford and the business arguments to a George Meany."[39] Businessmen who were drawn upon included utility executive Donald Cook, financier Robert Anderson, and Beverly Murphy of the Campbell Soup Company. Such persons could provide useful judgments and information on policy proposals, and their subsequent support could be helpful in securing the enactment or implementation of administration decisions.

It is not possible to determine with precision how much impact outside advisers had on the president's decisions and actions. Clearly they were important—they helped provide the president with the broad range of economic and political insight and information he needed and desired in making decisions. From some he sought trusted judgments, from others political reactions and insights, from others good economic information. They also provided him with an independent check on the feasibility and political realism of recommendations coming from administration officials. Presidents cannot afford to limit themselves to official aides and advisers in the exercise of their powers and responsibilities, nor will they when, like Johnson, they have a calculating and skeptical style of decisionmaking. It was sometimes remarked by White House staff members that "the only person Johnson trusts is Lady Bird; and then only 90 percent of the time."[40]

The Johnson Record: An Overview

In March 1961, following a period of recession, the American economy began an expansion that was to last for the remainder of the Kennedy administration, to continue throughout the Johnson administration, and to persist for the first 10 months of the Nixon administration. Lasting in all some 102 months, this was the longest continuous period of expansion in the history of the American economy. Some of the glow was taken off of the expansion after 1965 by increasing inflation, brought on largely by spending pressures generated by the Vietnam War. Nonetheless, this represents an impressive economic performance, and it did not just happen. Efforts by the Kennedy and Johnson administrations to stimulate the economy and then to maintain full employment conditions while seeking to moderate inflation clearly contributed to the expansion. Major macroeconomic actions by the Johnson administration will be discussed in this section. Since the decade of the 1960s was the heyday of the "New Economics," it seems advisable first to present some of the major "new economic" concepts employed by economic advisers during the Johnson (and Kennedy) administrations in analyzing the economy and framing economic policy proposals.[41] This will be done in nontechnical fashion. We turn first to a look at the New Economics.

The New Economics

The New Economics, as it came to be called, was a mixture of optimism and activism, of the belief that government could and should act to influence favorably the operation of the economy.[42] The new economists had considerable confidence in their ability to manage the economy; indeed, Walter Heller at one point spoke enthusiastically of their ability to "fine-tune" the economy. He was later to acknowledge that this was a gaffe.

The new economists wanted to do more than merely prevent "boom and bust" in the economy. Dissatisfied with the high levels of unemployment during the late 1950s and early 1960s, they targeted full employment (or "sustained prosperity") as their goal. This goal was stressed in their concepts of "potential output" and the "gap" in gross national product (GNP). Potential output was intended to measure the level of GNP that the economy could attain if it was operating at a full employment (4 percent or less unemployment) rate. The GNP gap measured the difference between actual output and potential output. If actual output was less than potential output, then economic resources were being wasted (not used) and an expansionary economic policy was called for.

Another concept of significance was that of the "full employment budget." This was intended to measure (at least more accurately than the actual budget surplus or deficit) the impact of fiscal policy on the economy. The budget both acts upon and is acted upon by the economy. A falloff in business activity, for whatever reasons, could reduce income and tax collections, and consequently produce a budget deficit, even though decisionmakers had not planned an expansionary fiscal policy. The full employment budget concept determines whether the budget would be in surplus or deficit given the existing set of revenue and expenditure policies. In assessing the impact of fiscal policy, it thus tries to hold the economy constant. At a high rate of unemployment the actual budget might be restrictive, even though in deficit, because if the economy were operating at full-employment conditions there would then be a budget surplus. It was this point of view that led the Council of Economic Advisers to advocate a tax cut in 1963, even though the budget was running a deficit, to stimulate the economy. The fiscal-policy target now became a balanced budget at full employment rather than a balanced budget every year or over the business cycle.

As economic activity expands and incomes rise, the existing revenue system, especially because of the operation of the graduated income tax, will bring in greater revenues. Indeed, revenues will tend to increase faster than employment declines. If government spending does not also increase, the result will be either a full-employment budget surplus or an increase therein, which will exert a restrictive influence on the economy and check the recovery. This condition is known as "fiscal drag." It is viewed as undesirable because it reduces growth of the economy, at least until the performance gap between potential and actual GNP is closed and inflation threatens.

To prevent fiscal drag from choking off recovery or growth of the economy, "fiscal dividends" should be declared. Those can take the form of either tax reduction or expenditure growth. As Heller has explained:

A central part of the job of fiscal policy is precisely this delicate one of declaring fiscal dividends of the right size and timing to avoid fiscal drag without inviting inflation. In an overheated economy, the fiscal drag that develops when fiscal dividends are *not* declared is a welcome antidote to inflation. When recession threatens, an extra dividend is appropriate. But in normal times we must close the fiscal loop by matching the annual $7 to $8 billion of revenue growth with tax cuts, increased expenditures (including social security benefits), and more generous support to state and local governments.[43]

The new economists were also concerned with the impact of wages and prices on inflation. They developed the view that to be noninflationary, wages and prices should be related to the growth in productivity in the economy. This found expression in the wage-price "guideposts," which will be dealt with in detail in Chapter 5. As formulated in 1962, the guideposts initially held that wages should not increase more rapidly than did the average rate of productivity in the economy. In 1965 and 1966 this principle found more concrete expression in the famous 3.2 percent wage increase guidepost, which was the average increase in productivity for the years 1960–64.

Mention also should be made here of the Phillips Curve, which, although it has now declined in influence, was an important concept in macroeconomic-policy discussion and deliberations in the 1960s. Essentially, the Phillips Curve suggests that there is a trade-off between the rates of unemployment and inflation in the economy: the higher the rate of unemployment, the lower the rate of inflation, and vice versa. The short-run challenge confronting policymakers was using monetary and fiscal policies so as to achieve the politically optimum balance between the unemployment and inflation rates. The long-run challenge, since the Phillips Curve was not stable, was creating conditions in which both low unemployment and little inflation existed. (The 1970s demonstrated that the opposite—high unemployment *and* a high rate of inflation—is also possible.)

The New Economics probably differed from the old economics more in spirit and emphasis than in kind; many of its concepts are drawn from mainline economics. The new economists were really distinguished by their optimism and activism, their confidence that the economy could be successfully managed, and their actual use of the concepts summarized here in making policy recommendations and managing the economy. And for a few years, as will be seen in the next section, they were generally successful in their actions.

Policy Actions

In January 1963 President John Kennedy requested that Congress enact a major reduction in personal and corporate income taxes, even though the national budget was in deficit, in order to encourage economic growth and reduce unemployment. The tax cut bill did not meet with an overly warm reception in Congress, and it was stalled there in late November when Lyndon Johnson succeeded Kennedy in the presidency. By using his powers of persuasion, pledging restraint in government spending, symbolizing thrift by turning down the White House lights, and producing an administrative budget of $97.9 billion (below the "magical" figure of $100 billion), Johnson was able to get Congress moving. In late February he signed the Revenue Act of 1964 into law.

The act permanently reduced income tax rates for all individuals and corporations. Individual rates ranging from 90 to 21 percent were lowered to 70 to 14 percent, while corporate rates were reduced from 52 percent to 48 percent. The reduction was made in two stages: most of the total reduction of $11.5 billion took effect immediately, but a small portion was delayed until 1965. The tax cut had the desired effect. Business investment and consumer spending increased and the unemployment rate, which had averaged 5.7 percent in 1963, dropped to 5.2 percent in 1964 and continued downward in 1965. Arthur Okun has stated that the long-run effect of the tax cut was to increase GNP by an annual rate of $36 billion.[44] It was, in all, a textbook example of a tax cut.

In its *Annual Report* of January 1965, the Council of Economic Advisers stated that the administration's fiscal program for fiscal year [FY] 1966 called for several expansionary actions in addition to the stimulatory effects of past actions, particularly the Revenue Act of 1964. These included a reduction in excise taxes, a liberalization of social-security benefits, and an increase in federal expenditures, mostly for grants-in-aid and transfer payments. These were necessary, according to the council, to offset the full employment growth in revenues and to decrease the full employment surplus during calendar year 1965.[45]

President Johnson recommended a $1.75 billion cut in excise taxes to Congress in January. When it became clear that there was strong congressional support for larger excise tax cuts, he increased his recommendation to $4 billion. (In 1964 Congress had reluctantly extended the excise taxes for another year at the president's request.) As enacted in June, the law provided for a $4.7 billion reduction in excise taxes on such items as appliances, radio and television sets, jewelry, automobiles, and telephones and communications services. The only major change made by Congress in the administration's proposal was a reduction in the tax on automobiles from 10 to 1 percent rather than the 5 percent that the administration had requested. Reductions totaling $1.8 billion took effect immediately, another $1.6 billion reduction was scheduled for 1 January 1966, and the remainder was to be phased in over the next three years.

Legislation enacted in July 1965 provided for a 7 percent increase in social-security benefits retroactive to 1 January 1965. This was financed by expansion of the social-security tax base from $4,800 to $6,600 and a small increase in the payroll tax rate, effective 1 January 1968. The administration believed that the retroactive benefits would give the economy a needed boost in the second half of 1965, and that financing them primarily through a tax base expansion would create less drag on the economy in the first part of 1966. By the time the higher base had begun to yield more revenue later in the year, medicare benefits, also authorized by Congress, would begin flowing out.[46]

As 1965 wore on, however, the concern of administration economists shifted from preventing fiscal drag to the possibility of an overheated economy. In the summer President Johnson committed the nation to increased involvement in Vietnam, and defense expenditures increased by over $3 billion in the second half of the year. In December the economy reached the interim goal of 4 percent unemployment. The Federal Reserve Board became concerned about inflationary pressures, and on 5 December they raised the discount rate from 4 to 4.5 percent. This action was criticized by administration spokesmen. (Hindsight has shown the FRB was correct.) There was, however, concern within the administration about the expansion in aggregate demand.

In December 1965, the president asked Ackley for his "private preliminary view of the policy implications of FY 1967 budgets of $110 and $115 billion." Ackley replied that "there is little question in my mind that a significant tax increase will be needed to prevent an intolerable degree of inflationary pressure" if the budget was $115 billion. The question was more difficult with the lower figure, but "a tax increase would probably still be necessary."[47] In another memorandum a few days later, Ackley concluded there was a need for an individual and corporate income tax increase. "Tactically, it may be feasible to propose higher taxes later in the year. From an economic standpoint, it needs to be done as soon as possible."[48] There was general agreement among LBJ's economic advisers that a general tax increase was necessary.

In his January 1966 State of the Union Message, however, the president chose to ask Congress only for a "bits-and-pieces" revenue package:

I believe it desirable, because of increased military expenditures, that you temporarily restore the automobile and certain telephone excise tax reductions made effective only twelve days ago. Without raising taxes—or even increasing the total tax bill paid—we should move to improve our withholding system so that Americans can realistically pay-as-they-go, speed up the collection of corporate taxes, and make other necessary simplifications of the tax structure at an early date.

I hope these measures will be adequate. But if the necessities of Vietnam require it, I will not hesitate to return to the Congress for additional appropriations or additional revenues if they are needed.[49]

The Congress responded quickly, passing the Tax Adjustment Act in March by substantial majorities. It temporarily restored excise taxes on automobile and telephone services to their pre-1966 levels (6 percent and 10 percent, respectively), provided for graduated withholding of personal income taxes, accelerated the collection of corporate income taxes, and required quarterly rather than annual payment of social-security taxes by the self-employed. Altogether, these measures provided for a one-time-only boost of $6 billion in revenue over the next fifteen months. Signing the measure, LBJ said it would provide funds to support the troops in Vietnam and "a careful measure of fiscal restraint to balance our economic expansion with reasonable price stability."[50] In actuality, it proved to be inadequate for either purpose.

The failure of the administration to seek a general tax increase meant that other stabilization measures would have to carry the burden. Efforts to induce business and labor to go along with the wage-price guideposts were intensified. A substantial effort to cut back on non-Vietnam spending was made. Much of the burden of restraining the economy was borne by the Federal Reserve Board, which acted to tighten the money supply. This led to the famous "credit crunch" in the autumn of 1966, followed by an easing of credit later in the year.

Within the administration discussion of the economic situation and the need for a tax increase continued. Ackley and Schultze were strong advocates of the desirability of a tax increase. In a memorandum to the president in May 1966, for example, Schultze indicated that expenditures for FY 1967 were going to be considerably higher than had been estimated in January. Noting the strong inflationary pressures that were developing, he said that "uncertainty over events in Vietnam is not sufficient reason to prevent a tax increase." His conclusion was unequivocal:

In short, under almost every conceivable circumstance—except a Vietnam settlement between July and November—a decision to raise taxes at least for the remainder of this year and early 1967 is clearly warranted. And even under that circumstance, the risks of serious inflation, in my view, far outweigh the dangers of having a tax increase extend a few months past the date of a possible Vietnam settlement.[51]

He favored a 10 percent income tax increase plus suspension of the investment tax credit and accelerated depreciation on buildings.

Not until September, however, did the administration propose action to restrain the surging economy. In a special message to Congress on fiscal policy on 8 September 1966 the president proposed a several-part program: (a) a reduction of $1.5 billion in spending for lower-priority federal programs, (b) suspension of the investment tax credit until 1 January 1968, (c) suspension of accelerated depreciation on buildings until the same date, and (d) an easing of monetary restraint by the FRB because of the use of fiscal restraint.[52] Congress again responded quickly and on 8 November, the president signed into law a bill suspending the investment tax credit and the accelerated depreciation allowance. He noted that he would promptly recommend their reinstatement if it became necessary before January 1968.[53]

In the fall of 1966, economic forecasts became less bearish because there was a discernible slowing down of economic activity. The December Troika review indicated that the first half of 1967 was going to be sluggish economically. The policy implications of this situation included a need for new stimuli from fiscal and monetary policy to prevent the slowdown from becoming a stall. Monetary ease, action to revive the housing industry (which had been hard hit by the credit crunch), and restoration of the investment tax credit and the accelerated depreciation allowance were recommended by the Troika. However, an upsurge in the economy by the middle of the year was foreseen. To contain this, the Troika proposed a surcharge of 5 percent on personal and corporate incomes, to become effective on 1 July 1967.[54]

In December 1966 and early January 1967, several of the president's economic advisers held meetings to develop a fiscal program. In a memorandum to the president on 9 January 1967, they recommended a 6 percent surtax on personal and corporate incomes, suspension of the investment tax credit when necessary, a speedup in corporate tax collections, continuation of the interest equalization tax, and continued pressure for easy money.[55] In his State of the

Union Message the president called for the 6 percent surcharge. His request elicited little favorable response and the administration did not push it for the time being.

The nagging problem of an unfavorable balance of payments worsened in 1967. Export sales declined while capital outflows to other nations increased. To deal with the capital outflow problem, the president recommended extension of the 1963 Interest Equalization Tax Act which had been designed to increase the cost of money for foreign borrowers. Congressional action extended the tax for the two years that the president requested. The legislation also authorized him to entirely eliminate the tax or to set it at any level up to the equivalent of an interest charge of 1.5 percent. This is probably the first instance of congressional delegation of discretionary authority to the executive to vary tax rates. Legislation was also extended in 1967 that permitted the executive to grant antitrust exemptions to financial institutions entering into voluntary agreements, under supervision of the attorney general, to reduce the flow abroad of U.S. dollars and credits.

Concern over continued softness in the economy was stirred in March by the Department of Commerce–Securities and Exchange Commission annual investment survey, which indicated a likely decline in business investments. On 9 March, a couple of days after Fowler, Schultze, and Ackley recommended consideration of restoration of the investment tax credit and accelerated depreciation allowance, the president sent a special message to Congress requesting their reinstatement. Their suspension, he said, had accomplished the purpose of economic restraint and hence they could be restored.[56] That this action was intended to stimulate the economy was soft-pedalled by administration officials. Once again, Congress acted. The necessary legislation, which was held up for several weeks because of an extraneous dispute over a presidential campaign fund, was enacted in June.

What various members of Congress, including some administration supporters, saw as the administration's on-again-off-again tax policy was beginning to produce strong rumblings of discontent. Liberal Democratic Senator Albert Gore of Tennessee, although not alone in some of his sentiments, seemed especially provoked:

> We are all Keynesians to some degree, and I am sure that every member of the Senate believes in the active use of the powers of government to help regulate the economy under certain circumstances. But are we capable of intelligently juggling our tax pat-

terns and tax rates? Are we not doing more harm than good with an on-again-off-again tax policy, the only constant being continuous and increasing deficits?

To begin with, forecasting is not sufficiently precise to allow policy to be pinpointed. And, second, timing will always be questionable when political activists must be counted on to arrive at decisions, and additional political forces must be called on to transform decisions into action.[57]

Gore preferred an "equitable tax system" with expenditure variations used for fiscal-policy action. Others, however, were more concerned that with a reduction of expenditures the economy would become resurgent in the second half of the year and a shift toward restraint in fiscal policy would become necessary.[58]

After much internal deliberation and consultation with outside groups and persons, a decision to seek a major tax increase was reached by the administration. A memorandum to the president initialed by Fowler, Wirtz, Trowbridge, McNamara, Schultze, Ackley, and Califano recommended a speedup in corporate tax collections, continuation of the automobile and telephone excise taxes, and a temporary 10 percent surcharge on corporate and individual income tax liabilities (to become effective on 1 July and 1 September 1967, respectively, and to continue until 30 June 1969, or as long as the Vietnam War required higher revenues).[59] These recommendations were incorporated in the president's special message to Congress on 3 August.

This touched off a ten-month struggle between Congress and the executive over the proposed tax increase. First, doubt was expressed in Congress that a tax increase was really needed at all. In the view of many members, since the economy was operating satisfactorily at the time, why monkey with it? Moreover, the public displayed no enthusiasm for a tax increase. Hearings were held, but no other action was taken by Congress in 1967. The necessity of action became clear after the turn of the year, as Arthur Okun reported:

> The need for economic restraint became clear to the Congress and the public early in 1968 when the horror stories of the economic forecasts began to come true. Prices accelerated to a 4 percent rate of increase; interest rates rose far above their 1966 peaks; and our world trade surplus again shrank. The economy moved into a feverish boom with a huge advance in GNP of $19 billion in the first quarter of 1968.[60]

Strong business support was expressed for the tax increase, but majority support in Congress could not be won until the administration agreed to couple it with an expenditure reduction. Enacted in June 1968 and quietly signed into law by the president, the Revenue and Expenditure Control Act provided for:

1. A 10 percent surcharge on individual income tax payments effective 1 April 1968, and on corporate income tax payments effective 1 January 1968. Individuals in the lowest two tax brackets were exempt from the tax. The surtax was slated to expire on 30 June 1969.

2. Continuation of excise taxes on automobiles and telephone service at existing rates until 1 January 1970.

3. Acceleration of corporate tax payments.

4. Reduction of budget expenditures by $6 billion in FY 1969.

In addition, there was to be a $10 billion reduction in appropriations (new obligational authority) in FY 1969, and a rescission of $8 billion in unspent prior-year appropriations at the end of 1969. Some spending and appropriations, such as for the Vietnam War, veterans' benefits, and interest on the national debt were exempted from the reduction requirements.

Congress subsequently reduced appropriations (new obligational authority) by $12.5 billion, or more than the act required. Expenditures (or outlays) were reduced somewhere between $3.5 and $4 billion during congressional action on the 1969 budget. The remainder was left to the administration to cut, which it did in such areas as non-Vietnam defense spending, government loan programs (lending was shifted to private markets), highway project postponements, and non-Apollo space projects.[61]

The Council of Economic Advisers expressed concern that the combination of tax increases and expenditure reductions in the 1968 legislation would provide too much restraint on the economy. A Troika memorandum in August 1968 viewed the prospective slowdown of the economy in 1969 as excessive and asserted that monetary ease was necessary to moderate it.[62] The FRB acted to expand the money supply, thereby offsetting the restraint of the Revenue and Expenditure Control Act. As Okun later put it: "This turned out to be wrong policy because it was the right policy for what turned out to be the wrong forecast."[63]

Inflation continued to plague the economy through the remainder of the Johnson administration and became a problem with which succeeding administrations had to contend.

A Concluding View

In many respects, the operation of the economy during the Johnson years was impressive (see Table 3). Prosperity reigned in the nation. GNP and per capita incomes expanded substantially (even when corrected for inflation). The economy operated close to its potential output level throughout the era. The rate of unemployment averaged less than 4 percent for 1966–69, and several million people were added to the labor force. Those who had predicted that high rates of unemployment would persist because of automation and structural problems in the economy were proven incorrect.

On the other hand, the rate of inflation in 1966–68 was the highest the nation had experienced since the Korean War years. This produced a decline in the net worth of large numbers of citizens and a loss of purchasing power for many others. When the Nixon administration took office in 1969, it confronted an inflationary economy. All, in short, was not rosy, although in retrospect the inflation of the Johnson years seems less severe than it once did, given the experience of the 1970s.

One can speculate that the Johnson economic record would have been better had there not been political resistance, based in part on opposition to the Vietnam War, to the administration's efforts at economic management, especially after 1965. Politics, however, constitute an important part of the environment of economic managers, as they should in a democracy. In the rest of this book we shall be con-

Table 3. *The U.S. Economy: The 1960s*

Year	GNP ($ Billions)	Consumer Price Index	Unemployment Rate	Labor Force (Thousands)
1960	503.7	103.1	5.5	72,142
1961	520.1	104.2	6.7	73,031
1962	560.3	105.4	5.5	73,442
1963	590.5	106.7	5.7	74,571
1964	632.4	108.1	5.2	75,830
1965	684.9	109.9	4.5	77,178
1966	749.9	113.1	3.8	78,893
1967	793.5	116.3	3.8	80,793
1968	865.7	121.2	3.6	82,272
1969	931.4	127.7	3.5	84,240

Sources: CEA, *Annual Report of the Council of Economic Advisers, 1970, 1971,* Washington, D.C., Government Printing Office, 1970, 1971.

cerned, among other things, with how the intermixture of economic and political considerations shaped and limited the actions of those involved in the development and administration of macroeconomic policy.

Walter Heller proclaimed that economics had "come of age in the 1960's." At the end of the decade, it still possessed growing pains; and things would get worse in the 1970s. But that is another story.

3. The Management of Fiscal Policy

A president will make only a few major fiscal-policy decisions in the course of a year, and perhaps not many more than that during his entire administration. To be constantly concerned about the economy is one thing, to take action constantly to shape its operation is quite another. The mental picture of a president and his advisers continually tinkering with the economy, maybe even fine-tuning it, is not accurate, as the discussion in Chapter 2 of the Johnson record clearly indicates. If presidents could by themselves take action to affect the economy, for instance if they had discretionary authority to raise and lower tax rates and were not constrained by the political environment in which they operate, then they probably would try to manipulate the economy more frequently. Such, of course, is not the case.

Primary responsibility for the development of fiscal-policy proposals rests with the president and the executive branch. This task has fallen to the executive as much by default as by design. Congress, characterized by the decentralization and dispersion of power, and lacking strong unified leadership, does not have the capacity to initiate well-conceived, unified fiscal-policy proposals. Because fiscal actions usually require the enactment of taxation and appropriations legislation, however, most of the ultimate authority over fiscal policy rests with Congress. In the fiscal-policy area, the president proposes while Congress disposes. There are some exceptions to this pattern. Some efforts to reduce expenditures for fiscal purposes, such as the Johnson administration's 1966 campaign to hold down expenditures, can be made largely within the executive branch, albeit with some concern for congressional sensitivities.

In the development and adoption of fiscal-policy proposals, the president must perform a number of management tasks. First, the president must secure the services of personnel and create or maintain structures and processes that will provide him with adequate and timely data, advice, and policy options. The macroeconomic subpresidency was discussed in Chapter 2, and in this chapter, the important Troika operation will be examined. Second, the president must see that actions are coordinated so that conflicts and divergencies do not occur among fiscal and other macroeconomic policies, with the resultant reduction of their beneficial effects. Coordination of fiscal and monetary policies is extensively dealt with in Chapter 4. Third, the president must act to secure cooperation and consent from others, both within the executive branch and Congress, for presidential alternatives. Some illustrations of this are provided in the case studies in this chapter. Fourth, the president must supply leadership in fiscal-policy development. Policy goals must be set, priorities articulated, action secured. The discussion of expenditure reduction in 1966 provides a good example of presidential leadership, although presidential leadership suffuses the entire fiscal-policy development process.

Some Preliminary Considerations

During the 1960s any reasonably capable student of economics could have provided an explanation of how fiscal policy should be employed to stabilize the economy on the basis of accepted theory. Tax cuts, expenditure increases, and budget deficits would be used to offset economic decline; tax increases, expenditure reductions, and budget surpluses would be used to combat inflationary situations. The goal would be to influence aggregate demand for goods and services in the appropriate direction. Economists might have argued about precisely how much stimulus or restraint was needed, or at what exact time action was required, but the basic policy prescriptions of Keynesian economics were generally agreed upon, and there was widespead acceptance of Keynesian economics. Even Milton Friedman in late 1965 was moved to proclaim that "we are all Keynesians now." The disarray currently afflicting the economics profession was a thing of the future in the 1960s.

The national government's taxation and expenditure policies are, of course, more than instruments of fiscal policy. They also finance governmental programs and allocate the costs and benefits of government. If taxes are to be raised, then an important question is, whose taxes will be raised? Likewise, expenditures are not cut in the abstract; rather, reductions must be applied to particular agencies and programs. (Few agencies or groups volunteer to assume such burdens.) Hence, the president must be concerned with more than what is economically desirable; he must also be concerned with what is politically and administratively feasible. Tax action, in particular, that the president wants may not be obtainable from Congress, or it may be enacted very slowly, or it may involve costs the executive would rather not pay.

Executive efforts in the 1960s to secure greater formal authority in fiscal-policy areas were usually unsuccessful. In 1962 President John Kennedy proposed to Congress that the chief executive be given discretionary authority "to make temporary counter-cyclical adjustments in the first bracket of the personal income tax." The proposal never got out of congressional committee. Walter Heller reports that in 1964 the Council of Economic Advisers (CEA) tried to write "a fairly strong standby tax power" recommendation into the president's *Economic Report*. However, President Johnson was not willing to accept it and it was watered down until "next to nothing" remained.[1]

In his subsequent economic reports to the Congress, President Johnson did make a number of mild recommendations pertaining to quicker action by Congress on taxes. In 1965 he suggested that Congress adopt procedures to speed up its consideration of tax legislation. The next year he urged Congress to undertake "background tax studies" which would facilitate "quick decisions and prompt action to accommodate short-run cyclical actions." In 1969, following the lengthy struggle over the income tax surcharge, he advised Congress to seek ways to respond more quickly to presidential tax requests. He then went on to express his belief that the president should be given "discretionary authority to initiate limited changes in tax rates, subject to congressional veto." None of these recommendations was actively promoted by the administration and no action was taken by Congress, which was strongly resistant to sharing its "power of the purse" with the executive.

One small breach in the congressional tax wall was made by the Interest Equalization Tax Act of 1963, as amended in 1967. The interest equalization tax was intended to increase the cost of foreign borrowing in the United States, thereby discouraging the flow of funds out of the country and reducing the continual U.S. balance-of-payments deficit. The 1967 extension legislation authorized the president to adjust the tax rate. By an executive order on 28 August, President Johnson reduced the equalization rate from 1.5 percent to 1.25 percent. As noted previously, this was probably the first instance in which Congress had authorized the president to make a discretionary tax change. It did not, however, serve as a precedent for further delegation of authority.

On balance it is probably easier to use fiscal policy to deal with recession than with inflation. Congress finds that it is politically easier to spend than to tax, and easier to cut taxes than to increase taxes. Moreover, a substantial portion of the national budget, being based upon laws and past commitments (e.g., contracts and entitlements, as for social security), is "uncontrollable" in the short run. All of this helps to build an inflationary bias into fiscal policy.

To be most effective, fiscal policy, along with the other instruments of macroeconomic policy, should whenever possible be used prospectively to prevent the development of economic problems rather than to remedy them after they arise. This requires action on the basis of economic forecasting. In the 1960s, forecasting was a fairly new and primitive art form. First President Kennedy and then President Johnson accepted the need for action based on forecasts, in considerable part because of the informational and persuasional activities of the CEA. The members of Congress, however, generally were not beneficiaries of these activities. They remained skeptical of policy recommendations, especially in the form of major tax action, based on what was likely to happen rather than on the "facts" of the situation. A difference of perspective thus contributed to legislative-executive differences in the fiscal-policy area. Add in such factors as the differences between Democrats and Republicans, liberals and conservatives, and labor and business on fiscal-policy matters and one realizes that fiscal policy preeminently is, and must be, a mixture of politics and economics, and a product of political bargaining. (The other areas of macroeconomic policy also manifest a blend of politics and economics.)

The Development of Fiscal-Policy Proposals

Presidential decisions, whether on fiscal-policy proposals or other matters, are customarily institutional decisions. The final say-so may rest with the president, but many people and organizations will be involved in the provision of advice, the development and evaluation of alternatives for dealing with a problem, and the fashioning and selection of a particular alternative. Institutional decisionmaking consequently becomes, *inter alia*, a problem in management. Structure and direction must be given to the process and its participants. Here then, our focus is on how the Johnson administration managed the development and selection of fiscal-policy proposals. Our attention turns first to what we will call the "Troika operation."

The Troika Operation

The Troika originated during the Kennedy administration. A tripartite mechanism for providing the president with economic information and advice, it was the basic component of the president's information system. Who was responsible for its development is not fully clear. Arthur Okun attributes a major role to Sam Cohn, a career official in the Bureau of the Budget (BOB) who wanted coordination among the agencies supplying the president with economic advice.[2] Walter Heller states that Secretary of the Treasury C. Douglas Dillon was its originator.[3] Robert A. Wallace, an assistant secretary of the treasury, says it evolved from the Tuesday Group of officials, so called because they met on any day except Tuesday to discuss economic policies.[4] There is probably some accuracy in all of these viewpoints. There does seem to have been general agreement that better coordination was needed in advising the president on economic matters.

The Troika was composed of the chairman of the CEA, the director of the BOB, and the secretary of the treasury. Together with their agencies they were responsible for preparing economic forecasts and developing economic advice for the president. The Departments of Agriculture, Commerce, and Labor, which previously had had important roles in economic forecasting, were now largely excluded. During the Johnson administration the secretaries of labor (Wirtz) and commerce (Connor) were decidedly unhappy about this situation. Although informal in the sense that it was not based on any statute or executive order, the Troika was a recognized and stable institution within the executive branch.

The division of responsibilities among the Troika agencies gave primary responsibility to the Treasury Department for estimation of revenues, the Bureau of the Budget for estimation of expenditures, and the Council of Economic Advisers for overall economic forecasting.[5] This was not a rigid division, however, and the agencies did sometimes challenge each other's estimates. Thus, the CEA might second-guess the Treasury's revenue estimates, while both the CEA and Treasury might question the BOB's expenditure estimates (especially after defense spending began to increase). Charles Zwick, Johnson's last BOB director, put it this way: "Everybody kibitzed on everybody else. We [BOB] questioned their [CEA] model. We always thought Treasury's revenue estimates were too low; they always thought our expenditure estimates were too low or something. So there was always a give and take on all aspects."[6]

The agencies also brought some policy biases to the Troika operation. The Treasury, for instance, was especially concerned with price-level stability because of its concern with debt management and the balance of payments and its relationship with the financial community. It tended to argue for more fiscal restraint. The BOB, in turn, showed little enthusiasm for expenditure reductions because the burden of such efforts fell on it and they were not easy to accomplish. The CEA had a clear preference for economic expansion. In practice, these policy biases were modified as the Troika agencies and officials sought agreement in their recommendations. Wallace, for example, saw the Troika as a means of offsetting what he called the "exuberance" of Walter Heller on the one hand and the conservatism of the Treasury on the other.[7]

The Troika was a three-level as well as a three-agency operation. The bottom or technician level consisted of individuals from the three agencies who had the responsibility of collecting statistical data and preparing the forecasts of future economic trends. Forecasts were prepared on a quarterly basis unless there were requests from the principals or White House for additional ones. The technicians were all economists and, while they did not entirely shed the policy orientations of their agencies, they did place strong emphasis on objective economic analysis and the production of accurate economic forecasts. As one account put it, "The Troika gets much of its organizational glue from the technicians who staff its bottom level. They have a strong group identification that at times seems to outweigh the institutional pull of their own agencies."[8] These technicians manifested considerable professional independence in performing the basic analytical work of the Troika. Okun, who at one time was a Troika technician, has stated that having a level of technicians in the Troika who knew that the best possible forecast was wanted made it very difficult for a principal to ask a forecaster "to take a dive" in order to meet some particular policy preference. To do so would have been to ask the person to violate the professional code and to behave contrary to the main job requirement—to be as correct as possible.[9] As a consequence there was an inhibition against manipulating the technical staff.

The middle level of the Troika, designated the option-framers, consisted of a member of the CEA, the assistant secretary of the treasury for fiscal affairs, and an assistant director of the BOB. At this level, political factors did enter into the forecasting process. When a forecast prepared by the technicians came to the option-framers, they reviewed it to determine whether anything appeared to be happening in the economy that needed attention. If everything seemed all right, the option-framers reported this to their principals, and the Troika exercise ended there.

If, however, some significant economic changes had occurred, these would be analyzed by the option-framers and technicians to determine their causes. Policy options that would counteract the problems revealed were then sought. A number of forecasts using alternative models of the economy would be made, a few of the optional policy forecasts selected as being most appropriate, and a report containing these prepared for the top-level Troika members. In some instances this report would recommend a particular policy alternative as most appropriate.

For the top level of the Troika, policy considerations predominated over technical forecasting, although one or more of the top officials may have been involved in the forecasting process from the beginning. There was, in short, interaction among all three levels of the Troika operation; no rigid separation of functions existed. The principals might send the option-framers' report to the president with a covering memorandum, perhaps requesting a meeting to discuss it if that seemed necessary. Or the Troika members might make policy recommendations to the president on the basis of the option-framers' report, with perhaps some additional analysis of the economic situation. We shall return to the matter of policy recommendations in a moment.

The Troika operation represented a regularized and systematic means of providing economic advice to the president. Okun has provided a general appraisal of its usefulness:

Here we had a procedure that assured that the President got at least a quarterly review regularly of what was new in the economy, whether there was any need to change the estimates of economic activity, employment, prices, gross national product, what had been carried in the budget or the last Troika memo, whether budget expenditures were outrunning the estimates, whether receipts were coming in stronger or weaker than had been anticipated. This forced all of us right from the staff level on up through the principal, indeed right up to the President, to focus at least that often on the fiscal policy question. And it also became a forum whereby you'd get a lot of contact and a lot of discussion among the various Troika people on how they saw the fiscal policy side of things. I think this turned it from a fire alarm system into a continuous watch, and I think it was really an institutional reform that fitted what I think was the key element in the whole of the New Economics, which was a shift of fiscal policy from meeting the problems to trying to plan and program and sustain prosperity for the country. We didn't just wait for a sign of recession and boom, and then say, "What shall we do about it?" We tried to think all the time, and on a regular basis, "How is the budget meeting the needs of the economy and to what extent are alterations in order?" I'm not saying we always answered these questions correctly, but we were asking the right questions, and I think that made a lot of difference.[10]

Hindsight enables one to say that, with one major exception, the Troika operation generated remarkably accurate economic forecasts for the Johnson administration. The exception was in 1968 when, following the passage of the Revenue and Expenditure Control Act, a forecast of excessive restraint on the economy led to an undue expansion of the money supply. A combination of skill and judgment, with a little luck, probably accounts for the Troika's success.

Sources of Economic Data

The Council of Economic Advisers and the other Troika members depended upon other agencies for much of the data needed in their forecasting and economic-analysis activities. Some major sources included the Federal Reserve Board (monetary and credit data, industrial production index), the Office of Business Economics (national income and product accounts, personal income), the Bureau of the Census (state and local finances), the Bureau of Labor Statistics (employment and price statistics), the Securities and Exchange Commission (business investment statistics), and the Department of Agriculture (farm prices). Over time a network of informal communications channels had been developed with the result that new data from these agencies were passed on quickly to the CEA. Ackley recalls that

> we had all the resources of the government's statistical agencies. We got them automatically; we had the systems set up which existed long before our time, and will probably last forever, in which all the economic information funnels in very quickly. It's still a horse and buggy operation, it's not computerized. We had a couple of employees who got these numbers over the phone or by messenger, and wrote them down by hand in black notebooks; but they were the best set of numbers in the whole government. And other agencies would always call on the Council to check out their numbers because these people were just sticklers for accuracy.[11]

The data collection system has become both more extensive and more modern in the last decade.

The data pipelines were kept open by informal contacts, usually at the staff level, but sometimes involving the heads of the various agencies. Economists in other agencies apparently found it to their advantage to cooperate with the council. This enabled them to share in its prestige, to feel involved in the development of fiscal policy, and to obtain hints about future policy.[12] Also, various people in the Departments of Commerce and Labor were asked to comment on and sometimes draft sections of the council's annual *Economic Report*.

Before the creation of the Troika, when the Departments of Agriculture, Commerce, and Labor were directly involved in forecasting and fiscal policymaking, one or another of them would sometimes withhold information from the others in order to strengthen its own position in making policy choices. With the loss of their policy formation roles, incentives of this sort for the withholding or biasing of data largely disappeared. But not entirely. Department secretaries might still resent being bypassed in the distribution of data. Thus in 1966 the secretary of labor directed the Bureau of Labor Statistics to give the CEA data on employment, the labor force, and prices only after it had been delivered to him, thereby delaying its transmission to the CEA. "Sometimes we have been able to pry them out sooner by a personal call from me or another member to one of [his] special assistants," Ackley wrote, "but we are tired of having to fight for vital economic information."[13] With Califano's approval, Ackley sent a letter to the secretary indicating that this withholding of data had caused some problems for the CEA, such as when the president had asked for an interpretation of some BLS data that the CEA had not received. He concluded with a proposed deal and a request:

> I have been quite willing to agree that we will . . . not report to the President any BLS data until you have reported them to him if that be your wish, and if you will specify which data you wish to so report and let us know when you have done so.
>
> I therefore respectfully request that BLS personnel be asked to resume their longstanding practice of making available to the Council all data that are generated by the BLS as soon as tabulation and checking are complete.[14]

This sufficed to reopen the information channels and end a bureaucratic conflict of less-than-titanic proportions.

Those involved in economic forecasting and fiscal-policy formation also needed information on monetary policies, which were under control of the independent Federal Reserve Board (FRB). Moreover, to be most effective, the use of monetary and fiscal policies needed to be coordinated in some way. Otherwise, they might be used in either a contradictory or excessive manner; that is, they might offset each other, or if both were used against inflation, for example, they might apply too much restraint on the economy. Thus, the Troika needed to know what the Federal Reserve Board was planning to do, and, since it was a two-way relationship, vice versa. A variety of arrangements, mostly informal in nature, were developed for the exchange of data and information between the FRB and the Troika agencies (these are discussed in Chapter 4).

Developing Policy Proposals

The Troika was the major source of fiscal-policy proposals for President Johnson. Whether LBJ accepted these proposals, either with or without modification, was another matter. More often than not, Troika proposals served as the beginning point for discussion and debate of what the administration should do, say, about inflationary pressures or the need to provide some stimulus to the economy. To illustrate, the economic program agreed to by a number of the president's advisers in January 1967 was not greatly different from that recommended by the Troika in its report a couple of weeks earlier.[15] Included in both were recommendations for a general tax increase (surcharge) at midyear, reinstitution of the investment tax credit, and continued pressure on the FRB for an easier money policy.

Through discussion and bargaining, the Troika sought to develop policy recommendations on which all the members could agree. Dissenting statements in Troika reports were rare. Differences were usually resolved by "negotiating the adjectives and adverbs" or by including statements of the risks associated with various alternatives in their memorandums.[16] The action and strategy of the Troika have been described by Ackley:

> On the vast majority of issues, the Treasury, the tax people in the Treasury, and the Budget Bureau and the Council saw things essentially the same way; and our strategy was so far as possible not to present the President with disagreements on which we had to give him divided advice. So far as we could, we tried to avoid that—particularly if the divided advice rested on different economic analyses or different forecasts. To ask the President to decide a question on the basis of an interpretation of economic data

or argument is really unfair. He's not as well qualified, certainly, as his advisers to make the analysis, to interpret the data.[17]

Such agreement was also likely to enhance the influence of the Troika.

The Troika was not always in agreement, however. In the spring of 1968 its members disagreed over the issue of accepting an expenditure reduction as a condition of winning congressional passage of the income tax surcharge. Okun has described the situation that developed:

. . . Fowler would have paid any price, taken any kind of cut in domestic spending. If he thought a repeal of social security was what was necessary to pass the tax bill, he would have been for it. Zwick really was dragging his heels on any significant expenditure cut, particularly on expenditure cuts which really required the President to make the cuts. The whole process there was really screwy—I mean it was Congress saying we're going to appropriate a hell of a lot of money and it's going to be even more than your budget but we're going to put a ceiling and you're going to have to commit yourself to come in under that ceiling. This was something the Budget Director found he couldn't live with, quite apart from what his sense of priorities were on the importance of federal programs—being ordered to make a slash and try to hassle [the cut] through all the agencies. . . . the agency heads whose programs would have been gored by a spending cut did not see the same urgency in the tax surcharge than Fowler and I did. Or that Zwick did.[18]

Zwick seems essentially in agreement with this account. He says the Treasury advocated expenditure cuts first in the name of fiscal responsibility, while the BOB and CEA were in effect saying that the tax increase had to be obtained while protecting the Great Society programs. Then, as pressure increased for the president to do something about the worsening economic situation, "the Council finally panicked and said, 'Let's cut out the programs, give up, pay whatever price we have to pay to get Wilbur Mills to go along with a tax increase.'"[19] Pressure in this instance produced a divergence among the Troika agencies and led to their taking policy positions consistent with their general institutional biases. More commonly, when divisions developed among the Troika, the CEA and BOB would line up in sort of an "executive office alliance" against the Treasury, although what conflicts there were among them were more matters of detail than of basic principle or policy.

Despite the advantages to be gained from broader knowledge of political factors, resistance to expanding the Troika to include additional agencies rested on two premises. One was that other agencies, like the Departments of Commerce and Labor, lacked skill in economic analysis even while they served as spokesmen for particular clienteles, which would inhibit their objectivity. The CEA and the BOB (at least the top-level personnel who were involved in the Troika operation) had no clientele other than the president, while the Treasury Department had a rather amorphous clientele in the "financial community." Second, it was considered to be hard enough to secure agreement among three agencies. Notwithstanding the pressures from Johnson for consensus among his primary economic advisers, especially on the technical or economic aspects of policy proposals, a larger group would have made the task even more difficult and increased the likelihood of disagreements. (In an interview, a former Troika member remarked on the unwieldy nature of the Carter administration's Economic Policy Group, which numbered half a dozen.)

The importance of the Troika is underscored by the fact that little if any fiscal-policy action was taken by the Johnson administration that did not reach the president through a Troika report. Thus, the 1965 excise tax cuts, the 1967 restoration of the investment tax credit and accelerated depreciation, and the 1968 recommendation for extension of the income tax surcharge were essentially Troika products. The ad hoc committees used by the president to fashion the 1966 suspension of the investment tax credit and accelerated depreciation, the January 1967 fiscal program, and the August 1967 request for a 10 percent income tax surcharge based their recommendations, reached through discussion and bargaining with the president, on Troika proposals.

Finally, it should be noted that Johnson was actively involved in the process of developing fiscal-policy proposals, whatever their sources. A Troika proposal, which itself might be initiated by a presidential request, was often merely the beginning of what might be an extended, and rather unstructured, decisionmaking process. The case of the 1966 suspension of the investment tax credit is illustrative. All during the spring and summer of 1966, Troika members had been hammering away at the president on the need for an income tax increase to offset the inflationary pressure created by increased spending for the Vietnam War. Finally in late August, the president, after telling them they could not get a general tax increase, acceded to suspension of the investment tax credit. This, according to Ackley, was "the best the Troika could get from him."[20]

Illustrations of Fiscal-Policy Management

In this section we move from a general analysis of fiscal-policy proposal development to an examination of three fiscal-policy decisions made by the Johnson administration. These are the decisions not to seek a general tax increase in early 1966, to undertake a major expenditure reduction exercise in 1966, and to request suspension of the investment tax credit in the late summer of 1966. In the second case we will also be concerned with the administration of the expenditure reduction exercise.

No claim is made that the decisionmaking processes in these instances have been fully reconstructed. These discussions, though, contain greater richness of detail than could be achieved in an overall analysis of fiscal-policy decisionmaking, and will convey insight into the management of the economic-policy process, the roles of various officials and agencies, and the use of information. Some of the problems involved in attempting to manage the economy will also emerge.

A Tax Increase Is Rejected: 1966

The chain of events that led to the Johnson administration's request in August 1967 for a general tax increase to combat inflation really began in the latter part of 1965. Thus, the issue of a general tax increase was a major aspect of macroeconomic policymaking for over three years. The 1966 expenditure reduction effort and the 1966–67 suspension and restoration of the investment tax credit are also integral parts of the story. The focus in this account will be on the president's decision in late 1965–early 1966 not to go for a general tax increase.

As American involvement in Vietnam increased after the decision in mid-1965 to significantly enlarge the U.S. commitment, defense spending began to move upward. This in turn put additional pressure on the American economy, which was then moving toward the full employment level. Wages and prices began to surge upward and inflation became a real threat.[21] With the exception of Treasury Secretary Fowler, the president's primary economic advisers apparently favored a tax increase. The president, however, rejected this advice, choosing instead to ask the Congress for a "bits-and-pieces" tax program: deferral of scheduled excise tax reductions, acceleration of corporate tax payments, and institution of graduated withholding of personal income taxes.

Two issues were central to the administration's consideration of whether a tax increase was needed in 1966. One concerned the level of defense spending, the other was the question of whether Congress would pass a tax increase if it was requested. These will occupy our attention in the present discussion.

On 19 December 1965, Ackley responded to the president's request for his "private preliminary view" of the effects of possible fiscal year (FY) 1967 budgets of $110 and $115 billion. Ackley reported that there was "little question" in his mind that a $115 billion budget would require "a *significant tax increase* . . . to prevent an intolerable degree of inflationary pressure." A budget of $110 billion would "probably" also require a tax increase. Moreover, he continued, "A budget of $110 billion could only be achieved—I assume—with a maximum of 'gimmicks.' These hold down the deficit in the Administrative Budget, but *don't lessen its economic impact*."[22] A week later Ackley followed this up with another memorandum in which, on the basis of a nearly completed Troika exercise on the state of the economy, he stated:

> The *only conclusion I can reach* is that an increase of individual and corporate income tax rates should be planned, *whatever the FY 1967 budget* may be (within the limits we have heard discussed). Tactically, it may only be feasible to propose higher taxes later in the year. *From an economic standpoint, it needs to be done as soon as possible.*[23]

Ackley also noted that "as late as last May, we were told that defense spending was not on the rise." He went on to say that "new surprises" could happen in defense spending, either upward or downward, in 1966.

Within the administration there were divergent views on the amount that should be requested for the defense budget. Secretary of Defense McNamara had informed the president in late 1965 that his review of defense needs indicated expenditures of $61.3 billion for FY 1967, "subject to further downward revision."[24] Subsequently, Califano told the president that he had discussed the defense budget with Undersecretary of Defense Cyrus Vance and with Schultze. Vance favored a $60 billion budget, while indicating expenditures could go as high as $65 billion in 1966. Schultze preferred a defense figure of $57 billion, believing that would permit him to bring in a total budget of $110–111 billion. (This was still within Ackley's tax increase figures.) Schultze also favored going for a large supplemental appropriation in May or June and a tax increase of some sort at that time. House Ways and Means Committee Chairman Wilbur Mills, Califano noted, favored a defense figure of $57 billion, while McNamara strongly favored $60 billion because he was "very concerned about our credibility both in budget terms and in terms of Vietnam if we go for the lower figure."[25]

Fowler and Assistant Secretary of Treasury Stanley Surrey had been dispatched to Little Rock on 22 December to discuss the economic situation with Mills. A few days later a Fowler memorandum to the president reported that Mills believed that FY 1967 civilian expenditures should not exceed those for 1966 and that the full impact of Vietnam expenditures should not be put in the 1967 budget because the people would be "startled" thereby. Mills opposed a general tax increase while being agreeable to such things as speeding up tax collections and retaining some excise taxes that were slated for reduction.[26]

On 27 December Schultze sent the president a memorandum marked "secret" in which he noted the need for an antiinflationary tax increase and proposed a "two-stage fiscal strategy" to secure higher taxes:

I agree with Secretary Fowler . . . that proposing a general tax increase in January would not be wise. At the same time, I am firmly convinced that with defense expenditures in the $60 billion range a general tax increase will eventually be necessary. In these circumstances, a *two-stage fiscal strategy appears to be most appropriate.*

I. *January Budget.*

1. *Estimate defense expenditures at $57 billion in the January budget.* This level of defense expenditures would have to assume that the armed forces return to their pre-Vietnam level by December, 1966.

2. This assumption can be defended on the grounds that no one knows how long hostilities will last;—we don't wish to ask for more appropriations than are absolutely necessary;—we will ask for supplemental funds when and if the situation requires, and will at that time propose the necessary means to finance the additional outlays; this approach was followed both in the second World War and in Korea.

3. Propose in January three *selective* tax measures:
—a graduated withholding plan;
—a further acceleration of corporate income tax payments;
—the restoration for 15 months of the pending reduction in telephone and auto excises.
These three tax changes will slow down the pace of expansion by perhaps $4 billion. *But this will not be enough to eliminate inflationary pressures.*

II. *Defense Budget Amendment*

If the fighting continues in Vietnam, a request for additional defense funds will be necessary in May or June. We don't know the magnitudes but a minimum of $6–8 billion in appropriations and $4–5 billion in expenditures is likely.
The Defense supplemental should be accompanied by a request for an across-the-board tax increase on personal and corporate incomes. It is too early to settle on the magnitude of this increase, but a minimum would probably be $5 billion.[27]

Schultze believed this strategy would help protect Great Society programs against congressional cuts. A major disadvantage would be sharp criticism of the $57 billion defense figure as "phony" and the like. In all, he believed the two-stage strategy offered "the best chance of getting the kind of fiscal policy needed to restrain inflation." It combined political expedience with a realistic view of the defense-spending situation.

Confronted with this varying advice, and acting on the basis of his political judgment, the president decided to go for a FY 1967 administrative budget in January that included total expenditures of $112.8 billion and defense expenditures of $60.5 billion. The "bits-and-pieces" tax program mentioned at the beginning of this section rather than a general tax increase was requested. Although Ackley and Schultze rejoined forces in the spring of 1966 to advocate a general tax increase (and Fowler swung to their viewpoint), the president continued to refuse to follow this part of Schultze's two-stage strategy. Actual defense expenditures for FY 1967 were $70.1 billion; total expenditures ran $127 billion. Inflation gained momentum.

Were the president's advisers misled, as some have contended, concerning the likely level of defense expenditures?[28] Perhaps they were when defense spending first began to accelerate following the decision in mid-1965 to increase the U.S. military commitment to Vietnam. Ackley has stated that his advice to the president from July until October of 1965 was based on "an incomplete or incorrect understanding" of future defense expenditures.[29] By late in the fall, however, that no longer seems the case. By then Johnson's advisers knew that increased spending was great enough to require a tax increase to offset inflationary pressures.

The memorandums quoted above indicate that there was a prevailing notion that the $60 billion defense figure was too low. Concerning the $110 billion and $115 billion budget figures in his December memorandum, Ackley has stated that "we knew damned well that neither of these figures was in the least bit relevant, and the real figure they were talking about—that military program which had been approved—was represented by a substantially larger figure.[30] Also, Schultze's "two-stage strategy" memorandum recognized the economic need for a general tax increase while doubting the political wisdom of seeking it in early 1966. Further evidence that Washington officials were not long misled concerning Vietnam spending estimates is supplied in anecdotal form by Walter Heller, who notes that the Federal Reserve Board in mid-1965 was quite skeptical of the accuracy of Vietnam expenditure estimates, which were purported to be "harmful if swallowed."[31] The magnitude of defense expenditures was simply not something about which knowledgeable Washington officials could long be misled, even should a president desire to do so (as Johnson apparently did). Whether they should have "gone public" with their knowledge is another matter.

Could President Johnson have gotten Congress to increase taxes generally if he had requested this in early 1966? Johnson himself has indicated no in his memoirs.

Early in 1966 I discussed a possible tax increase with my Cabinet officers. I asked for their opinions. Only one Cabinet member, Secretary of Commerce John Connor, spoke in favor of higher taxes. A vote showed the Cabinet to be in overwhelming opposition.

On March 30, 1966, I invited more than 150 leading businessmen to a dinner at the White House. After dinner, I outlined our economic situation and asked them:

How many of you would recommend tomorrow a tax increase to the Congress for the purpose of restraining our economy? Those of you that would, I wish you would raise your right hand.

Not a single hand went up. Not one of those businessmen supported a tax increase to dampen the rising inflation. A few weeks later I met with a group of labor leaders. I posed a similar question. I got a similar answer . . .

> I sounded out the congressional leadership on a tax increase, and their answer was painfully clear. The House leadership reported late in the spring of 1966 that of twenty-five members of the House Ways and Means Committee, the most support I could then expect was four votes. Chairman Mills' vote was not among them. . . .[32]

Joseph Califano recounts a meeting the president had with the joint leadership of Congress and the chairmen and ranking minority members of the Ways and Means and Finance committees. After Ackley outlined in detail the need for a tax increase, the president "spoke heartily" in favor of it. He then asked those present what the chances were of passing it. "I remember Carl Albert saying, 'Mr. President, you will get about 15 votes combined in both houses,' and Jerry Ford saying, 'Mr. President, you won't even get that.'"[33]

On the other hand, a month after Johnson's dinner meeting with the businessmen, Otto Eckstein, who had recently left the CEA, conveyed an insight to the president gained from his discussions with several businessmen: "And why did their friends just sit there when you asked them about tax action at your dinner? . . . They were caught *flat-footed*, with their *tongues tied*. If a candid man-to-man poll had been taken a clear majority would have favored a tax rise."[34] A reporter who was a close observer of the administration later claimed that Johnson offered no suggestion to the businessmen that expenditures would be considerably higher than indicated in the January budget.[35]

Charles Schultze has speculated that Johnson could have gotten a tax increase in early 1966 if he had "wrapped himself in the flag," tied the tax increase to the Vietnam fighting, asked for wage-price controls, and so on. Johnson was not willing to do this, according to Schultze, because he was concerned with fending off the hawks and with holding down the generals who were pressing him to expand involvement in Vietnam.[36] (That, of course, happened later anyway). Also, Schultze believed increasing taxes at this time would have adversely affected the effort to secure more Great Society programs from Congress. Ackley has said that the president never disputed the economic correctness of Ackley's advice that a general tax increase was needed in 1966; however, he did not think it was politically feasible.[37]

Okun provides some additional insight into the president's thinking: "He kept telling us, he was for a tax increase at the earliest possible moment that he thought it conceivably could be taken seriously, that you couldn't sell it on the basis of a forecast, you had to wait for a little bleeding to take place before you volunteered to sew up the wound."[38] Indeed, even in the fall of 1967, when Johnson did seek a general tax increase, there was substantial resistance in Congress because the "facts," as contrasted to the administration's forecast, did not seem to indicate severe economic problems.

The decision not to seek a general tax increase in 1966 can be viewed as the first defeat of the New Economics by the old politics. Had the administration been able to get the tax increase fairly quickly from Congress when it eventually did decide to go for it, and had the increase's impact, when finally achieved, not been offset by the loosening of monetary policy, the "defeat" would not have been especially significant.

Reducing Expenditures to Fight Inflation: 1966

Following the decision not to seek a general tax increase in January, part of the Johnson administration's program to hold down inflationary pressures in the 1966 economy included a strong effort to reduce government expenditures. This effort, which really began before the budget for FY 1967 (1 July 1966–30 June 1967) was sent to Congress in January, extended throughout the 1966 calendar year. It was given increased impetus by the president's special message to the Congress on fiscal policy in September 1966. Responding to the need for additional restraint on the economy, the president proposed a four-part economic program consisting of suspensions of the investment tax credit and accelerated depreciation on industrial buildings, a request that the Federal Reserve Board cooperate with the administration to ease the "inequitable burden of tight money" (this was the time of the famous "credit crunch"), and "strong measures to reduce lower priority federal spending." Noting that he had already directed that lower-priority federal programs be reduced by $1.5 billion in FY 1967, he estimated that an additional $3 billion reduction would be required "in that portion of the 1967 budget under direct presidential control." This would be done by requesting appropriations for federal programs at levels below those authorized by Congress, by withholding appropriations provided above the president's budget recommendations whenever possible, and by reductions or delays in using program appropriations requested in the 1967 budget.[39]

At a news conference on 29 November 1966, President Johnson announced that he had approved "the recommendations of the Cabinet and the agency heads" for a budgetary cutback of $5.3 billion in federal programs (i.e., obligational authority, which permits agencies to commit themselves to the expenditure of funds). This, he said, would permit a reduction of over $3 billion in federal expenditures during the remaining seven months of the 1967 fiscal year. Moreover, he indicated that efforts to further reduce federal expenditures would continue.

In this section, we will discuss how this reduction in appropriations and expenditures was accomplished and what happened to it subsequently. Variation in expenditures, of course, is one of the instruments of discretionary fiscal policy. When it comes to reducing expenditures to stabilize the economy, however, this is far easier to recommend than it is to achieve. Reductions have to be implemented in particular programs, and those officials and private citizens who support a particular program, whether as believers or beneficiaries, are not likely to be enthusiastic about a reduction in its funding. An alternative, although a not very realistic or responsible one, would be an across-the-board (or meat-axe) approach to reduction. Many Republicans and conservative Democrats in Congress in 1966 (and subsequent years) were advocates of this approach, but they were generally unsuccessful in their endeavors, which were concentrated on domestic and Great Society programs.

At this point, a few numbers can provide a context for understanding the budget reduction effort, its scope, and its problems. The administrative budget for FY 1967 sent to Congress in January 1966 called for expenditures of $112.8 billion, with $58.3 billion for defense and $54.5 billion for civilian programs. The budget reduction effort was focused on civilian programs. In June BOB examiners estimated that nondefense expenditures and new obligational authority would run $57 billion and $63.8 billion, respectively, for FY 1967. It was further estimated that $33.5 billion of civilian expenditures were "uncontrollable" on the basis of existing law or past commitments.[40] Thus, only $23.5 billion in expenditures, or about one-fifth of the budget, were readily controllable by the administration; this substantially narrowed its discretion in identifying reduction targets. We turn now to the budget reduction campaign.

In mid-January the president requested an analysis of the programs that would have to be cut to take $2 billion of expenditures out of the budget. On 24 January, Budget Director Schultze had the analysis prepared and sent to the president, noting that "since we have so many fixed commitments, and since the Government is faced with growing workloads in a number of old-line activities, much of the cut would have to come out of the newer, high priority programs." Targets for cuts identified included the poverty program, water-resource construction programs, the National Institutes of

Health, the supersonic transport, some space programs, and financial assistance to public schools and universities.[41]

In March the BOB provided a more detailed analysis of areas where budget cuts could be made. This list differed somewhat from the January list. Since Congress was only in the initial stages of its consideration of the 1967 budget, the possible reductions or reserves identified by the BOB did not take into account possible congressional cuts, which might include items on the executive's list; possible congressional add-ons, which would be good candidates for reductions; the political controversy that might be created; or the legal basis for reduction, it being assumed that any needed statutory authority would be obtained. Moreover, it was noted that many of the reduction possibilities on the current list (e.g., the supersonic transport, higher-education facilities construction, Farmers Home Administration loans) had been on the "B list" in December and the president had decided not to propose them at that time. (The "B list" included agency projects or programs regarded as desirable but which exceeded spending targets.) The interest of the BOB in reducing the budget seemed clearly restrained.[42]

A study undertaken by the attorney general indicated the president had broad authority, more subject to political realities than legal inhibitions, to control the expenditure of funds (including impoundment) to curb inflation. Two statements from the study illustrate this viewpoint. The study opined that "the expenditure of appropriated funds is not a mere ministerial function. It is instead a highly discretionary function requiring the exercise of sound judgement." Also, the study stated that "the faithful execution of appropriation acts requires that they be interpreted and administered in the context of other laws and in accord with the Constitutional powers and responsibilities of the President." Action by President Dwight Eisenhower in the fall of 1957 to stay within the national debt limit by controlling expenditures was cited as an example, as were the impoundments of military funds by Presidents Eisenhower and Truman.[43]

Presidential interest continued to exist and in June the reduction campaign developed momentum. The Bureau of the Budget had combed through the budget and identified a variety of programs where reductions, deferrals, or stretch-outs of expenditures were either "realistic," "realistic but painful," or "unrealistic to consider." The staff calculated that if the reductions in the first two categories were made, the relatively controllable portion of the administrative budget expenditures could be reduced by a billion dollars. Reduction or deferral of construction contract awards for highways, which came out of the highway trust fund, could reduce expenditures another $200 million. Schultze noted that these proposals had been developed entirely within the BOB and did not reflect the views of the various affected agencies. He continued:

> In order to take the actions necessary to reduce budget expenditures along the lines indicated above, it would *not* be sufficient for the President merely to ask Federal agencies to "do their best" in reducing expenditures. Specific program cuts would have to be undertaken, and agreed upon in advance by BOB and the agencies.
> To get such an exercise underway would require a Presidential directive to the agencies (which could be handled either through a formal memorandum or be done orally at a Cabinet meeting). In no event could such an exercise be handled "quietly." Many of the items which would have to be cut relate to particular projects or grant programs whose recipients would quickly become aware of the reduction.[44]

Since most of the appropriations bills were then still before the Congress, there was also a problem of timing in budget reductions. If the president announced a budget cutback before the Congress completed budgetary action, it might react by reducing some programs (e.g., rent supplements and foreign aid) below desirable levels, or requesting that budget reductions be submitted in the form of budget amendments to afford an opportunity for congressional review. To prevent this, Schultze suggested that formal budget reduction action should not be taken until most of the bills had at least gone through the Senate Appropriations Committee. This, however, would not prevent the president from indicating earlier an intention to take action to moderate the increase in expenditures, nor preclude project deferrals which could be done quietly.[45]

Acting on Schultze's advice, the administration scheduled a cabinet meeting on 16 June to deal with the problem of expenditure reduction. The president discussed congressional action and other factors which threatened to cause expenditures to exceed the levels proposed in January, emphasized the need for action to offset the expenditure increases, and called on the departments and agencies to see what could be pared from their budgets. Reduction targets of $2 billion in obligational authority and $1 billion in expenditures were set for the civilian agencies. The budget director was instructed to set a savings target for each agency. He and Joseph Califano were requested to begin meeting weekly with the heads of major spending agencies (like the Departments of Housing and Urban Development; Agriculture; Commerce; Health, Education, and Welfare) and to report to the president on their progress. (A number of other agencies were asked to make reductions but were not involved in the weekly meetings.) The secretary or agency head, or the second in command, were asked to attend the meetings and to be prepared to speak and make decisions for their department or agency.[46]

A letter from the budget director was subsequently sent to each agency involved, providing it with two savings targets—for obligational (or program) authority and for expenditures. The Department of Health, Education, and Welfare (HEW), for instance, was given a program target of $475 million and an expenditure target of $288 million; the Department of the Interior, $155 million and $83 million, respectively; and the Department of Justice, $15 million in each category. In each instance the target represented a very small fraction of the agency's total budget. Thus, the expenditure reduction exercise got underway.

The first meeting of the major-spending agency representatives was held at the White House on 24 June. Joseph Califano opened the meeting by describing the project and its importance because of the economic and Vietnam situations. Presidential interest in expenditure reduction was stressed. Budget Director Schultze then outlined the exercise. The BOB had allocated the president's expenditure objective among the agencies without consulting them in order to get things started quickly. Schultze acknowledged, however, that the agency heads would have to make many of the basic decisions. BOB staff would be available to help in handling the cutbacks.

Each agency was requested to prepare a report consisting of three elements: "(a) preliminary program to reach the target reduction, with that target divided into two priority bands, (b) a statement of the implications of each of the reductions suggested, and (c) a description of the actions necessary and the possible public response to such actions." Priority was to be given to the least sensitive and least controversial expenditure reductions; that is, "agency lists should not be 'loaded' to emphasize the political sensitivity or public outcry that could result from actions against very popular programs." The agencies were asked to have their reports ready within a few days.

The agency officials present were cautious and conditional in their responses to the reduction exercise. Some replied that they would review the "possibilities"; others indicated problems in making reductions. James Webb, director of the National Aeronautics and Space Administration (NASA), said he thought he might be able to do what the president had asked. However, he feared his problems were not understood. He did not know, he explained, how he could "request the apportionment of less funds than he [had] urged on the Congress and still keep (a) his credibility on the Hill and (b) his staff and contractor teams going." In somewhat different fashion, Wilbur Cohen, undersecretary of health, education, and welfare, wanted to be credited with the amounts by which he could reduce new spending legislation currently being considered by Congress. And so it went.[47]

The minutes of the meeting were sent to the president. "As you can see," Califano remarked in his covering memorandum, "it is going to be a long hard road."

Three additional meetings with the agency representatives were held. The second meeting focused on the possibilites for procurement deferrals and stretchouts. Generally the agency representatives thought they could make some small reductions in procurement expenditures (the Commerce Department came up with a figure of $100,000 to $150,000) while discussing various programs or financial commitments which limited their discretion in reducing purchases of supplies and equipment.[48] The third meeting dealt with reductions in agency personnel and overtime payments. Agency representatives discussed the need for overtime payments to meet emergencies, seasonal workloads, and the need to hire additional employees. An employment freeze was undesirable, but some personnel reductions were considered possible. The agencies again emphasized problems and limitations: Secretary Fowler of the Treasury Department indicated that "a freeze on employment would cut the payroll by $10 million; a 50 percent vacancy replacement, in addition, would cut payroll by $35 million. Most of this reduction would be in the Internal Revenue Service where it would delay the master file and reduce enforcement, possibly reducing revenue collections much more than the amounts saved."[49] He did not explain why the Treasury's reduction would have to be concentrated in the Internal Revenue Service.

Fowler, incidentally, was one of the stronger advocates of general expenditure reduction to fight inflation in the administration. A few days after the final agency meeting, he sent the president a memorandum proposing that the president urge Congress either to cut back the budget by an across-the-board percentage reduction sufficient to offset its additions to the budget or to pass a resolution telling the president to reduce nondefense appropriations to a point where the budget would be no larger than when it was presented in January. Schultze, in response, characterized both alternatives as "impractical," the first because add-ons were concentrated in narrow areas of the budget and could not be compensated for by across-the-board action, the second because of the large amount of cutbacks suggested. Schultze thought the president should limit himself to a $1 billion to $2 billion reduction. The president did not act on Fowler's advice.[50]

The fourth and final agency budget meeting was held on 15 July and concerned the implementation of budget cutbacks. Schultze asked the agency representatives to estimate how many of their recommendations could be done quietly and how many would require a government-wide order that would probably have to be public. Wilbur Cohen of HEW, for example, thought that 80 percent of their reductions could be done internally while the remainder would cause "an external storm." A program for carrying out the reductions was then outlined and agreed to. It involved the following elements:

1. *Each agency will proceed to make those deferrals and reductions that it can make* without a Presidential order and without provoking a hornet's nest.

2. Bureau of the Budget (either at agency head level or top staff level or both) will raise any necessary questions directly with the agencies about the agency action programs to achieve the reductions the President directed.
—The agencies should pinpoint *specific actions* (rather than organizational units and general areas) and state the effect or implications of each.

3. *The Bureau will then prepare for the President a paper setting forth each agency's specific program* to meet the President's 1967 reduction goals of $2 billion in program level and $1 billion in expenditures (below the amounts we estimated would be approved by Congress).
—The paper will divide the actions into 2 groups: (a) the least controversial, which are already being effectuated (per 1, above), and (b) those which would require a Presidential (as distinct from an agency head) general order or would raise *major* squawks or political problems.
—The implications of the actions (i.e., effect on program, policy, clientele groups, and the public or political relations) will be set forth; in terms of some representative examples for the least controversial group, but in full detail for the tough items.
—Presidential guidance on these actions will be sought by the Director, and word will be passed to the agencies as needed.

4. Whenever possible and applicable, the reductions should be considered in 2 stages: first, a deferral from the first to the second half of fiscal 1967; second, on the basis of a decision made this fall or winter, a continuation of the deferral to fiscal 1968, a cutback or a moving ahead with the item.[51]

The memorandum concluded by specifying that budget reductions and deferrals "should be *real* rather than bookkeeping gimmicks or gadgets." Moreover, leases were not to be substituted for purchases. Confidentiality and sensitivity were to be observed in the conduct of the expenditure reduction program.

Schultze sent the president a progress report on the budget reduction exercise in August. The results are shown in Table 4. The agencies had already been instructed to proceed with the less controversial reductions, Schultze reported. The more controversial reductions were referred to the president for consideration. Most were subsequently put into effect; some controversial reductions that were not made were the elimination of city mail deliveries on Saturdays and a general program cutback in the Justice Department.

The Troika in its report of 22 August stated that if action on taxes was not scheduled before January 1967, then it was important to take additional action soon on expenditure cutbacks.[52] Expenditures were estimated to be running $12 billion higher than first-of-the-year estimates. To hold expenditures at a reasonable level they recommended action "to hold down nondefense outlays by $2 to $3 billion, beyond the cutbacks already submitted" to the president. Schultze registered a dissent to this recommendation on the grounds that such a cut was not feasible in addition to what had already been done. Many of the increases in the 1967 budget were "uncontrollable, for example, the G.I. bill, pay increases, and interest on the debt. He did not see how other programs could practically be reduced by sufficient amounts to achieve the new reduction target specified (a total cut of $3–$4 billion). Schultze's views did not prevail within the administration, however.

Throughout the summer of 1966 the administration had been wrestling with the problem of devising an economic program to meet the threat of inflation.[53] Activity picked up following the August Troika report, and on 2 September the president and a group of advisers reached agreement on an economic program which the president presented to the Congress on 8 September (outlined at the beginning of this section). The memorandum from his advisers stated in part that the president should "announce that you have

Table 4. *Fiscal Year 1967 Proposed Budget Reduction ($ Millions)*

Degree of Controversy	Program Reduction	Expenditure Reduction
Less Controversial	1,075	667
More Controversial	1,196	722
Total	2,271	1,389

taken and are taking actions to reduce the Fiscal 67 budget by $1.5 billion" and should "instruct Budget Director Schultze to prepare a program for an additional reduction of $2 billion, should this become necessary, with a caveat on programs that help the poor and needy." By 8 September not only was the program necessary, but the president had upped the additional ante to $3 billion.

At a meeting of various department and agency officials on 15 September, the president discussed the importance of the expenditure reduction program, which was comprised of five parts: immediate budget reductions; further budget reductions, which would involve more difficult and sensitive cuts; delay or postponement for the next three or four months of every possible expenditure and contract; a cutback for overtime payments; and holding down 1968 budget requests. A Schultze memorandum to the president prior to the meeting indicated he was having difficulty getting some agencies to cooperate. "It would be helpful to me," he wrote, "if, at some point in your remarks you casually indicated that you wanted *every* program to be examined for possible expenditure cuts, from *space* to agriculture. I am having some trouble with NASA and this reference would help."[54]

Unlike the earlier budget reduction exercise, this second wave of reductions was not accompanied by agency meetings in the White House; rather, it was handled substantially within the BOB, with some consultation with the departments, agencies, and the White House. In late October Schultze sent word to the president: "We are in the process of a *detailed* appropriation-by-appropriation reestimate of the 1967 budget." He noted that there were 1,250 separate appropriation items for perhaps twice that many programs or activities.[55] Out of this activity came a detailed list of possible budget reductions along with their political implications.

To build congressional support, or reduce opposition therefrom, discussions were conducted on the budget cutbacks with thirty-two congressional leaders. Schultze reported that they were pleased to be consulted, mostly agreed that budget reductions were necessary, and sympathized with the problems involved in making reductions. They also conveyed some advice as to how cuts should be handled, namely: (a) new programs should be cut ahead of old and ongoing programs; (b) painful cuts must be shared equally between Congress and the administration; and (c) cuts should be kept in balance across the board. No one was to have a case that his program was cut while others were not cut.[56]

Joe Barr, undersecretary of the treasury, was sent as an emissary to Representative Wilbur Mills, probably the most influential advocate of spending reduction in the Congress and someone whose cooperation was needed on tax legislation. Barr reported that Mills' "only advice was the President should meet his $3 billion target—he was committed and one way or another he should meet it." Mills, said Barr, did not object to any of the proposed cuts, he just kept insisting that the $3 billion target be met.[57]

Congressional action on the 1967 budget requests had not made the administration's task any easier. Notwithstanding appeals from the president at White House meetings and through the media to be careful in adding to the budget, congressional add-ons to the budget provided the basis for an additional $2.5 billion in expenditures in FY 1967.[58] As is well known, there is often a divergence between congressional rhetoric and action on budgetary matters.

The results of the overall expenditure reduction campaign were announced by the president at an Austin press conference on 29 November, a few weeks after the general elections.[59] He stated that he had approved "the recommendations of the Cabinet and the agency heads for a fiscal 1967 budgetary cutback of $5 billion 300 million in Federal programs. . . . With this approved reduction, we then plan to achieve a $3 billion plus cut in Federal spending for the next 7 months of this fiscal year." In response to a reporter's question he provided some examples of the reductions. It is, however, difficult to determine from the president's statement exactly what was reduced. Much of the reduction took the form of delays, deferrals, and stretchouts of expenditures rather than of outright terminations. Some of the savings were questionable, for example the $25 million Department of Labor reduction involved funds not spent for government employees and veterans' unemployment compensation because of a lack of need. Also, $800 million of program reduction came from the administration's refusal to accede to unwanted congressional increases in program authorizations. Johnson did not lack skill in the art of budget gimmickry.

Table 5. *Fiscal Year 1967 Budget Reductions: A Partial View (\$ Millions)*

Agency	Program Reduction	Expenditure Reduction
Highway construction	1,100	—
Housing and Urban Development	987	546
Health, Education, and Welfare	530	275
Corps of Engineers	436	60
Department of Agriculture	400	350
Department of Interior	206	110
General Services Administration	100	30
Department of Commerce	65	12
Federal Aviation Agency	35	—
Small Business Administration	50	30
Department of Labor	25	25
Department of Treasury	20	11
Veterans Administration	15	7
National Aeronautics and Space Administration	60	30
Office of Economic Opportunity	32	100

Source: *Public Papers of the Presidents of the United States: Lyndon B. Johnson, 1966*, Vol. II (Washington D.C.: Government Printing Office, 1967), p. 1406.

This action did not fully sate the president's appetite for budget reduction. On 8 December, the beleaguered Schultze wrote that "on the basis of our conversation over the past week, I have reviewed the 1967 budget to see where an *additional* \$1 billion in spending could be cut." To accomplish this, he told the president, cuts would have to be made quickly and this would mean cutting many Great Society and politically popular programs. "I don't believe these cuts are feasible" was his conclusion.[60] This appears to have marked the end of the FY 1967 budget reduction exercise.

The concern of the president's economic advisers shifted in late 1966 from inflation to a possible economic slowdown in the first part of 1967. On the basis of its December analysis of the economic situation, the Troika advised: "No additional net restraint on demand is needed, now or in the near future. Indeed, for the coming months we need new stimulus, both from fiscal and monetary policy, to minimize the risk of a dangerous stall." The possible need to release some of the funds earlier "impounded" was noted.[61]

In February 1967, the administration began to release some of the appropriations withheld. By the end of the 1967 fiscal year (June 30), or early in the next fiscal year, most of the funds previously deferred or withheld had been released. One explanation for this action was provided by a presidential statement in March 1967, in which the release of some deferred funds for highways, low-cost housing, flood control, and other purposes was announced:

> These programs provide important benefits for the American people. Otherwise, I would not have proposed, and the Congress would not have enacted them. The deferrals and reductions undertaken last fall were put into effect as a necessary means of reducing the overheating which then threatened the American economy—not because the programs themselves were in a sense undesirable.
>
> The deferral of Federal contracts and the other economic measures adopted last fall have had the desired effect. Inflationary pressures have subsided. As a consequence it has been possible, in a careful and orderly manner to release some of the funds which had been deferred.[62]

Thus, the funds now could be used for their authorized purposes.

Second, members of Congress, agency officials, and others were interested in securing the release of funds for favored programs, from a few hundred thousand dollars for fire ant eradication to hundreds of millions of dollars for highway construction.[63] The release of the funds referred to above was not unrelated to a meeting held at the White House a few days earlier between administration officials, congressional leaders, and committee chairmen. The topic: discussion of priorities and timing in the release of cutback funds. Given the president's need for congressional support for a variety of purposes in 1967, and the view that release of the funds was not only noninflationary, but needed to stimulate the economy, he could well afford to be responsive to their interests.

Efforts at expenditure reduction continued through the remainder of the Johnson administration. In August 1967, Budget Director Schultze testified before the House Ways and Means Committee in support of the administration's tax bill. There he stated that the administration was currently making efforts to achieve reductions and deferrals in the FY 1968 budget in order to offset the increase in "uncontrollable" programs and the release of funds withheld in the 1967 budget.[64] There is some irony in that.

Suspending the Investment Tax Credit, 1966.

The Kennedy administration in 1962 had secured the adoption of a 7 percent tax credit for investments in equipment and machinery to encourage the modernization and expansion of productive facilities. Although its enactment had been opposed by most business groups, the business community soon learned to like the investment credit and became firmly attached to it.

In the spring of 1966 the Council of Economic Advisers, Budget Director Schultze, and Chairman Martin of the Federal Reserve Board all advised the president of the need for a general tax increase to restrain the economy.[65] This was a continuation of the effort begun in late 1965 (see the discussion below of the 1968 tax surcharge). Fowler was apparently not as strongly in favor of an increase, while McNamara counseled delay. The council also favored suspension of the investment tax credit as a "rifle shot technique" to postpone investment demand to a time when it would be more needed.

Indecision prevailed, and for a time no policy action was taken. However, several of the president's advisers recommended in May that a number of economic studies should be undertaken to help provide the president with information needed to make a decision. These included:

1. Program for future decision making designed to reduce our non-Vietnam budget expenditures—Bureau of the Budget.

2. A memorandum from the Secretary of Defense giving his best judgment on the magnitude and time pattern of FY 1967 defense expenditures and orders for purposes of *internal* planning and decision making.

3. An analysis of outlook for business fixed investment, housing, consumer spending, state and local government expenditures in the light of April and May developments—together with the materials in items 1 and 2 this would constitute a supplement to the Troika memorandum of April 8.

4. An analysis of outlook for financial institutions assuming tax increase and no tax increase. Joint study by Troika plus Federal Reserve Board and Federal Home Loan Bank Board.

5. Study by Federal Reserve Board of implication for monetary policy assuming tax increase and no tax increase.

6. Balance of payments outlook and its bearing on tax increase issue.

7. Economic consequences of tax increase—short-term and long-term.

8. Various alternatives for increasing taxes.

9. Outlook for prices and voluntary restraint on wage-price decisions assuming tax increase and no tax increase.

10. Combinations of fiscal, monetary and debt management policies assuming tax increase and no tax increase.[66]

The president approved the recommendation.

The need for and form of a tax increase were debated within the administration during the spring and summer of 1966. By the middle of August, several of the president's major advisers—Schultze, Ackley, Fowler, Walter Heller, and Kermit Gordon—were agreed on the need for a general tax increase. All except Fowler also favored suspension of the investment tax credit and accelerated depreciation on industrial structures. Fowler opposed the suspension of the investment tax credit because, as Ackley put it, he seemed to feel "a sort of constitutional commitment" to the business community about it and also believed it should be a permanent tax provision.[67] The president had become convinced suspension was necessary to slow down excessive business investment.

On 22 August, Ackley, McNamara, and Califano were scheduled to attend a meeting in Cambridge with a group of economists from MIT and Harvard.[68] This group (most of whom had some previous involvement with the administration) was meeting at the instigation of the administration to develop recommendations for a 1967 tax program. At the president's suggestion, Fowler was taken along so that he could be "educated" on the need for suspension of the investment tax credit (it was known that this would be one of the group's recommendations). Johnson wanted Fowler to understand that suspension of the tax credit was "a considered decision" and that "a lot of good economic minds thought it was a good decision."[69] Johnson was aware that if Fowler was really in favor of the suspension he would work harder on its enactment and implementation. We will have more to say on implementation subsequently.

A memorandum from Ackley to Califano on 29 August, which was sent on to the president, indicated that an "informal group" of advisers favored sending an "immediate and comprehensive new economic program" to the Congress. This included a corporate tax increase (the president apparently had already ruled out a personal income tax increase), suspension of the investment tax credit and accelerated depreciation (Fowler was still opposed), holding down of nondefense spending, and efforts to strengthen the wage-price guidelines.[70] This memorandum and other materials were discussed at White House meetings during the next two days. The proposal for a

MEMORANDUM

BES
FI 11
F I 1-2
FG 110
FG 115
September 2, 1966 FG140
Friday, 2:20 p.m. FG11-1
FG 11-3
FG 135
FG 11-6
FIS

THE WHITE HOUSE

WASHINGTON

FOR THE PRESIDENT

FROM   Joe Fowler, Bob McNamara, Nick Katzenbach, Larry
O'Brien, Charlie Schultze, Gardner Ackley, Dave
Ginsburg, Joe Califano

We are now in agreement on the following economic package:

1. A statement of your intention to ask, at an appropriate
time in the future, for whatever tax measures are necessary to
raise the money to cover add-ons to the budget by Congressional
action or by the Generals in Vietnam.

2. Announce that you have taken and are taking actions to
reduce the Fiscal 67 budget by $1.5 billion.

3. Instruct Budget Director Schultze to prepare a program
for an additional reduction of $2 billion, should this become neces-
sary, with a caveat on programs that help the poor and needy.

4. Suspend temporarily the investment credit for an
appropriate fixed period of time, unless sooner terminated by
a Presidential finding that the national defense effort no longer
requires the suspension.

5. Suspend the accelerated depreciation law for buildings
for the same period of time.

6. Announce that Federal agency and participation certificate
paper will not be sold so as to add new capital requirements to the
private market for the remainder of Calendar 66, unless market
conditions improve sufficiently to warrant it.

Figure 1. *Memorandum of Agreement: The 1966 Tax Proposal*

corporate tax increase was dropped in favor of a statement that the president should ask "at an appropriate time in the future, for whatever tax measures are necessary to raise the money to cover add-ons to your budget by congressional action or by the Generals in Viet Nam."[71] The final economic package agreed upon by the president and his advisers included suspension of the investment tax credit and accelerated depreciation, expenditure reduction, and a possible future tax increase (see Figure 1).

According to Ackley this package was the product of negotiations between Johnson, the CEA, and the Troika, and was the most they could get from him in the way of final action. The signatory group was more of a "ratifying" than a decisionmaking body. The signed memorandum, which was written by Califano after the fact, was designed to protect the president from "betrayal," that is, from one or more of his advisers subsequently opposing something in the agreed-upon package.[72]

The suspension of the investment tax credit recommended to the Congress and readily enacted into law in October 1966 was not a simple either-or sort of decision; rather, it required implementary rules: this is why the wholehearted support of Fowler and the Treasury Department was needed. As enacted, the suspension did not apply to investments of less than $20,000 or the purchase of air- and water-pollution control facilities. It applied to equipment ordered as well as received during the suspension period (October 1966 through December 1967), but not to equipment placed on binding order prior to the suspension.[73] The Treasury bore the major responsibility for drafting the suspension legislation, presenting it to the Congress, and supporting its enactment. The exemptions in the suspension legislation were added by the House or Senate and agreed to in Conference Committee. How did the exemptions come about? Okun provides an explanation that focuses on the role of the Treasury Department:

The real power of the Treasury, of course, lies in the fact that it manages most of the legislation in nuts and bolts form to certainly implement the revenue side of the budget. You can fight like hell about whether you want the line on equipment drawn here or there with the Treasury, and then they come back and say, "Well, we followed the party line, but in this conference committee we just couldn't sell it." There was always a tendency to find that the initial position of the Treasury was more saleable to the Congress than any other position, and you have every reason to suspect that they were using their power in this nuts and bolts kind of negotiation on the marking up and amending of legislation to try to push their own preferences.[74]

A few months later, in March 1967, the administration recommended reinstitution of the investment tax credit and accelerated depreciation to offset a slowdown in the economy. Congress passed the necessary legislation in late May.

These actions on the investment credit made sense from the administration's perspective, given its economic forecasts, and they represent part of its effort to fine-tune the economy. They were not without political and other costs, however. According to Joseph Barr, Russell Long, the chairman of the Senate Finance Committee, and Wilbur Mills were "really very upset" by them, and thought they indicated the "lousy" quality of the administration's economic forecasting. "So when we came up with our proposal in the fall of '67 for a big heavy increase in the surtax, they were very skeptical as to whether or not our forecasts were correct."[75] This was an important but by no means the only problem the administration had to contend with in seeking enactment of the surtax.

Improving the Fiscal-Policy Process

Those involved in the development and administration of public policies will by experience become aware of various problems—inadequate operating authority, cumbersome administrative arrangements, insufficient or inadequate data and information on which to base decisions, and so on. A matter of continuing concern for those involved in fiscal-policy management during the Johnson administration was the need for better data and information with which to make fiscal-policy decisions, especially given the activist orientation of the administration.

Two efforts—one successful, the other really not—to improve the informational bases for fiscal decisions will be treated in this section. The successful effort was the replacing of the administrative budget with a unified budget in the budgetary process in 1967. The unsuccessful effort (although it is not clear from the documentary record how much action there actually was) involved the proposal to establish a national data center. Neither idea received much attention, whether in the form of interest, support, or opposition, but the budget reform succeeded because the president became committed to it. The national data center lacked the strong advocates ("change agents" in the jargon of modern public administration) necessary to bring it into existence. Proposals can falter from lack of support, even in the absence of strong opposition.

Budget Reform

Until 1968, three different budget formats were used for various purposes. The one most referred to was the *administrative budget,* which was presented annually by the president to the Congress for its consideration. This budget excluded all government trust funds (e.g., for social security and highway construction), which by the late 1960s involved tens of billions of dollars in revenues and outlays. Another was the *national income accounts* (NIA) *budget,* which handled government receipts and expenditures on the same basis as did private businesses and individuals. These data were used for computing GNP and national income statistics. The national income accounts budget included trust fund operations but excluded government lending programs. It was the most useful of the formats for measuring the economic impact of the government's taxation and expenditure programs. Third was the *consolidated cash budget,* which included all of the government's cash transactions, including lending operations. This was viewed by the Bureau of the Budget as the best basis for making decisions on federal programs other than concerning their economic impact.

In a November 1966 memorandum to the president, Charles Schultze noted that he and Henry Fowler had recently discussed the national income accounts budget with the president. He then went on to argue in its favor, saying tht it was most useful for economic policymaking and that the administrative budget was "misleading as a guide to fiscal policy."[76] He acknowledged the need for a campaign to win acceptance of the NIA budget. The president proved receptive to the recommendation for budget reform.

In his budget message to the Congress in January 1967, President Johnson used the NIA budget in explaining the economic impact of the proposed budget for FY 1968 (1 July 1967–30 June 1968). Noting that "some of our traditional budget concepts do not adequately portray the Federal Government's activities," he went on to state:

> For many years—under many Administrations—particular aspects of the overall budget presentation, or the treatment of individual accounts, have been questioned on one ground or another.
>
> In the light of these facts, I believe a thorough and objective review of budgetary concepts is warranted. I therefore intend to

seek advice on this subject from a bipartisan group of informed individuals with a background in budgetary matters. It is my hope that this group can undertake a thorough review of the budget and recommend an approach to budgetary presentation which will assist both public and congressional understanding of this vital document.[77]

In March, Johnson announced the appointment of a presidential Commission on Budget Concepts. Chaired by David M. Kennedy, who later became secretary of the treasury in the Nixon administration, its sixteen members included members of Congress, administration officials, university economists, and businessmen.[78] A variety of former and present public officials, scholars, research organizations, and others provided the commission with information and advice. The commission held fairly extensive deliberations and was unanimous on most of its recommendations. The most time-consuming topic considered by the commission, eventually decided in the affirmative, was whether to include loan programs in the budget.

In its report, which was released in October 1967, the commission recommended that "a unified summary budget statement be used to replace the present three or more competing concepts that are both confusing to the public and the Congress and deficient in certain essential respects."[79] The unified budget was to include information on appropriations; receipts, expenditures, and lending; means of financing; and national loans and securities outstanding. All federal programs were to be included in it, including loan programs and trust funds. A variety of other recommendations were also made. The commission obviously believed that the unified budget would facilitate sound government decisionmaking on both programmatic matters and fiscal policy. Almost all of the commission's recommendations were put into effect by the Johnson administration. As a consequence, the national budget is now a much better document for use in fiscal-policy formation.

The budget for FY 1969 sent by the president to the Congress was a unified budget. In the view of the administration, there were four major components to this new budget concept: First, it was comprehensive, including both federal funds and trust funds; second, lending programs were separated from spending programs within the total of federal outlays, because lending programs were less direct in their effects on income and output in the economy; third, receipts for government business-type activities were treated as offsets against expenditures by the agency or function to which they related; and fourth, more prominence was given to actions requested of the Congress, including appropriations and tax or other actions of a fiscal-policy character.[80]

There appears to have been little pressure on President Johnson, at least from outside the administration, to undertake budgetary reform. Why then did he? One explanation is provided by a White House staff official:

> The Commission on Budget Concepts was created just because the public numbers were such an unrealistic representation to the American people. This was an interesting thing that Johnson did. There was no pressure to change the budget concepts. We would get nothing out of it. It made our budget $200 billion rather than $150 billion. Johnson just thought it was good for American government. To do something like this you needed a President who really understood the budget and appropriations, not someone who had been a military leader like Eisenhower. Johnson loved and understood the budget.[81]

It has also been suggested that Johnson found the unified budget attractive because the trust fund surpluses, when included in it, somewhat reduced the size of the overall budget deficit (from what it would have been under the old administrative budget). Moreover, Johnson had generally committed himself to accepting the recommendations of the commission.[82]

Improving the Data Supply

The collection of statistical data during the Johnson years was handled by a score of federal bureaus—among others, the Census Bureau, Federal Reserve Board, Office of Business Economics, Office of Emergency Planning, Business and Defense Services Administration, and the Bureau of Labor Statistics. Coordination of all this activity was the responsibility of the Office of Statistical Standards in the Bureau of the Budget, which was also authorized to seek to improve the collection and storage of statistical data. It had not, however, proved fully adequate to its task.

The CEA was constantly concerned with improving the supply of economic data. In a 1967 statement it noted that while improvements in the quality of statistical data during the past decade had been made, problems did remain, including large volumes of data that were not fully comparable. Problems involved in the measurement of productivity and unit labor costs were cited as illustrative:

These statistics are necessarily derived from statistics on employment, man-hours, employee compensation, and output. Currently, these series, in turn are obtained from different samples and different reporting units and are compiled by different agencies, using varying statistical techniques and even varying definitions. Additional problems of comparability arise because measures of productivity and unit labor costs need to be made analytically in combination with information on capacity utilization, prices and investment.[83]

Problems of this sort were the consequence of decentralized statistical systems set up over time to meet the varying needs of different agencies.

The case for better data was ably presented by the Presidential Task Force on the Quality of Economic Data in its 1968 report. First, as the concerns of economic policymakers had shifted from merely limiting the severity of booms and recessions to preventing "wide swings from a path of balanced growth," more detailed and accurate data were necessary to guide policy efforts. Second, because the economy was operating at close to the full-employment level, fine measurements of resource capacity utilization and tightness in labor markets were necessary. These had been less needed when the economy was generally characterized by slack. Third, structural changes had occurred in the economy. The service and trade sectors had expanded, but knowledge of their financial and investment activities had not kept pace. Fourth, the public's interest in the government's economic performance had soared. Thus "the occasional glaring failure of our statistical information gets wide public attention and can impair confidence in our economic policies as well as our statistical agencies." An example was the wide disparity between advance reports and "final estimates" on monthly retail sales. Half of the time in recent months the advance reports had indicated changes in retail sales in the wrong direction.[84] The task force indicated that there was a need for additional data on such items as inventories, retail sales, actual business transaction prices (as contrasted to list prices), construction prices and activity, and the competitiveness of U.S. prices in international markets.

One avenue for improving data quality and collection was suggested by Gardner Ackley—namely, more money. Administration experts, he said, were aware of the data weak spots and had well-defined priorities for improvement. The coordination of structural programs was adequately handled by the Bureau of the Budget. The real problem was that the appropriations committees in Congress were "stingy in funding statistical programs." In 1967 the government was spending $85 million on regular economic statistics programs. The expenditure of another $20 million would, in Ackley's opinion, strengthen many weak spots and fill many of the gaps in the government's statistical programs.

A more sweeping and spectacular reform, first proposed by the Bureau of the Budget internal task force, was the establishment of a national data center. The Heineman Commission, which was set up in 1966 to study the organization of the executive branch, recommended in its final report on organization for economic policy that immediate action to create a National Statistical Data Center in the Department of Commerce be taken.[85] To this end all responsibility for the government-wide coordination and unification of statistical data would be transferred from the Bureau of the Budget to the Department of Commerce. The secretary of commerce would be given responsibility for developing plans to reconcile data series and would be directed "to publish an annual report on the availability and uses of various government data series, and on progress toward integration and more accessible storage of series for wider use within the government and by the interested public." Transfer of the data collection activities of the Bureau of Labor Statistics to the Commerce Department was also advocated. The commission thought this might contribute to a broader consolidation of the Departments of Commerce and Labor into a more broad-gauged Department of Economic Affairs. (The president had proposed merger of the two departments in January 1967, but this proposal had been abandoned because of strong opposition from the bureaucracy and organized labor.) We should note in passing that the Heineman Commission thought that the proposed Department of Economic Affairs could become an effective major participant in economic-policy development and administration, because of the independence from special interests and the analytical capacity it would have, and so urged the president to keep the proposal alive until it was politically realizable.

Improvement of the government's economic statistics was also a concern of the Joint Economic Committee in Congress. In testimony before one of its subcommittees, Arthur Okun presented a rationale for a national data center:

> It would establish someone whose job was to offer statistical services. This is a limitation that we find today in making requests to other agencies for the kind of data we want. We know we can get what we want from them, we know they will try to help us,

but we know we are asking them to try to do something which is a diversion from their main task and a new and added burden on them. If we had a statistical service center or a national data center, we would have a group which is enthusiastically ready, able, and willing to meet our needs. That would be their job and they would welcome our requests as part of their main activity.[86]

He also thought the data center should be able to develop strong ties with private research organizations, which were an important source of economic data.

The Johnson administration ended without the establishment of the data center. Substantial opposition to the concept of a national data center developed because of concern that it might lead to intrusions on privacy. Those who saw a need for a data center to support economic-policy development were unable, whether because of the lack of intense interest, the pressure of other concerns, or sheer inertia, to overcome this opposition. Unlike budgetary reform, the documentary record does not indicate much presidential interest in improved data collection in the form of a data center or anything else.

Concluding Comments

President Johnson was actively involved in the strategic management of fiscal-policy development during his administration. Not only did he set goals and priorities, he was also deeply immersed in the actual shaping of policy proposals, calling for information, initiating action, exerting pressure for consensus among his advisers, and making decisions. The process of policy development reflected his style, the substantive outcomes reflected his preferences (for better or worse, one might add). The need for consent emerges as an important factor constraining presidential leadership, and reflects the limited legal authority of the president in the fiscal arena. Control of most fiscal-policy actions ultimately rests with Congress.

The Troika, which was inherited from the Kennedy administration, was the primary mechanism used by the Johnson administration to generate both technical information and fiscal-policy advice and alternatives. Informally arranged, with no official basis, the Troika provided structure, continuity, and coordination in the development of fiscal-policy proposals. Although some policy disagreements did exist among the principals on the Troika, these proved neither insoluble nor disruptive. It is noteworthy that almost all of the Troika's forecasts and policy recommendations were agreed to, through bargaining, by all three principals. This clearly eased the president's decisionmaking task by eliminating the need for him to resolve conflicts among his advisers or to choose from among divergent policy proposals (a problem that appears to plague the Reagan administration). He still, however, faced the important tasks of appraising the feasibility of the Troika proposals and deciding whether they were likely to secure the needed political consent—whether from within the administration, Congress, or the nation.

Other advisers, from within and outside the government, were used by the president, either individually or as members of groups, to help him assess the utility of Troika proposals, to appraise their political feasibility, and to develop strategies for securing their approval. Advisers in this category were selected more because of presidential confidence in them and their abilities than because of their formal positions.

The implementation of fiscal-policy decisions showed much variation. Sometimes the activities involved were relatively routine and noncontroversial, as in developing the administrative regulations necessary to put the suspension of the investment tax credit into effect. This was handled by the Treasury Department and presidential involvement was minimal. In contrast, implementation of the 1966 expenditure cutback was a complex, conflictual, and lengthy process. Many agencies and officials were involved, mainly without enthusiasm. Central direction of the cutback effort by officials from the Executive Office of the President was required to secure spending reductions, which had to be made with one eye on their programmatic effects and the other on their possible political consequences. Members of Congress became involved because the reductions affected their constituents, their pet programs, or both. The expenditure reduction effort was initiated by the president, involved continual interest and supervision from him, and succeeded only because of his strong interest and support.

Fiscal-policy management was hampered during the Johnson years by the lack of adequate economic data. Consequently, some efforts were made to improve the quantity and quality of available economic data. These seemed likely to win ready general support, but such was not the case. The shift to the unified budget succeeded because of firm, continuing presidential interest and support. In comparison, the creation of a national data center lacked a strong advocate (there is no evidence of presidential interest) and was unable to stir sustained interest, either within the executive branch or Congress. It consequently failed to win approval.

In all, the fiscal-policy development process was well managed by the Johnson administration. Although at the presidential level it is not possible to distinguish easily between management and policy matters, the fiscal-policy problems of the administration are attributable more to incorrect policy decisions than to management failures. Managerial practices here, on the whole, provided the president with adequate and timely economic data, advice, and fiscal-policy alternatives. Good management processes can help protect against bad policy decisions; they cannot ensure that all policy decisions will be substantively correct. The Johnson experience demonstrates this.

It can be contended that decisions on when to request tax increases from Congress are management decisions because they involve the "management of timing." In our view, however, much more is involved in a request for a tax increase than simply the issue of timing. Thus, President Johnson's decision in early 1966 not to seek a general tax increase (which many cite as a mistake), but rather to rely on various other macroeconomic actions was essentially a policy decision. It directly and importantly affected the nature and content of policy and clearly went beyond the management of macroeconomic institutions.

4. The Management of Monetary Policy

Monetary policy is concerned with controlling the supply of money and credit to achieve the goals of national economic policy. In the United States, authority over monetary policy is vested in the Federal Reserve System, the central bank established by Congress in 1913. The Federal Reserve exercises control over the supply of money and credit through the application of three major policy instruments: changes in member bank reserve requirements, open-market operations, and discount policy.

Since monetary and fiscal policy are functionally interdependent, the president must develop mechanisms for coordinating their formulation and implementation. In the Johnson administration, the formal coordinating mechanism employed was the Quadriad, whose members consisted of the Troika, described in the previous chapter, and the chairman of the Federal Reserve Board. Numerous informal methods of coordination also were used.

Since the Federal Reserve System is an independent agency of Congress, the president must use his powers of persuasion to ensure that the monetary policy being pursued by the Federal Reserve is consistent with the administration's macroeconomic objectives and policies. In addition to the symbolic power of his office, a president also may use his power of appointment of the members, chairman, and vice chairman of the Federal Reserve Board to influence the attitude of the board toward cooperation with the administration.

This chapter begins by describing the structure of the Federal Reserve System and examining the practical significance of its structural independence from the administration. This is followed by a review of the coordination efforts made during the Johnson years and President Johnson's use of his power to make appointments to the board. To illustrate the problem of coordination, a case study of the 1965 discount rate decision is presented. Finally, the issue of reform of the Federal Reserve structure is considered.

The Structure of the Federal Reserve System

The statutory organization of the Federal Reserve System is characterized both by formal decentralization and by a unique blending of public and private authority.[1] The authors of the congressional enabling legislation deliberately sought to diffuse power within the Federal Reserve System over a broad base—geographically, between the public and private sectors, and even within government—so that no one person, group, or sector, either inside or outside of government, could exert sufficient leverage to dominate the determination of monetary policy.[2]

The Federal Reserve Board of Governors consists of seven members appointed by the president with the advice and consent of the Senate. Each member is appointed for a nonrenewable term of fourteen years, with one term expiring in January of each even-numbered year.

The chairman of the board is selected from among the seven members by the president and appointed for a four-year term. The term, however, is not concurrent with the presidential term, so an incoming president might have to serve most of his first term in office with a chairman appointed by his predecessor.

The Federal Reserve District Banks are dispersed across the nation in twelve geographic districts. Each bank is privately owned by the member commercial banks in its district. The profits accruing to ownership, however, are limited by law to a six percent annual dividend on paid-in capital stock. (The earnings largely come from interest income on the district banks' large holdings of U.S. government securities.) The member bank stockholders elect six of the nine directors of their district bank, and the remaining three are appointed by the Board of Governors. These nine directors, in turn, choose the president of their district bank, subject to the approval of the Board of Governors.

Statutory authority for the execution of monetary policy is similarly dispersed, even with respect to the exercise of any single one of the instruments available. Member bank reserve requirements are set by the Board of Governors within specific and rather narrow limits established by Congress. Open-market operations, that is, the purchase and sale of financial instruments, typically short-term U.S. government obligations, are controlled by the Federal Open Market Committee (FOMC), which consists of the seven members of the Board of Governors plus five voting members drawn from the twelve Federal Reserve District Bank presidents. Discount rate changes, that is, changes in the cost to member banks of borrowing from the Federal Reserve, usually are initiated by the directors of the Federal

Reserve District Banks, but are subject to "review and determination" by the Board of Governors.

In practice, however, there is a high degree of centralization within the Federal Reserve System in the application of the three control instruments. The Board of Governors plays the central role in formulating and implementing monetary policy. Sherman Maisel, who spent nine years as a member of the Board of Governors (1965–73), estimates the relative influence on monetary policy of the various actors within the Federal Reserve System to be as follows: chairman—45 percent; staff of the Board of Governors and the FMOC— 25 percent; the other members of the Board of Governors—20 percent; and the Federal Reserve District Banks—10 percent.[3]

When the Federal Reserve was created, its principal functions were viewed as supplying currency when needed, clearing checks, and providing a discount mechanism for the convenience of member banks. There was no conception of monetary policy as an active contracyclical force. Open-market operations were unknown and reserve requirements were fixed by law, with no flexibility permitted.

In time, though, aided by the Banking Acts of 1933 and 1935, the Federal Reserve began a transformation from a passive service agency to an active regulatory agency charged with implementing an important share of national economic policy. This shift in function was accompanied by a rise in the power of the centralized Board of Governors and a corresponding decline in the role of the regional Federal Reserve District Banks and their "owners," the commercial banks.

Without question, the dominant figure in the Federal Reserve System is the chairman of the Board of Governors. The chairman is by far the most visible member of the board, the most influential member of the FOMC, and is generally regarded, by Congress and the general public, as *the* spokesman for the Federal Reserve. As advisor to the president, negotiator with Congress, and chief administrator of the Federal Reserve System, with influence over all aspects of monetary policy in his capacity as chairman of the board and the FOMC, the chairman is in practice the embodiment of the central bank in the United States. The other six members of the Board of Governors also exercise a much more substantial amount of authority over monetary policy than is indicated in the formal structure of the Federal Reserve System.

The staff of the Board of Governors and the FOMC are almost all professional economists. They serve as a major link between the Federal Reserve and the economics profession, and they help shape the technical character of the board and FOMC deliberations.

Besides the chairman, other members, and staff of the Board of

Governors, the only other body playing a major role in monetary policymaking is the FOMC. It is through their periodic participation in the FOMC that the presidents of the twelve Federal Reserve District Banks have their primary influence on monetary policy. Out of the twelve members of the FOMC, a majority of seven are members of the Board of Governors. Four of the other five members are chosen on a rotating basis from among eleven of the district bank presidents. The remaining member is the president of the Federal Reserve Bank of New York, who is a permanent member of the FOMC.

While statutory authority for the FOMC is confined to the direction of open-market operations, in recent years the practice of bringing all policy matters under review at FOMC meetings has developed. Although only five of the district bank presidents are entitled to vote at any one time, all twelve attend every meeting and participate in the deliberations. While potential changes in reserve requirements and the discount rate are discussed in FOMC meetings, the Board of Governors retains ultimate authority over their determination.[4]

While the FOMC decides on the appropriate open-market policy for the coming period, the execution of this policy is in the hands of the Federal Reserve's manager of the Open Market Account. The manager, with a staff of about eighty, operates the Open Market Desk at the Federal Reserve Bank of New York. A similar staff is also engaged in foreign-currency operations for the FOMC.

The FOMC instructions contained in the policy directives adopted at each meeting are generally couched in rather broad language, for example, conduct open-market operations so as to attain "somewhat firmer conditions." Thus, the account manager has to translate this rather imprecise language into daily transactions, namely, purchases and sales of financial instruments. In the process, the manager can exercise a modest amount of discretion and personal interpretation.[5]

Independence of the Federal Reserve

Given the central role of the Board of Governors and its chairman in the formulation and implementation of monetary policy, the structural independence of the Federal Reserve both from Congress and the administration is a matter of continuing concern.[6]

Representative Patman Raises the Issue

Shortly after President Johnson assumed office, Representative Wright Patman (Dem. Texas) raised with him the issue of the independence of the Federal Reserve System. In a speech to the United

States Chamber of Commerce on 27 April 1964, the president had referred to the Federal Reserve as "a very non-partisan organization and a very sound organization."[7] The following day, the president had spoken of the "independent Federal Reserve."

Not surprisingly, perhaps, press accounts of the president's comments drew the attention of Representative Patman, a longtime critic of the Federal Reserve. Writing to the president on 4 May 1964, Patman tactfully indicated that he was deeply disturbed by the president's comments: "If such statements have been reported correctly, it would appear that you favor a completely independent Federal Reserve."[8] Referring to hearings under way before the Subcommittee on Economic Stabilization of the Joint Economic Committee, which he chaired, Patman stated, "I had hoped that you would wait until all our testimony is available before taking a stand on this very, very important issue. . . ." He requested a meeting with the president to discuss this "vital subject" and, in words calculated to evoke the populist sentiments deeply ingrained in the Texas roots which he and the president shared, observed in closing that "it would be just as reasonable to make the goose the guardian of shell corn as to make New York bankers the guardian of the peoples' interests on interest rates."

A month later, Representative Patman again expressed his concern about the Federal Reserve to President Johnson, noting, "Time and time again they have defied presidents and the executive branch, even under Herbert Hoover, who called them 'a weak reed to lean on.'"[9] In the meantime, the president had asked Walter Jenkins, special White House assistant, to obtain the views of Robert Anderson, secretary of the treasury under President Eisenhower, on Patman's charges about the Federal Reserve.[10]

Anderson subsequently submitted to the president an eight-page memorandum in which he concluded, "The Federal Reserve is not now, nor has it ever been, independent of Government. . . . Correctly used, the term independence relates to the System's independence *within* Government."[11] The language employed by Anderson was similar to that used by Walter Heller, chairman of the Council of Economic Advisers (CEA), when he commented in an earlier memorandum to President Johnson that the Federal Reserve "is properly described as 'independent' *in* but not independent *of* the Administration."[12]

However, the difference in the two characterizations is far more than semantic. Independence within *government* and independence within *the administration* are quite different concepts, and this difference goes to the heart of presidential concern about the Federal Reserve.

Independence from Whom?

Anderson's views of the Federal Reserve's independence within government were based on the fact that Article I Section 8 of the Constitution gives Congress the "right to coin money and to regulate the value thereof," thus making monetary management a congressional responsibility. Anderson reasoned:

> There can scarcely be any question, however, as to Congress' right to discharge this responsibility by delegating the actual job to an agency of its own creation and for which it remains continually responsible. . . . Nor can there be any room for doubt that Congress can, if it so desires, embue one of its agencies with a relatively high degree of independence from the executive branch and erect safeguards to protect it from the day-to-day pressures which can emanate from the Congress itself.[13]

Thus, the ultimate check on Federal Reserve independence is the power of Congress to alter its structure or to call it to account for any of its actions.

Sherman Maisel has indicated that the Federal Reserve is well aware of the conditional nature of its independent status:

> Congressional presence is felt at each meeting on monetary policy. The Federal Reserve Board believes that its flexibility, its ability to hire good staff and to generate new ideas are important. It recognizes that to continue to operate as it does, it must satisfy a majority of Congress. Thus, what concerns individual congressmen in the monetary field automatically concerns the Federal Reserve.[14]

However, a recent analysis by political scientist John Woolley emphasizes that the Federal Reserve itself is not without political power: "Rather than being passive before congressional power, the Federal Reserve has some formidable political resources of its own."[15] Woolley contends that Congress' failure to check the Federal Reserve's power can be attributed as much to the weakness of Congress as to the acceptability of the Federal Reserve.

In the short run, political interest in Federal Reserve policy is linked to the performance of the economy. Congressional concern about monetary policy rises with interest rates. Conflicts about policy objectives with an administration are likely to occur around the turning points of the business cycle—in particular, administrations become concerned about "premature" tightening of monetary policy choking off a recovery, or about "undue" delays in easing monetary policy postponing an economic upturn.

Woolley points out, though, that the short-run political forces focused on the Federal Reserve seldom are mobilized simultaneously or consistently.[16] The interests of the financial community in combating inflation are diffused by its concern with other areas of policy. Members of Congress are seldom concerned with the technical aspects of monetary control—only with their results, as expressed in politically sensitive indicators like interest rates and credit availability. Economists tend to focus almost exclusively on the technical issues of monetary policy (over which they are strongly divided), but lack a continuing and substantial political base.

Nonetheless, the fact that the Federal Reserve clearly recognizes that Congress has the authority to force major changes on it has at times motivated defensive actions on its part. Woolley concludes that while Congress can punish the Federal Reserve for actions it dislikes, "it is doubtful whether the Federal Reserve will permit the necessary conditions to last long enough to provoke that kind of congressional anger."[17]

The Federal Reserve thus walks a delicate line. In the short run it must sometimes sacrifice part of its capacity to act independently— thereby running the danger of reducing its technical credibility—in order to enhance its political credibility and preserve its capacity to act independently in the long run.

For example, observers of Federal Reserve behavior have noted that it tends to avoid making changes in monetary policy prior to election time.[18] This is demonstrated in a memorandum from CEA Chairman Walter Heller to President Johnson in September 1964 on the subject of preelection monetary policy.[19] Heller informed the president that the chairman of the Federal Reserve Board, William McChesney Martin, Jr., had assured him that the Federal Reserve would not tighten monetary policy before the November 1964 election, but might wish to take a fresh look thereafter.

While the Federal Reserve is ultimately responsible to Congress, there can be no question that it is legally independent of the Treasury Department. As early as 19 December 1914, an opinion by the attorney general of the United States held that the Federal Reserve Board was an independent bureau, or establishment, of the government and as such was not under the jurisdiction of the Treasury.[20]

Practical independence from the Treasury, however, was not achieved until the famous "Accord" of 4 March 1951, which marked the end of inflexible pegging of the prices of Treasury securities, obligating the Federal Reserve to purchase all securities offered it without regard for the needs of monetary policy. Since that time, the Federal Reserve has given no special consideration to the Treasury's demand for funds when selecting its monetary targets. Its general policy has been that the Treasury must pay the going market interest rates.

But can or should the Federal Reserve be completely independent of the president? A Federal Reserve totally independent of presidential authority could potentially conflict with the administration's responsibility for formulating and implementing an overall macroeconomic policy for the nation. As expressed by another one of the CEA chairmen under President Johnson, Arthur Okun, there is "widespread recognition that a totally independent Central Bank is inappropriate in a democracy, and in practice the Federal Reserve has tended to follow a line that is independent within but not of the administration currently in office."[21]

Beyond the advisability of the central bank attempting to maintain complete independence from the administration, there are practical limitations to its ability to act independently. Maisel notes that "in time any president can make certain that his views prevail," explaining:

> Even if he did not have the power to appoint new members to the Board as vacancies occur, it is clear that no body—even a private one—can continue to function well under an all-out attack by the Administration. The White House holds too many cards in any direct showdown.[22]

In what he has termed the "scapegoat theory," Edward Kane argues that presidents recognize the pragmatic value of having a macroeconomic-policy tool that can operate more or less solely in response to the technical requirements of the economy in the face of political opposition, and that Congress appreciates the value of the Federal Reserve's autonomous structure as a means of shifting the blame for unpopular policy choices away from elected officials to an "independent" central bank.[23] In essence, Kane argues that the Federal Reserve's independence is a useful sham.

Woolley, however, points out the difficulties that would be inherent in the Federal Reserve's attempting to preserve the illusion of independence while always acting in concert with the wishes of the political authorities. He also notes that the numerous instances of conflict and frustration, as well as the generally recognized power of the Federal Reserve and its chairman, argue against easy acceptance of a theory of tacit collusion.[24]

Thus, the key issue is one of reconciling the structural independence of the Federal Reserve with its political dependence on congressional good will and its practical responsibilities to work with the nation's chief executive. While George L. Bach has concluded that it would be "intolerable" to permit an independent central bank to negate the basic macroeconomic policies developed by the executive and legislative branches, he observes that "independence, looked at practically, is a matter of degree, not just black and white. The real question, then, is the terms on which the Federal Reserve participates in governmental policy making and execution."[25]

In the final analysis, the Federal Reserve's effectiveness in making monetary policy lies in its ability to work with the administration without surrendering its authority to act independently on occasion, while the president's effectiveness rests, at least in part, on his ability to influence the actions of the Federal Reserve and to mesh its judgments and responsibilities with those of his economic advisors without incurring the political costs of an open break. This *mutual interdependence* characterizes the uneasy relationship that most presidents have with the Federal Reserve.

Taken as a whole, the record does not support the view that the Federal Reserve attempted to operate independently from the Johnson administration. Rather, with one major exception, namely, the decision to raise the discount rate in December 1965 (discussed in detail later in this chapter) the Board of Governors worked closely with the administration throughout both of President Johnson's terms of office.

Coordination of Monetary Policy

The principal concern of any president in dealing with the Federal Reserve is to develop an acceptable basis for the effective coordination of its monetary-policy actions with the execution of fiscal and debt management policies by the administration. In the Johnson years, as in previous administrations, both formal and informal coordinating mechanisms were used.

Formal Coordination: The Quadriad

Since the well-publicized "Accord" between the Treasury and the Federal Reserve in 1951, coordination of monetary policy with the national economic policies being pursued by an administration has been a matter of continuing concern.

In 1953, early in the first Eisenhower administration, a high-level Advisory Board on Economic Growth and Stabilization (ABEGS) was created under the chairmanship of the CEA Chairman Arthur Burns. Other members of the board included representatives of the secretaries of the treasury, agriculture, commerce, and labor, the director of the Bureau of the Budget, and the chairman of the Federal Reserve Board, as well as Gabriel Hague of the White House staff. The purpose of the board was to keep the president "closely informed about the state of the national economy and the various measures necessary to aid in maintaining a stable prosperity."[26]

In its early years, the weekly meetings of ABEGS are reported to have assured "easy and regular contact among Burns, Humphrey (secretary of the treasury) and Martin (chairman of the Federal Reserve Board)," with the result that they "consulted actively."[27] Another observer notes that "outside contacts made at first through ABEGS and then in other ways involved the staff in some degree of policy operations."[28]

In the latter years of the Eisenhower presidency, ABEGS became dormant. However, Burns is reported to have retained his views of its usefulness and to have recommended that it be formalized in the guise of an economic-policy board to relate to economic matters in much the same manner as the National Security Council relates to matters of national defense.[29] This was never done, but in the period 1958–60, following Burns' departure from the administration, Secretary of the Treasury Robert B. Anderson took the lead in establishing regular informal meetings with the chairman of the CEA, the director of the Bureau of the Budget, and the chairman of the Federal Reserve Board.[30]

ABEGS was abolished on 12 March 1961 by order of President Kennedy. However, the *Annual Report* of the CEA for that year noted: "The Chairman of the Council served with the Secretary of the Treasury, the Director of the Bureau of the Budget, and the Chairman of the Federal Reserve System in an advisory group which met periodically with the President to review monetary developments, issues, and policies."[31] Walter Heller, the CEA chairman under President Kennedy, states that this group was initially called the Fiscal and Financial Advisory Committee. Dissatisfied with the resulting acronym, FIFAC, Heller took to the dictionary and found the term "Quadriad" (an act which should have earned him the plaudits of a grateful public).

In an early memorandum to President Johnson, Heller explained the role of the Quadriad:

> You met Monday night with the budget "Troika" of Dillon, Gordon, and Heller. When we add Bill Martin of the "independent" Federal Reserve, it becomes the financial "Quadriad"— which Webster defines as "A union or group of four—*rare.*"
> That's us.
> President Kennedy met with the Quadriad every four to ten weeks. Typically, we reviewed (1) the economic outlook; (2) Federal Reserve money policies and Treasury debt-management; and (3) the balance-of-payments situation. The main purpose was to coordinate monetary policy—to make sure that the Federal Reserve was managing the money supply and interest rates in a way that serves overall administration policy.
> The Quadriad has (with one exception) met at my call, after checking with the President. We met for 20 minutes to one hour. Our last meeting was on September 12.
> If you want this group to continue—which I strongly urge—an early meeting seems desirable. . . . If you say the word, I'll arrange a meeting.[32]

President Johnson accepted the suggestion of his chief economic adviser and the Quadriad was continued, meeting three times in 1964, six times in 1965, four times in 1966, three times in 1967, and twice in 1968.[33]

Concerning the influence of the Quadriad in the Johnson years, Bach has observed:

> President Johnson, unlike his predecessor, had little interest in detailed discussion of economic issues. The quadriad, which had thrived under President Kennedy, gradually atrophied, not by design but because it did not well serve the Johnson administration's style. While there were no serious rifts, contacts between the Treasury and the CEA, on the one hand, and the Federal Reserve, on the other, became less and less frequent.[34]

The comments of those who chaired the CEA during the Johnson administration, though, suggest other reasons for the decline in the frequency of Quadriad meetings, and note a corresponding *increase* in the informal contacts and cooperation between the institutions involved.

Walter Heller succinctly compares the attitudes of Presidents Kennedy and Johnson toward economic issues, noting that both were inclined to fiscal caution, if not conservatism. President Johnson shared with his predecessor a growing impatience with the performance of the economy and a willingness to explore the potential of new economic ideas. The major difference between the two, according to Heller, was that "actual *performance,* the hard evidence of results flowing from policy action, looms larger in President Johnson's economic thinking."[35] Heller also notes that "President Johnson (who had once described his economics to me as 'old fashioned') turned quickly, smoothly, and effectively to the use of modern economics."

Heller's successor as CEA chairman, Gardner Ackley, views the Quadriad meetings from 1962 through 1965 as largely ineffective.[36] While he observes that Heller had been more favorably inclined toward them, Ackley complains that the Quadriad meetings had no real agenda (only a list of questions) and no prepared background papers (in marked contrast to the Troika exercises). "The President would ask Martin questions. Martin would talk at length without saying anything meaningful or committing himself to anything."[37]

Ackley states that while meetings of the Quadriad declined after 1965, staff coordination between Troika participants and the Federal Reserve increased: ". . . certainly we didn't have anything like a Quadriad until late 1966 or 1967, when we really began to work together other than through an occasional high-level meeting."[38] Ackley goes on to say that during the last two years of the Johnson presidency, the Federal Reserve moved from being a "distant observer" in the economic-policy exercise to being a fourth member of the team:

> Although I don't think we ever got a joint memorandum to the President on economic policy, signed by the Secretary of the Treasury, the Budget Director, the Council Chairman, *and* the Chairman of the Federal Reserve, on several occasions we got Martin to send a separate communication to the President , along with ours, saying that he had participated in the discussion, and that in general the Fed concurred with the point of view expressed, or something of that sort. Which was a great accomplishment.[39]

Arthur Okun, who succeeded Ackley as CEA chairman, also observes that in the first two years of the Johnson administration, the Quadriad met more frequently than it did in the last three years, because the earlier period was marked by disagreements between the Federal Reserve and the administration on the proper direction of monetary policy. The watershed in this relationship, according to Okun, was the decision by the Board of Governors in December 1965 to raise the discount rate, an action not concurred in by the administration. "There was much less relationship with the Federal Reserve prior to that even than there was after that event or than there was with other agencies."[40]

Quadriad Meetings in the Johnson Years

The record of Quadriad meetings early in the Johnson administration suggests that the Quadriad was viewed by the administration as a means of bringing pressure to bear on the Federal Reserve to comply with economic-policy decisions already made by the Troika rather than as a mechanism for coordinated macroeconomic-policy formulation. Thus, in his first memorandum to the president calling for a meeting of the Quadriad, Heller stated as one of the meeting's three purposes "to put the Federal Reserve on gentle notice that it's important to keep giving the economy enough monetary elbow room for expansion."[41]

The next meeting of the Quadriad, on 18 March 1964, also appears to have resulted from a concern by the administration that the Federal Reserve would tighten credit, with Heller noting that "Bill Martin's fears of prospective inflation seem to be mounting to a fever pitch."[42] In recommending a third meeting of the Quadriad in 1964, Heller suggested, "This is a good idea substantively, and would also make a good news item."[43]

The administration and the Federal Reserve were in basic agreement on the major directions for economic policy during the last half of 1964, and there were no meetings of the Quadriad. As noted previously, this period of inaction preceded the November elections, and Martin had informed the administration that there would be no change in monetary policy.

Early in 1965, however, Gardner Ackley, who had taken over as chairman of the CEA, wrote the president warning of Federal Reserve plans to tighten money as part of the balance-of-payments program, and pointed out the importance for prosperity of keeping the tightening modest: "This is a matter for discussion between you and Bill Martin. (In the past, such discussions have involved the 'quadriad' . . . But, if you prefer, a private meeting with Martin could provide the opportunity."[44]

The following day, the FOMC moved to tighten credit and the administration responded by scheduling a meeting of the Quadriad for early February (later postponed to 10 March). Prior to this meeting, Ackley cautioned the president:

> Bill Martin's recent testimony to the Joint Economic Committee was not wholly reassuring.
> —He second guessed his own 1964 policies as perhaps being too easy (and certainly not too tight).
> —He judged that we're "sailing close to" inflation (I would note that we are on the troubled seas of too much unemployment).
> —He stated that, if the voluntary balance of payments program should fail, "we must be prepared to take whatever additional measures are needed, including of course, a less expansive overall credit policy." [45]

The Quadriad meeting, however, was said to have "solidified the understanding that monetary policy ought to remain basically accommodative." [46]

The gap between Federal Reserve and administration views of the overall economic outlook and the prospects for inflation gradually widened during the next two months. Monetary policy continued to be basically accommodative, and Quadriad meetings in early May and June were reported to have ended on a "generally harmonious note." [47] Nonetheless, concern persisted within the administration that the Federal Reserve might strike a course independent of the president's policies. Thus, in reporting an increase in wholesale prices in June, Ackley informed the president that the price news was bad and added a handwritten postscript: "The reaction of the press, public, and the Fed is something that worries me." [48]

By August, the CEA was becoming more concerned about the economy. Interest rates were beginning to rise under the impetus of the delayed effects of the monetary tightening of the previous spring and speculation of further tightening. At the 26 August meeting of the Quadriad, the Federal Reserve was urged to head off the upward movement of interest rates. [49]

Throughout the fall, the administration was deeply concerned that the Federal Reserve would take an independent course and move to tighten credit prematurely, that is, before the administration had decided that restraint was warranted. A Quadriad meeting on 6 October resulted in an uneasy truce with the Federal Reserve, but concern that monetary policy might be tightened persisted. The deterioration in the relationship between the administration and the

Federal Reserve, which culminated in the decision by the Board of Governors in early December to increase the discount rate and tighten credit, is discussed later in this chapter.

The final Quadriad meeting of 1965 occurred at the Johnson ranch on 6 December, three days after the board's decisive discount rate increase. Its decision to act independently of the administration appears to have been cathartic. Beginning with the 6 December meeting of the Quadriad, and continuing throughout the remainder of the Johnson presidency, relations between the administration and the Federal Reserve became much closer. While Quadriad meetings were held less frequently, there was much more staff contact and cooperation. At the same time, the emphasis of the Quadriad meetings shifted away from trying to persuade the Federal Reserve not to take action undesired by the administration to assisting it in implementing policies agreed to by both parties.

The new supportive stance of the administration emerged in the early months of 1966. The CEA on several occasions, both in writing and in person, defended the Federal Reserve's strategy within the government and to the press. This was the position taken at the Quadriad meeting held on 2 March 1966.[50]

The Federal Reserve appears to have reciprocated by expanding its direct communication with the administration. Thus, on 14 May, the president received a memorandum from Martin giving the Federal Reserve's views on the current economic situation and promising, "I will let you know if there are any comments that come out of our Open Market Committee meeting tomorrow which might be of interest."[51]

Martin, recuperating from an operation, was away from the board during most of the summer, and in his absence Vice Chairman J. L. Robertson continued to keep the administration informed of Federal Reserve thinking. On 13 July, Ackley reported to the president that Robertson "came to see us today to tell us about some decisions the Board has taken and about its divided views on raising the discount rate."[52] The memorandum indicated that Ackley and Robertson had discussed in some detail the views and divisions of opinion within the Board of Governors.

During the summer of 1966, there was increasing concern within both the administration and the Federal Reserve over the failure of the tight credit policies to reduce bank lending and overall spending within the economy. It became apparent that a very rapid expansion in business loans was being financed by liquidation of other banking assets, particularly municipal securities. As a result of bank selling, the securities market became, in the jargon of Wall Street, "somewhat disorderly."[53] Apprehension grew that individuals seeking to acquire liquidity by selling bonds would find no market for them or would discover prices so low that they would be unwilling to take the capital losses. This "credit crunch" led to pressures in Congress for legislation to force a rollback of interest ceilings on time deposits.

The next meeting of the Quadriad on 27 June was aimed at assessing the dimensions of this problem. "The CEA began suggesting ways to achieve further restraint without bringing undue damage to the already beleaguered financial system."[54] At the same time, the administration withstood pressure to criticize the Federal Reserve. Joseph Barr, undersecretary of the treasury for monetary affairs, urged the administration in a memorandum not to criticize the Federal Reserve, and on 29 July Ackley wrote the president to concur: "It is essential that the Administration not join Congress in beating the Fed over the head for its policies. . . . While we feel strongly that the timing of the Fed's action last December was a blunder, we cannot fault them for their general policy position since."[55]

As the summer drew to a close, concern continued within the administration and the Federal Reserve over the expansion in business loans and the chaotic conditions in the securities market. The board met with the twelve Federal Reserve District Bank presidents to consider possible actions. The board favored acting through the discount window, seeking a change in Regulation A, which governs loans to member banks. The conference of presidents was unanimous in its opposition to any change in Regulation A. A compromise was worked out, and the presidents agreed to a less formal action. On 1 September, the Federal Reserve wrote to each member bank, diplomatically suggesting:

> The System believes that the national economic interest would be better served by a slower rate of expansion of bank loans to businesses within the context of moderate overall money and credit growth. Further substantial adjustments through bank liquidation of municipal securities or other investments would add to pressures on financial markets. Hence the System believes that a greater share of member bank adjustments should take the form of moderation in the rate of expansion of loans, and particularly business loans.[56]

Access to the discount window would be based on bank cooperation with this informal directive.

This action, which amounted to a gentle form of credit rationing through the operation of the discount window, marked a significant break with past procedures. The CEA gave "wholehearted support" to it.[57] At the last meeting of the Quadriad in 1966, on 23 September, "signals for judging when monetary easing might appropriately be taken" were a topic of discussion.[58]

As 1966 came to a close, the relations between the Federal Reserve and the Johnson administration appear to have moved even closer. On 11 November, the Troika reported to the president that "in close cooperation with Chairman Martin" they had been reviewing policy goals, the basic forecast for the economy, and related policy matters. Attached to this memorandum was a report to the Troika from its technical advisers appraising the economy, which noted, "We have been over this paper with Chairman Martin and he concurs generally."[59] On 23 November, Ackley informed the president that he had received a phone call from Martin in which he had reported that the FOMC had shifted its policy slightly toward easier money. Ackley observed, "Perhaps it's a means of telling us—if we do move on taxes—the Fed is ready to move on money."[60]

The year ended on a harmonious note. Ackley reported to the president on 23 December that the three members of the CEA had met on the previous day with the entire Board of Governors (except Martin), "and strongly urged that a signal be given of the shift toward easier money." Ackley also noted that the next day the board sent a telegram to each of the Federal Reserve District Banks authorizing them to say, in response to inquiries, that the 1 September credit restraint letter had been withdrawn.[61]

In 1967, the two meetings of the Quadriad in June and July were concerned with the appropriate role for monetary policy pending action by the Congress on increasing taxes. Thus, in a memorandum to the president on 27 May, Ackley stated that the market needed to be convinced that the administration would seek and get a tax increase when restraint was needed and that the Federal Reserve would not jump the gun and provide monetary restraint before fiscal action was taken. He suggested that this message be conveyed at a press briefing following a Quadriad meeting. The president could announce that his fiscal and financial advisers believed that restraint was not currently needed, but would be required later in the year, and that there was agreement that restraint should be in the form of a tax increase, not monetary tightening. Ackley proposed that the president report that he had requested a "coordinated economic alert" by the Quadriad when the time was right for initiating tax action. He also suggested that there be a meeting of the Quadriad principals prior to the Quadriad meeting with the president "so that we don't seem to be fencing Martin into a surprise treaty in your presence."[62] Clearly,

Ackley was anxious to avoid a repeat of the December 1965 independent action taken by the board.

By fall, Congress had shelved the proposed tax bill and concern shifted to maintaining the availability of credit. The 10 October meeting of the Quadriad led to such an agreement. However, growing signs of overheating in the economy in the last quarter of 1967 resulted in a progressive firming of monetary policy as indicated by a December increase in reserve requirements and two hikes in the discount rate in the spring of 1968. All of these actions were concurred in by the CEA.[63]

The 24 June meeting of the Quadriad followed passage of the tax surcharge bill. This meeting had been preceded by a staff exercise to prepare a full financial projection consistent with the basic economic outlook. Agreement was reached that monetary policy should begin moving toward ease, though the speed of the shift was left open.[64] On 15 August, with the full support of Chairman Martin, the board reduced the discount rate.[65] The final meeting of the Quadriad came near the end of the Johnson presidency, on 12 December 1968.

Informal Coordination: A Moveable Feast

In addition to the formal coordinative mechanism of the Quadriad, there developed over time several informal methods of coordination that tended to strengthen communication between the Federal Reserve and the administration. One such practice was a series of informal luncheons. Every Monday, the chairman of the Federal Reserve had lunch with the secretary of the treasury and half a dozen of his staff. This was followed by a private meeting between the two principals. On Wednesdays, the staff economists of the Treasury Department went to the Federal Reserve for lunch with its staff economists.

The disagreement between the administration and the Federal Reserve in December 1965 over the discount rate hike also appears to have led to more direct communication between the Board of Governors and the CEA. Okun relates that "the sense of failure of communication and some personal unpleasantness on both sides from this split on policy led to a very determined and much more formalized effort at coordination."[66] Starting in February 1966, at the invitation of Chairman Martin, the entire Board of Governors and the three CEA members met for lunch every second Thursday. The president frequently received reports from the CEA chairman describing the highlights of these meetings, which generally were described as "pleasant and cordial."[67]

Opinions differ as to the value of these meetings, however. Okun observes that the Thursday luncheons often led to additional contacts between the members of the CEA and the board: "You'd get into a luncheon conversation; somebody would follow it up; and there'd be phone calls and such."[68] Ackley was less enthusiastic about the meetings, observing that although "we sparred around the edges of what policy was and would be and ought to be, communication just didn't exist in terms of really hard talk about questions like these: what are you going to *do*; what *ought* you to do; and *why, when,* and *how much.*"[69]

At a professional level, there was a good deal of informal contact between the respective staffs of the Federal Reserve, Treasury, CEA, and Bureau of the Budget. While during the Johnson presidency there generally was no joint staff effort in preparation for Quadriad meetings, on several occasions a joint Troika–Federal Reserve exercise was mounted. According to Frederick L. Deming, undersecretary of the treasury for monetary affairs, there was "just constant conversation between Budget, Council, Federal Reserve, and Treasury around-the-horn."[70]

In assessing the significance and effectiveness of informal coordination of economic policy, it is important to recognize that the principal staff economists in these institutions, and in some cases the top officials themselves, came from quite similar backgrounds and shared a common professional perspective. This served to mitigate institutional loyalties. Economists were recruited from the same set of academic institutions. A number of Treasury staff members came from positions in the Federal Reserve System or from banks and other financial institutions that dealt closely with the Federal Reserve. The common professional orientation of staff members served to facilitate a system of coordination that relied on informal contacts and personal initiatives. In the later Johnson years, the appointment of professional economists to the Board of Governors contributed to closer contact between the Federal Reserve and the CEA.[71]

In summary, both formal and informal methods of coordination were widely employed in the Johnson presidency to ensure that Federal Reserve policies were consistent with the administration's overall macroeconomic goals and policies. Bach suggests that the Federal Reserve is least effective when it is most isolated from the president and from coequal working relationships with the administration. "Extreme independence is, unfortunately, likely to mean splendid isolation from the decisions that matter."[72] Here, Bach appears to be referring to the possible impact of Federal Reserve isolation on its capacity to influence overall macroeconomic policy.

The experience of the Johnson years, however, provides little real evidence that Federal Reserve independence leads to isolation. To the contrary, the use of its independence in December 1965 appears to have enhanced its influence with the Johnson administration. Woolley has emphasized that the capacity of the Federal Reserve to act independently can be a useful bargaining chip.[73] Overt conflict, as evidenced by the Federal Reserve's independent action, reflects a breakdown in negotiations—not an absence of influence. Even when the Federal Reserve fails to take independent action, it may nonetheless be exercising influence on the administration.

But the concern of the president is to develop mechanisms for exerting influence on the Federal Reserve. During the Johnson years, the role of the Quadriad and the frequency of Quadriad meetings varied directly with the degree of tension existing between the administration and the Federal Reserve. In the first two years of the Johnson presidency, the administration was concerned that the Federal Reserve would move independently to tighten money, choking off expansion in the economy. Quadriad meetings were aimed at conveying to Chairman Martin the administration's views and seeking to gain his commitment to them.

After the Board of Governors took independent action in December 1965 to raise the discount rate, relations between the administration and the Federal Reserve appear to have relaxed. While Quadriad meetings were held less frequently, informal contact and cooperation between the administration and the Federal Reserve greatly increased.

Of course, the need for formal coordination of the type provided by the Quadriad format is much greater when the Federal Reserve and the administration are in disagreement over the direction and pace of economic activity and the appropriate policy response than when they are in agreement. Thus, the easier relations of the latter years of the Johnson presidency were due in no small measure to the fact that the Federal Reserve and the administration were in agreement that— in the absence of action by Congress on the requested tax increase— monetary restraint was required. In this regard, it also should be recognized that by the later years of his administration, President Johnson was dealing with a Federal Reserve Board more amenable to his macroeconomic viewpoint.

The Role of the President

In addition to the opportunity provided by periodic Quadriad meetings, a president can attempt to influence the Federal Reserve through appointments to the Board of Governors as well as through his relations with its chairman.

Appointments to the Federal Reserve Board

Federal Reserve Board members are appointed for fourteen-year, nonrenewable terms, with one vacancy occurring each even-numbered year. Thus, at a minimum, a president is able to appoint two members to the board during a term of office. In practice, however, vacancies occur more frequently, as board members often do not serve a complete fourteen-year term. During the Johnson presidency, two reappointments and three new appointments were made to the Federal Reserve Board.

Early in the Johnson presidency, consideration was evidently given to establishing a formalized procedure for selecting members of independent agencies. Myer Feldman, a presidential assistant, wrote the president on 8 January 1964 describing a proposed selection procedure: potential candidates would be requested to complete a detailed questionnaire which would be submitted to a "panel of lawyers, economists, and political scientists, representative of all sections of the Nation, for an appraisal."[74] The goal was to develop a screening procedure similar to that used for selection of federal judges. Feldman indicated that the benefits of this formal mechanism would be both to buffer the presidency from the inevitable political pressures generated by appointment opportunities and to provide for an independent professional evaluation of potential candidates.

Feldman appended to the memorandum a long list of disadvantages of a formal screening process for presidential appointments. In particular, he emphasized the difficulty of selecting appropriate review panels for members of independent agencies that were not professionally unique, pointing out that this situation was not comparable to the selection of members for the federal bench. He also noted the problem of keeping the deliberations and findings of the review panels secret, particularly since many of the potential candidates might not be aware of or agree to being considered.

The record does not indicate if this concept was given serious consideration by the president, but it was never implemented. As with other major appointments, the president relied on John W. Macy, Jr., chairman of the Civil Service Commission, to screen likely candidates for administrative agencies and to make recommendations. A number of presidential assistants were also engaged in the process.

In the case of Federal Reserve Board appointments, the president's economic and financial advisers were actively involved. Names of potential candidates were frequently submitted by members of Congress and others inside and outside the administration, including Chairman Martin, often with the active encouragement of the candidates themselves. In addition to the normal background check by the FBI, the screening of candidates involved soliciting the views of the banking and business community.

Shortly after assuming office, President Johnson had his first opportunity to make an appointment to the board when the term of J. L. Robertson expired on 31 January 1964. The president was informed on 30 November 1963 of the pending vacancy by Ralph Dungan, a presidential assistant, who noted that President Kennedy had intended to give the next board appointment to Seymour Harris of Harvard University. Dungan concluded by noting, somewhat cryptically, "I would be glad to fill you in on all of the by-play surrounding this one which is complicated."[75]

Professor Harris had made it known to the press that when President Kennedy had named Dewey Daane to the board in November 1963, he had promised to appoint Harris to the next board vacancy. This generated considerable opposition from the financial community. Harris may well have removed himself from consideration by his efforts to get the job.

After the first of the year, President Johnson heard directly from Harris when he received an unsolicited letter from him containing a general discussion of economic-policy issues. The president responded with a polite acknowledgment expressing gratitude for "your crisply stated comments on monetary policy."[76]

Senator Edward Kennedy (Dem. Mass.) had recommended Harris for the board in December, noting that his brother had intended to give him the next vacancy, and the senator repeated his recommendation in a letter to the president on 29 January.[77] About the same time, the president also received a letter from Adlai Stevenson mildly supporting Harris for appointment to the board.

The publicity surrounding the consideration of Harris had drawn substantial opposition to his appointment. Thus, on 10 January, in a letter to presidential aide Lawrence O'Brien, Senator Willis Robertson (Dem. Va.), chairman of the Senate Banking Committee, noted that he had expressed to President Kennedy his opposition to the appointment of Harris, and observed that the *New York Times* of that day contained a statement by Harris that he had been promised the appointment.[78] Several times during January, Senator Robertson forwarded to the president letters from a number of bankers opposing the Harris appointment.[79] A close friend of the president, Abe Fortas (later to be named a justice of the Supreme Court), also had written to presidential assistant Bill Moyers noting that while he had "no personal judgment about Seymour Harris," he was forwarding a letter from a prominent Boston banker expressing opposition to Harris by "a large segment of Boston's business and financial community."[80]

The key blow to Harris' appointment, however, may have been the publicity surrounding his aspirations. Robert Roosa, undersecretary of the treasury for monetary affairs in the Johnson administration, relates that he was sitting in the Cabinet Room waiting for a meeting with the president when Johnson entered carrying a ticker tape and said, "Who's this Seymour Harris? This professor at Harvard who just appointed himself to the Federal Reserve Board this morning?" Roosa said that he recognized right away that this was the end of Harris' chances for the appointment.[81]

For whatever reason, attention shifted to reappointing Robertson to the board. On 22 January, Macy wrote the president noting that Robertson was eligible for reappointment (since he had not initially been appointed to a full term) and observing that "he was a strong Kennedy supporter on the Board, expansion-minded in terms of fiscal policy, and would like to be reappointed."[82] While some consideration was given to appointing Frederick Deming, then president of the Federal Reserve Bank of Minneapolis and later to become undersecretary of the treasury under President Johnson, the decision was eventually made to reappoint Robertson.[83]

The next opportunity for President Johnson to make an appointment to the board came in the spring of 1965 with the expiration of the term of A. L. Mills, Jr. As early as 12 November 1964, Heller had written the president informing him of the forthcoming vacancy on the Federal Reserve Board and of a possible opening on the Federal Home Loan Bank Board. Heller stated that he was writing "to express CEA's *strong interest in filling these jobs with people who will help, not hinder, you in sustaining prosperity.*"[84]

On 4 January 1965, Mills submitted a formal letter of resignation to the president, indicating that he would step down on 1 March. On 10 February, Chairman Martin suggested three candidates to Macy from the San Francisco Federal Reserve District for Mills' replacement, adding, "I am very anxious to get a younger man over here."[85] The board vacancy was included on a list of pending appointments sent to the president on 12 February.

On 2 March, Ackley informed the president that Mills was no longer participating in Federal Reserve decisions. He urged prompt action in finding a suitable replacement for him:

At today's Open Market Committee meeting, there was a minority of 4 (out of 11) that wanted to move to even tighter money. One or two others are wavering. . . . This makes it particularly important that a decision be reached as quickly as possible on a new appointee whom we can count on.[86]

Consideration appears to have been given once again to Seymour Harris. Presidential assistant Jack Valenti informed the president on 31 March that he had received a call from Secretary of Commerce John Connor reporting on his sounding of the business community on the possibility of appointing Harris to the board. Connor had found a unanimous reaction that Harris would be "a disaster."[87]

Initial support for the appointment went to Leslie C. Peacock, vice president and chief economist of the Crocker-Citizens National Bank. In a memo of 22 February, Macy submitted four names to the president for consideration, indicating that Peacock was his own preference as well as that of Chairman Martin.[88] However, consideration soon focused on the third choice submitted by Macy, another professor, Sherman Maisel of the University of California.

Maisel had been recommended for appointment to the Federal Home Loan Bank Board by Governor Pat Brown of California.[89] Maisel had written Macy and arranged for an interview in late January. Subsequently, on Macy's recommendation, Maisel received the appointment to the Federal Home Loan Bank Board.[90]

On 27 March, Macy recommended to the president that Maisel be given the Federal Reserve Board position, observing that Ackley had spoken with Maisel, "closely cross-examined him regarding his philosophy of monetary policy," and certified that "he supports your position in this area all the way."[91] Maisel indicates that on 1 April he met with the president, who asked if he would be willing to serve as a member of the board. He recounts:

. . . it was clear that they [the administration] had reviewed my speeches and publications and believed that on the Federal Reserve Board my approach to problems, my analysis and decisions would probably fit the economic patterns and programs the Administration was trying to foster.[92]

Maisel accepted the appointment and it was announced within the hour.

The third, and most controversial, appointment to the board by President Johnson came a year later, when Cranby Balderson completed a full term of office on 26 February 1966. With fresh memories of the December 1965 schism between the board and the administration, when Balderson had joined with three other members in approving an increase in the discount rate, the president and his advisers were extremely careful to make certain that Balderson's replacement would support the administration's economic policies.

On 29 December 1965, John Clinton, a Macy aide, related a conversation with Governor Maisel concerning the Balderson replacement.

> In his opinion the most important question to be resolved is the one of dependability. The President would be served best by selecting someone upon whom he could count to be on his side on monetary policy when a crisis comes. This is a matter not worth bargaining over.[93]

Maisel went on to observe that it would be "an ace in the hole" if the appointment forced the resignation of Martin from the chairmanship.

On 14 January, Representative Wright Patman wrote the president strongly recommending Seymour Harris for the board, again noting that President Kennedy had promised to appoint him.[94] The president, however, appears to have already made up his mind on Harris: the next day, when asked by presidential assistant Marvin Watson if he wanted further checking on Harris, the president indicated that he did not.[95]

Macy initially favored the appointment of Hugh D. Galusha, Jr., who had replaced Deming as president of the Federal Reserve Bank of Minneapolis, to the Balderson slot on the board. Macy wrote to the president indicating that he had discussed the appointment of Galusha with Heller, Ackley, Budget Director Kermit Gordon, and Treasury Secretary Fowler, and observing, "He is a sound liberal and can be expected to vote for the administration's views."[96] However, Galusha was reported to be not interested in an appointment to the board.

Macy suggested that another possible candidate might be Andrew Brimmer, an assistant secretary of commerce and one of a handful of recognized black economists. Noting that he had discussed Brimmer with Fowler, Ackley, and Heller but not with Chairman Martin or Senator Russell Long (Dem. La.), who had his own candidate, Macy observed:

> Although it is not governing in my recommendation, I believe it would be highly salutory for a strongly qualified Negro to assume a position of leadership in the banking community which to date

has been less than totally affirmative in its equal opportunity program. . . . Brimmer would be the ideal Negro professional to make this breakthrough.[97]

Macy also noted that Brimmer "would be completely loyal to your economic program in the Federal Reserve post."

On 25 January, Heller wrote the president, "As you instructed I phoned Brimmer." He was "clearly interested" in the Federal Reserve Board appointment.[98] Heller reported that Brimmer "felt the *timing of* [the] *discount rate* [decision] *was 'atrocious'*—that it should have waited until the President had reviewed the whole economic and fiscal situation." Brimmer was said to have described himself as "in the middle, leaning toward Main Street, not Wall Street." Heller concluded that "He is *clearly a 'Johnson man' but might jump the traces once in a great while.*"

At Heller's suggestion, Brimmer provided the president with copies of speeches he had made in support of the president's economic policies.[99] Three days later, Clinton reported to Macy that he had received favorable comments on Brimmer from Undersecretary of the Treasury Joseph Barr, Budget Director Kermit Gordon, and Okun, but he also referred to Brimmer's "unabashed efforts to get the job."[100]

On 5 February, Heller provided the president with additional comments on Brimmer. Under "Loyalty," he noted:

Brimmer describes himself as a 100% Johnson man who has been preaching the gospel (especially to Kennedy men) . . . that the achievements of the Johnson Administration didn't just happen . . . that they are the direct product of the leadership and skill of President Johnson.[101]

Heller noted that those in the CEA and other agencies who had worked closely with Brimmer described him as "able, articulate, effective, and diplomatic." In a postscript, Heller indicated that a key consideration in selecting the next board member would be how he would have voted on the December discount rate hike and, in reference to another candidate for the board, reported:

LBJ hunch verified: on the plane today, a CED [Committee for Economic Development] man said Les Chandler [Princeton] told him he'd have voted *with* Bill Martin in December. (Bill thinks otherwise and told me yesterday that he doesn't want Chandler on the Board.)

On 1 February, Treasury Secretary Fowler informed the president of a conversation with Chairman Martin in which they had discussed the board vacancy.[102] Martin favored the appointment of Atherton Bean, chairman of the board of International Milling and a director of the Minneapolis Federal Reserve District Bank. Fowler reported that "Chairman Martin says Bean is not a 'Martin man' but one who would exercise independent judgment." However, Fowler indicated that he believed that Bean would have voted with Martin on increasing the discount rate. Martin was said to have indicated that if the appointment was to go to an academic, he preferred Brimmer. After commenting on a number of other candidates, Fowler concluded by saying that Martin had told him that "he continues to be an LBJ man and wants to help. . . . If there is any desire for him to go, someone can give Mr. Martin a quiet nudge and he will resign."

On the same evening, the president met with Chairman Martin. The meeting resulted in a long letter on the following day in which Martin strongly supported the appointment of Bean, noted that "his only objection" to the appointment of Brimmer was the fact that he was an economist and "each of the last three appointees in succession has been an economist, and appointment now of a fourth would mean constitution of a majority of the Board from the membership of a single profession."[103] All the same, Martin went on to comment disparagingly on Brimmer's qualifications for the board, noting that his appointment would result in

> the creation of widespread doubts within and without the System that would damage confidence and gravely impair the ability of the Federal Reserve to carry out functions of vital importance to the economy and the government alike.

Somewhat charitably, Martin added that Brimmer "may at some later time . . . become universally recognized as indisputably qualified for appointment to the Federal Reserve Board."

Martin proposed another meeting with the president, and this was held on 6 February. However, Martin remained unconvinced of the desirability of Brimmer's appointment and the following day sent the president still another memorandum strongly urging the appointment of Bean, who would "enhance the stature of the Board, establish the integrity of the Federal Reserve System, and assure continued confidence in its work, both at home and abroad."[104]

Treasury Secretary Fowler appears to have shared Martin's concern about appointing yet another economist to the board. On 7 February he sent the president an outline of the statutory requirements for board membership and the backgrounds of the current board members.[105] Fowler noted that industrial and commercial interests were not represented on the board, and while there was no requirement for this, he felt it would nonetheless be useful to have such a member.

Meanwhile, Heller wrote the president still another memorandum on the board vacancy listing a number of advantages if the president were to decide to appoint Bean rather than Brimmer, whom Heller described as his "sentimental favorite":

1. Blame for tight money—and for a while it has to be tighter than we like—*stays firmly on Martin.*

2. *You avoid the danger of a Martin resignation.* Bob Anderson and Julian Baird both called yesterday to say that the Brimmer appointment *would risk Martin's (plus one other's) resignation.* They say they have heard he is very able, but they object because:
—He hasn't got "statute" [*sic*]
—He is an all-out easy money man
—The world would say it's a political appointment.

3. If you appoint Bean I think you would get a little more willing cooperation *from the business and banking communities on your financial guidelines and price guidelines.*

4. Bean would vote your way *a very high proportion of the time* and we would help, along with the Fed staff, in keeping him on a Johnsonian expansion path.[106]

Faced with this conflicting advice, the president requested that Macy talk further with Brimmer. On 22 February, Fowler reported to the president on a conversation with Brimmer, in which Fowler had been joined by Ackley and Heller, which he termed "very satisfactory."[107] Nonetheless, Fowler recommended that the president consider Paul Volcker, deputy undersecretary of the treasury, for the board vacancy. Two days later, Macy recommended to the president that Brimmer be given the appointment, noting, "He advises me that he strongly supports your economic position" and "assures me that he would be prepared to get along with Chairman Martin."[108]

Convinced at last, President Johnson decided to select Brimmer. He notified Martin by phone of the decision and announced the appointment. Two days later, Martin informed the president through Marvin Watson that the appointment of Brimmer had worked well at the Federal Reserve System and that Johnson was "to be highly congratulated for the way you have handled this appointment."[109] As will be discussed below, Martin's reaction may well have been related to the fact that his own appointment as chairman was coming up for renewal and would be the subject of a presidential decision the following month.

It has been suggested that President Johnson selected Brimmer in order to punish Martin for the board's decision on the December 1964 discount rate hike.[110] However, given the extensive deliberations on this appointment, the fact that the president met twice with Martin to hear his views firsthand, and Martin's indication through Fowler that if the appointment was to go to an academic his choice would be Brimmer, it appears more likely that Brimmer's appointment was motivated by two factors: Brimmer's strong support for the administration's economic policies, and the opportunity for Johnson to appoint a qualified black professional to an important post.

In his account of his presidential years, President Johnson wrote of his appointment of distinguished black men and women to the highest offices in the land, noting that Brimmer and other blacks had been appointed

> for their competence, wisdom, and courage, not for the color of their skins. But I also deeply believe that with these appointments Negro mothers could look at their children and hope with good reason that someday their sons and daughters might reach the highest offices their government could offer.[111]

President Johnson's next appointment to the board came in 1967, when Governor Charles N. Shepardson's term prematurely expired because he had reached the mandatory civil-service retirement age. On 20 February, Macy had written the president that "here is an opportunity to place a strong and effective Johnson man on the Fed at a time of normal term expiration."[112] A few days later, the president received a letter from Heller offering "Further Thoughts on Fed Appointments."[113] Heller remarked that, while he realized that "the eyes of Texas" were upon him (alluding to Shepardson's Dallas roots), he still thought the president should consider a number of individuals from the Minneapolis Federal Reserve District, including Atherton Bean.

The president, however, turned to a Texas banker, William Sherrill, for the Shepardson replacement. Sherrill had long been supported for a major appointment by presidential assistant Jack Valenti, who described him as "one of the ablest men I know."[114] According to Valenti, Sherrill was "a brilliant man . . . your man . . . LBJ all the way . . . active in your campaign . . . totally loyal without doubt."[115]

Late in 1965, Valenti had urged the president to appoint Sherrill to the board of the Federal Deposit Insurance Corporation (FDIC), describing him as "my close friend from Houston," and as being "tough, smart, discrete, and of course, totally our man."[116] The president named Sherrill to the FDIC board on 26 February 1966.

In a series of memorandums in early 1967, Macy recommended Sherrill for the Shepardson position on the Federal Reserve Board. One point in Sherrill's favor was that he was favorably viewed by the banking industry. Thus, Macy emphasized Sherrill's "current stature in bank supervision and his ability to communicate effectively with representatives of the regulated industry."[117]

As with other Federal Reserve Board appointments, the candidate had been evaluated by a number of economic and financial advisers within the administration. Thus, on 17 April Macy had forwarded to the president favorable reviews of Sherrill by Joseph Horne and K. A. Randall of the FDIC, Comptroller of the Currency William Camp, Undersecretary of the Treasury Joseph Barr, and Governors Maisel and Brimmer of the Federal Reserve.[118]

Nor were the views of Chairman Martin ignored. On 21 April, Macy related to the president a discussion with Martin. While Sherrill was not Martin's first choice for the job, he was said to have indicated that Sherrill "looks all right," and to have described him as a "likeable fellow" who would work well with the other members of the board."[119]

President Johnson named Sherrill to the board on 22 April. Three days later, in a letter to Macy, Martin said that the appointment would "work out all right" and commented on the "very good visit with the president" about the appointment.[120] In January 1968, when Shepardson's term came to an end, President Johnson reappointed Sherrill to the board.

The selection process for Federal Reserve Board appointments in the Johnson administration was open, thorough, and deliberate. Woolley has said of the board appointments:

> Candidates must have the support, or at least the respect, of some constituency, and they must not be vigorously opposed by any of the major groups. They must be known quantities. They must not be thought to be erratic, whimsical, radical, or unwilling to compromise. Preferably, they should have demonstrated success in business, finance, or economics.[121]

One would expect similar criteria to apply to most, if not all, presidential appointments.

The record also indicates that the Johnson administration placed a high priority on finding candidates who would be supportive of the president's economic program. The Maisel and Brimmer appointments added to the board two economists sympathetic to the New Economics favored by Heller, Ackley, Okun and others among the president's economic advisers. In placing Sherrill, the president added to the board a man who was well respected by the banking community and was known to be politically supportive. The influence of these appointees should not be overlooked as one source of the improved relations between the Federal Reserve and the administration during the last two years of the Johnson presidency.

Reappointment of Chairman Martin

In addition to appointing members to fill vacancies on the board, a president also has the opportunity to name the chairman of the board. The chairman serves a four-year term that, as pointed out previously, is not concurrent with the presidential term. Thus, it was not until 1967 that Martin's term came up for renewal. To many, William McChesney Martin, Jr. epitomized the Federal Reserve System, having already served as chairman of the Board of Governors for fifteen years. (Martin served out the term of a previous governor and was then appointed to a full fourteen-year term.) A strong and dominant personality, Bill Martin is a man about whom few people can remain neutral.

Governor Maisel has described Martin as a "fun-loving Puritan," observing that he could best be characterized as a "money moralist."[122] Martin strongly believed that the role of the Federal Reserve was to see that there was not too much money created, although he recognized that the system should accommodate normal growth in the economy. A product of Wall Street, Martin prided himself on his skill in interpreting money markets. This led to his placing his faith in the "tone and feel" of financial markets rather than relying on specific quantitative measurements. Martin sought to keep the Federal Reserve completely nonpartisan and viewed with suspicion intanglements with other groups that might serve at critical times to prevent the Federal Reserve from exercising its independent responsibilities to halt inflationary pressures.

The very attributes that made Martin attractive to bankers both at home and abroad led many economists to suspect him. Gardner Ackley has stated that "Martin was absolutely zero as an economist. . . . He has no real understanding of economics."[123] A bit more charitably, Arthur Okun characterized Martin as "honest and conscientious" and indicated that he developed "good personal relations with Martin, and came to respect [him]—although I'm not sure I understand the guy a great deal."[124]

In the spring of 1964, shortly after coming into office, President Johnson made concerted efforts to develop a closer relationship with the Federal Reserve chairman. In typical Johnson style, these initiatives began with clear and highly publicized indications of the high regard which the president had for the Federal Reserve as an independent agency and for Chairman Martin as its leader. These assurances of support conveniently came in the wake of a series of major hearings by the House Committee on Banking and Currency under the chairmanship of Representative Wright Patman. At the outset of these hearings, Patman had made clear his intention to introduce legislation to severely restrict the independence of the Federal Reserve System.[125]

In a speech to the United States Chamber of Commerce on 27 April, President Johnson, as noted earlier, referred to the Federal Reserve as "a very nonpartisan organization and a very sound organization" and observed that it was "led by a very able man."[126] The next day, in a meeting at the White House with sixty corporation executives, the president continued the treatment:

> But let me assure you: if the balance of payments turns sour or inflation starts rolling, I will look to the independent Federal Reserve as our second line of defense. I would have said "first," but you in this room are the first line. . . . Right behind you is Bill Martin—a man to whom I give full faith and credit as an inflation fighter beyond compare.[127]

The message was not lost on the banking community. In an article entitled "President Refers to 'Independent' Fed: ABA Opposes Changes in Fed," a leading Washington financial publication linked testimony by the American Bankers Association opposing changes in the Federal Reserve System proposed by House Banking Committee Chairman Patman to the president's reference to an "independent" Federal Reserve.[128]

President Johnson's comments were quickly followed by a face-to-face and highly publicized meeting with Chairman Martin. Prior to this meeting, Heller had provided the president with a long list of suggestions as to points that might be covered in the discussions. Noting that the Federal Reserve had great control over interest rates, though Martin might claim otherwise, and that medium- and long-range interest rates had eased off in recent weeks, Heller suggested, *"You may wish to compliment Martin on the improved 'tone' of the bond market*—without being too specific about what you think his contribution has been—and encourage him to help *keep it that way."* [129]

Thus armed, the president met with Martin on 5 May. The press reported:

> In the White House gardens last week, two familiar Washington figures strolled about, deep in conversation on a subject Americans dearly love—money. The meeting was not without irony. Pres. Lyndon B. Johnson, whose Texas background makes him lean towards cheap money, does not want to see the present U.S. business upswing choked off by an early move toward tighter credit. The man with whom he talked, William McChesney Martin, Jr., Chairman of the Federal Reserve Board, had just that power. [130]

The article pointed out that "there is a new readiness at the Fed to accommodate itself to government policy" and "it will be Martin's job over the next few years to bring the Fed closer to government— without losing the Fed's sense of independence."

The results of this private meeting between President Johnson and Chairman Martin were not long in coming. On the following day, Martin told the Advertising Council that he saw "no immediate prospect of a rise in interest rates." The implications of his remarks were impressive and readily apparent to the administration. Heller wrote the president, "The outlook is now good—especially after Bill Martin's good statement today at the Advertising Council. . . ." [131] A week later, Heller reported to the president that there had been a further easing of market yields, observing that "Martin's statement gave a *final blow to the recent expectation of higher interest rates* immediately ahead." [132] In another memorandum entitled "Chairman Martin's Impact on Interest Rates," Heller noted the "power of the jaw bone," suggesting, *"You may well wish that your words had as much impact on prices of goods and services as Bill Martin's words have on the price of money."* [133] The memorandum went on to cite comments in the *New York Times,* the *Wall Street Journal,* the *American Banker,* and two private bond letters attributing the improvement in the bond market to the confidence instilled by Martin's comments to the Advertising Council. Heller concluded by observing, "There is now a new secret weapon in the arsenal of Government economic policy—a walk around the South grounds ('down the garden path?') with the President."

Relations with the Federal Reserve remained smooth in the ensuing months. In reporting on one of the periodic luncheons between the CEA and Chairman Martin, Heller commented that Martin "cited several times the good conversations he had had with you not so long ago. He was most generous in offering to cooperate with CEA—he always has been, but was particularly warm and insistent about it on this occasion."[134] It would be almost a year before relations between the Federal Reserve and the administration again became a matter of concern.

President Johnson met with Chairman Martin outside of the Quadriad format on a number of occasions, though none of these meetings received the publicity of the first meeting with the chairman. Martin was a frequent visitor at the White House, attending meetings and social gatherings. The president took care to include Martin along with other administration economic advisers when he was hosting dinners for business executives.[135] Ackley suggests, however, that the president found it difficult to bring Martin aboard as a member of the economic-policy team:

. . . he found Martin one who—quite surprisingly—was pretty much immune to "The (Johnson) Treatment." He had worked him over on more than one occasion without appreciable results, and he certainly had expected people in his administration—the Secretary of the Treasury and members of the Council, and so on—to work on Martin and his Federal Reserve colleagues. I guess he came to see that Martin was just there in the way, and that there wasn't any way to push him aside, so that he had to try to work around him.[136]

In spite of the difficulties they may encounter in attempting to influence Federal Reserve chairmen, presidents often find it difficult to replace one who has earned the confidence of the banking and financial communities. Early in 1967, when Martin's term as chairman was nearing an end, Macy succinctly summarized for the president the case for his reappointment:

I would recommend your reappointment of Martin as Chairman. . . . Although Martin's independence and occasional disagreements with Administration fiscal policy may constitute negative factors in his retention, he does enjoy high prestige with the banking and business communities in this country and with fiscal leadership in other parts of the world. The designation of a successor who could draw the confidence of these elements would be difficult and the consequences might be disruptive at a time when further unnecessary problems should be avoided.[137]

While Martin had indirectly offered to resign if given a "quiet nudge," it was clear that he wanted to remain as chairman until the expiration of his membership term on the board. In a letter to the president commenting on candidates to replace Governor Shepardson, Heller had dwelt at some length on the question of whether Martin should be reappointed. He remarked that he had heard reports from Federal Reserve economists that Martin was "running for re-election."[138] Heller also indicated that he had received word from Brimmer "out of the blue" that he strongly favored keeping Martin as chairman and he felt confident that he was reflecting the views of five board members (that is, all except Martin and Shepardson).

Judgment of Martin's reelection aspirations stemmed from his efforts to push the Open Market Committee to greater monetary ease. For example, Fowler reported to the president on 11 October 1966 on one of his periodic luncheons with Chairman Martin. He noted that Martin had informed him that the most recent FOMC meeting had resulted in a decision to maintain an "even keel" policy which would lean a bit toward the easing side, and that while several members of the FOMC had wanted to hold a tight rein, Martin had persuaded them to a modified course in the direction of ease.[139] Fowler concluded, "I think this represents some progress and, more importantly, the fact that Bill is trying to help." CEA Chairman Ackley was sending similar reports to the president, noting that on several occasions Martin had convinced the FOMC to go along with a proposed action "because the President wanted it."[140]

In the face of strong support from his colleagues on the board, his high standing in international and domestic financial circles, and Macy's recommendation, President Johnson, like his predecessor, bent to the political winds and reappointed Martin for a final term as chairman of the Federal Reserve Board.

Chairman Martin had earned the esteem of the business and financial communities because he had demonstrated his determination to use monetary policy to resist inflationary pressures, even at the price of acting independently of the president and his advisers. While the Federal Reserve under his guidance generally cooperated with the Johnson administration and supported its economic policies, the one time it acted independently gave substance to Martin's symbolic standing as the guardian of the nation's financial integrity. This was the decision in December 1965 to increase the discount rate. Of this action, Governor Maisel has said, "It was the end of the age of innocence; the Fed would not be the same again."[141]

The December 1965 Conflict

During early 1965, relations between the Federal Reserve and the administration became somewhat strained. In February, much to the consternation of the administration, the Open Market Committee moved cautiously to tighten credit. In an attempt to resolve some of the issues, CEA Chairman Ackley met with Chairman Martin. He reported to the president on the results of the luncheon, which he characterized as "quiet and friendly," noting that Martin "emphasized that he wants to be a 'team player,' and to work out a unified position with you on all issues . . . and it is clear he doesn't expect to win them all."[142] Explaining that Martin liked the idea of regular Quadriad meetings every three to four weeks with the president at which monetary issues could be threshed out, Ackley stressed that he had indicated to Martin that if he wanted to be on the team, he would have to guard against actions or statements that appear to commit the administration, or even the Federal Reserve, to a position before it is discussed with the president and agreed upon. Ackley lamented, "I don't know whether he really got the message, but I tried."

In March, the Open Market Committee moved toward slightly tighter money. In reporting this action to the president, Ackley complained that he had learned of it through "unofficial channels"; in the past, Chairman Martin had sent word to the president through the CEA when a change in monetary policy was made.[143] He added, "Perhaps he has informed you through other channels. In any case, it seems *reasonable to me to expect that he should notify you in some way.*"

Over the ensuing weeks, monetary policy remained basically accommodative, with no further tightening of credit by the Federal Reserve. The Quadriad met in March and again in May. There is evidence that the president instructed his financial advisers to maintain close contact with the Board of Governors during this period: in April, Fowler wrote the president, "I appreciate very much the suggestions you have made on several occasions about keeping close to Bill Martin and others in areas of common concern."[144]

The Crisis Approaches

On 1 June, speaking before a commencement-day luncheon of the Columbia University alumni, Chairman Martin observed "disquieting similarities" between the prosperous conditions of the present and the situation in the 1920s. While the main theme of his remarks was the need for further improvements in the U.S. balance of payments, the newspapers headlined the implicit crash warning. The Dow Jones Average fell nineteen points in the three days following the speech and about sixty points over the next three weeks.

Martin's address was widely assumed to constitute an attack on the Johnson administration's economic policies, and many observers feared that it signaled a shift from accommodation to restriction in monetary policy. Sherman Maisel, only recently appointed to the board, notes that he found himself in the "middle of an economic donnybrook" as the "Federal Reserve entered a period of tense relations with the Administration."[145]

Martin's comments reinforced concern within the administration that he was encouraging a change in monetary policy. Two weeks earlier, Ackley had complained to the president of an earlier statement by Martin which he termed "another of his frequent declarations *clearly implying the need for tighter money*—if not now, soon."[146] Ackley wasted no time in criticizing Martin's drawing of parallels between recent events and those of the 1920s, arguing that "it reveals again his *abysmal failure to comprehend the results of 30 years of progress in economic research and economic policy.*"[147] He suggested that the president *"might wish to indicate privately to Bill that some of his recent pronouncements seem unnecessarily disturbing to business confidence in the American economy and in your economic policies."*

The following day, after further reflection on Martin's speech, Ackley concluded that it did not signal a new strategy by the Federal Reserve: "It is hard to know what Bill was driving at in his speech. Some people—especially central bankers—just can't stand prosperity, and keep looking under the bed for ghosts. Bill has taken to conducting the search in public."[148]

Secretary Fowler suggested six reasons for holding a Quadriad meeting, noting, "I have not found in Martin any different view from that he expressed in the last meeting with you."[149] Nonetheless, Fowler felt that "if we are all singing in tune at that meeting on the stable outlook for the continuance of the expansion, it might be worth risking another press conference at which the Quadriad could become a quartet singing in tune a cheery note." The Quadriad meeting was held on 10 June, but the transcript of the press conference that followed indicates that Martin, while endorsing the prosperity of the day, refused to be drawn into speculating on future monetary policy.[150]

On 25 June, Martin gave another commencement address. Maisel observes, "The speech was optimistic and stated clearly that the Federal Reserve would continue to furnish the funds needed by American business for expansion."[151] Whether by coincidence or not, within a day or so of Martin's second speech the decline in stock prices ended and the market rebounded.

Martin's 1 June speech appears to have led the White House to inquire into whether the president had the power to remove a member of the Federal Reserve or to designate another chairman prior to the expiration of the current chairman's term of office. The results of this inquiry were not reassuring. White House aide Jake Jacobson wrote the president on 6 July 1965:

> Attached is a memorandum from Ramsey Clark [the attorney general] holding that the President can remove members of the Board of Governors of the Federal Reserve System only for cause and that the Chairman of that Board, once designated, cannot be removed from the chairmanship prior to the expiration of his four year term. The "cause" which might permit removal does not include disagreement with policies but only neglect of duty or malfeasance in office.[152]

Attached to Jacobson's memorandum were two memorandums written by Clark. In the first he noted, "Since the Board is an independent agency, lack of confidence or disagreement with policies or judgment would not be in itself 'cause' for removal."[153] In the second memorandum, Clark observed, "The question has been raised whether the President has the power to dismiss a member of the Board of Governors of the Federal Reserve System other than for 'cause.'"[154] Clark concluded that the president did not have that power, nor would a constitutional challenge to so limiting a president's removal power likely be sustained. He concluded, "Throughout the 50 years of its existence, the independence of the Board has been universally acknowledged and . . . despite the numerous differences that have arisen . . . no attempt has ever been made to remove a board member."[155]

By August, interest rates had begun to rise. Administration forecasts of the economy still pointed to only moderate advances; the impact of escalation in Vietnam expenditures was not foreseen. For example, on 30 July, Ackley sent the president a memorandum on

"Economic Aspects of Vietnam," in which he indicated that the Vietnam situation had affected speculative commodity and financial markets, but was unlikely to significantly impact overall prices, output, or employment in the coming months.[156] Ackley recognized, however, that if expenditures followed the path projected by Secretary of Defense Robert McNamara, they *"could provide a significant stimulus to economic activity during the first half of next year."*

The CEA's Administrative History asserts that "there was no indication that the Fed's assessment of the domestic outlook differed from the Troika's."[157] Anecdotal evidence, however, suggests otherwise. Heller notes that the board was aware by mid-1965 that the Vietnam expenditure figures were incorrect:

> Everybody had to use the official projections of Vietnam expenditures, and the Fed, among others, in their Green Book—their confidential Green Book [used for Open Market Committee briefings]—had to plug in Lyndon Johnson's forecast for Vietnam expenditures and of course they were way off the track. So the Fed did it with a footnote which said, "For internal use only, but dangerous if swallowed."[158]

Following a Quadriad meeting on 26 August, it was agreed that if the Treasury was approached by bankers seeking an administration response to a possible hike in the prime rate, they should be encouraged to talk to Martin (who had agreed to this approach).[159] Nonetheless, Ackley remained concerned about possible interest rate increases. He observed to the president on 10 September, "When Bill Martin talks about higher interest rates as the product of 'natural forces,' it sounds like the blossoming of daisies."[160] He noted that financial columnist Sylvia Porter's recent bond letter had, however, put it more accurately: "The squeeze of recent weeks reflects policy."

In a series of memorandums to the president in the last two weeks of September, Ackley continued to warn of a pending break with the Federal Reserve. Thus, in mid-September, he cautioned that *"the upward pressure on interest rates is intensifying every week"* and *"the demand for funds is pushing ever harder against a Federal Reserve policy which does not fully accommodate it."*[161] Prophetically, he asserted:

> If there is to be a showdown with the Fed on monetary policy, it probably cannot be delayed much longer. You may conclude that

the wisest course is to stand aside and accept a somewhat higher rate level. But *the Fed has the power to prevent it, and the decision should be made consciously rather than by default.*

On 29 September, Ackley told the president that if the prime rate were to increase, the Treasury bill rate would probably rise to 4 percent, enabling the Federal Reserve to say that it was technically no longer possible to hold the discount rate. "The only way I see this threat can be removed is if *Bill Martin learns you are concerned about what's happened since our last meeting.*"[162] Two days later, noting that a New York bank had raised its rate to finance companies, he told the president that this was the "*inevitable result of the tightening that the Fed has engineered* over the past few months, and the knowledge that many in the Fed . . . are *pushing for an increase in the discount rate.*"[163]

Concern about a discount rate hike was not limited to the CEA. On 4 October, Budget Director Charles Schultze informed the president that when the Federal Reserve staff prepared its economic forecast for the board, the Bureau of the Budget usually tried on a confidential basis to keep it abreast of BOB thinking in a general way. Schultze said that he had instructed his staff *not* to discuss the budgetary outlook with the Federal Reserve, reasoning, "Quite apart from security considerations, I'm afraid that *the budgetary outlook would be used as an excuse to tighten up on monetary policy.*"[164] Schultze noted that this matter had been discussed with the CEA and with Secretary Fowler.

Ackley summarized the growing gap between the administration and the Federal Reserve in a memorandum prepared for the Quadriad meeting of October 6. Explaining that decisions by the Federal Reserve in the next few weeks would determine whether the nation got a new structure of higher interest rates across the board and a new design of monetary policy to restrain rather than support economic expansion, Ackley said that the choice was between a sizable jump in interest rates and a rollback of the recent increases.[165] He warned that "monetary policy stands at the crossroads," and concluded that the best course would be "*to head off a jump in interest rates now, and to take another careful look at the start of 1966* when we can get a better reading on the Budget, the price outlook, and key elements of private demand such as autos and business investment."

Chairman Martin responded to the administration's criticism by writing a long memorandum to the president.[166] He pointed out that too much emphasis was being placed on interest rates when the real problem was to keep funds flowing "freely and effectively" to sustain healthy progress in the economy. If interest rates were not permitted to respond to market pressures, credit availability would be reduced. Ceilings on rates paid on the deposits were the real problem, but if these were raised, it would require a simultaneous increase in the discount rate and would probably lead banks to charge more for new loans or show less interest in meeting new-loan demand. He argued that a higher rate structure would expand, not constrict, credit availability.

In an off-the-record talk to the Business Council a week later, Martin made the same argument, leading Ackley to remark that his statement constituted a clear "declaration of independence" for the Federal Reserve.[167] Thus, the difference of opinion between the administration and the Federal Reserve was clearly understood. The problem faced by the administration was how to get the Federal Reserve to go along with its desire to postpone action until after the first of the year. It is significant that no further Quadriad meetings were held in the critical months of October and November. On Labor Day weekend, the president suffered a gall bladder attack, and on 8 October he entered the hospital for an operation. He spent much of the remainder of the fall recuperating from the operation. Governor Maisel reports that

> Chairman Martin . . . told me that the disruption due to President Johnson's operation had made coordination both with the Quadriad and within the Fed extremely difficult. Given the developing situation in Vietnam and the President's penchant for secrecy, Martin never felt sure how much of what he was told was in confidence, or what positions taken by members of the Quadriad reflected positions acceptable to the President.[168]

Attempts at Coordinated Policy Formulation

Arthur Okun has detailed one approach made by the administration to the problem of bringing about coordination of monetary and fiscal policy.

> Now in '65, Dan Brill got promoted at the Federal Reserve Board. . . . He worked very closely and was very friendly with members of the Council, and I think that improved coordination. . . . There was an agreement in September '65 . . . to start

some coordinated staff work. We asked the President to ask a set of questions—I'm not sure to what extent this was suggested to him by someone else—"what are the expert's views on where the economy is going; and what's the threat of inflation; would tighter money help on the regulatory supervisory front; or should we be doing these things there? If our effort is really to tighten up on the abuse of credit markets, do you want to just cut the total flow, or do you want to pin-point the abuses."[169]

Okun stated that in response to these questions, Chairman Martin agreed to a joint staff effort. A special Quadriad research group was formed that included Paul Volcker, deputy undersecretary of the treasury; Charles Zwick, assistant director of the Bureau of the Budget; Dan Brill of the Federal Reserve staff; and Okun representing the CEA.

The Quadriad research group reported the results of their analysis to the Quadriad members (i.e., Fowler, Schultze, Martin, and Ackley) on 6 November, noting that "this memorandum is intended to summarize our discussions and staff work in the past three weeks in response to your request for an appraisal of the outlook for economic activity, prices and costs, and the balance of payments as it relates to decisions for economic policy."[170] The analysis emphasized that economic policies in the closing months of 1965 should be formulated within an environment dominated by "the prospect of continued economic expansion, at about the same pace as has prevailed since mid-year; continued strong demands for credit on banks and capital markets; moderate but continuing upward pressures on industrial prices; and a balance of payments situation which, while improved, is falling far below earlier hopes and expectations."

Against this background, the analysis concluded that the short-term policy mix with the "best chance of achieving desired goals" involved "continued watchful waiting by the monetary authorities," "a prompt and public condemnation of price increases not warranted by cost developments," and "development and announcement of an improved program to inhibit direct investment funds flowing abroad soon enough to forestall a swelling of anticipatory outflows." Looking to 1966, the research group foresaw no need for monetary stimulus and possibly a "need for restraint" which might be reinforced to a degree by balance-of-payments considerations.

Stripped of their protective coloring, the findings of the Quadriad research group essentially supported the position being taken by the administration. Zwick observes that "Brill's general viewpoints probably came closer to the Administration's than the Fed's, and he had personal problems, but we finally all signed this to our principals."[171] Okun thought the memorandum "went somewhat beyond our mandate" and commented:

> I thought Brill was living dangerously in taking the position he did. It was really a policy recommendation saying we ought to keep monetary policy about where it was, should not tighten for the remainder of the year, consider in light of the budget where we would be for 1966; and if the GNP outlook exceeded seven hundred and twenty billion or so, that would be a signal for tightening-up of policy which might call for higher taxes or for a tightening of monetary policy. Basically the judgment would have to be made at that time of the degree and the choice of instruments used for restraint. . . . I remember when we signed the document, Brill said, "I'll bet we've made monetary policy for the rest of the year." He said, "Well, Martin's going to feel obliged to distribute this, and it's a pretty reasonable position for arguing against taking action now. A lot of guys on the Board are predisposed not to take action anyway; it gives them a good excuse for doing this."[172]

Ackley apparently agreed with Brill. When he forwarded a summary of the joint Quadriad analysis to the president, he concluded, "Bill Martin is apparently ready to buy the report."[173]

The Quadriad analysis had used a set of budget projections provided by the Bureau of the Budget which estimated that the rate of federal purchases would rise from $67.3 billion in the third quarter of 1965 to $71.3 billion in the second quarter of 1966. The Troika analysis, presented on 1 November, contained both this projection and a second estimate showing $1.5 billion more of an increase in federal purchases over the period.[174] However, Joseph Barr points out that both forecasts were seriously understated: "The Defense Department figures [the source of the Bureau of the Budget data for defense spending] were off 12 to 15 billion dollars [a year]."[175] Barr also notes that the Federal Reserve was using the higher estimates of defense spending internally, observing that "they were paying attention to what Senator Russell and Senator Stennis were saying in the area of military spending and weren't paying any attention to what the Defense Department was saying."

By the end of November, the CEA was projecting a slightly higher GNP increase, that is, to $710 billion by the end of the second quarter as compared with $708.8 billion estimated in the Quadriad analysis and $709.3 billion projected in the Troika analysis. Ackley advised the president, "As you well know, the timing and pace of the defense build-up cannot be gauged exactly at this time but this uncertainty is not of major proportions for the period between now and mid-1966."[176]

By late November, the administation recognized that the Federal Reserve would likely move to tighten credit before the end of the year. Thus, on 29 November, Ackley alerted the president that "as Joe Fowler has informed you, the Federal Open Market Committee at its meeting last week made no change in monetary policy," but also that "Chairman Martin expressed his intention to vote to approve an increase in the discount rate if it is proposed by any regional Federal Reserve Bank."[177] Noting that three of the regional bank boards were scheduled to meet on 2 December and that one or more would propose such an increase, Ackley concluded that Governor Daane represented the swing vote needed for approval of the discount rate increase by the Federal Reserve Board. He suggested:

> Governor Maisel believes that Daane's vote against a discount rate increase can be obtained, although he now probably leans in favor of it.
>
> Daane represents the administration in a number of international forums, including the Group of Ten. Secretary Fowler could point out to Daane that it would be inappropriate for him to continue to represent the administration if he votes against a clear administration policy position.
>
> If this fails, Maisel believes that a clear communication of your views to Daane—personally or through an intermediary (e.g., Doug Dillon, who recommended Daane's appointment as Governor)—could persuade him to wait until the situation clarifies in January.

Ackley concluded that it might be desirable to schedule a Quadriad meeting on 3 December to give the president a direct opportunity to persuade Martin to hold off voting for a discount rate increase, but observed that "it is prudent to take out insurance by working on Governor Daane." The following day, the president was informed that Fowler had talked to Daane and had reported that "he got his point across and Daane was sympathetic; however, he is still uncertain as to how Daane will vote."[178]

On the same day, President Johnson received a memorandum from

Governor Maisel containing excerpts from a statement he had made to the other governors in which he generally opposed an increase in the discount rate at this time, arguing that a discount rate hike or a sharp tightening of credit "could be interpreted only as a vote of no-confidence by the Federal Reserve Board in the national goal of growth at full employment."[179]

On 1 December, the president received an updated Troika report which concluded that the case for monetary action was not persuasive at that time, but noted: "It might well become so in January—particularly if the budget is large—as part of an integrated package of fiscal-monetary policy actions."[180] The Troika noted that Martin could act in January with or without consensus, and concluded, "The suggestion for delay is not a devise to stall action but rather to coordinate it and make it more understandable, should action prove necessary." At the suggestion of the Troika, a Quadriad meeting was called for 6 December:

> We want to make clear that the need for monetary policy action, as part of an integrated monetary fiscal stabilization program, could become desirable within the next four to six weeks. The case for monetary policy action early in 1966 should not be ruled out—it may, in fact, become persuasive. . . . One technical but important point must be noted. The necessary scheduling constraints of the Treasury financing program give only a narrow time margin for monetary-policy actions in January. The only feasible time for such action is, roughly, from January 13 to 20.[181]

The Board Acts "Independently"

On Friday, 3 December, the Federal Reserve Board voted 4 to 3 (with Governors Robertson, Mitchell, and Maisel dissenting) to increase the discount rate from 4.0 to 4.5 percent on 5 December, with the action to become effective on Monday, 6 December. Governor Maisel has described his surprise at the action:

> I was dumbfounded when I appeared at a special meeting of the Board of Governors called to deal with a minor regulatory matter . . . to find that a request from the New York bank for a discount rate change had been added to the agenda. No staff studies were before us; no statements by the Board; no opinions from other government agencies were available. In contrast to the reams of paper and studies that accompanied most actions of the Board, this crucial step was handled informally and without documenta-

tion. . . . So much stress was laid on intuition that the question was considered to be primarily one of timing of the move. What it was expected to accomplish or what target would be sought was not part of the discussion.[182]

Given the extensive discussions that had been going on for over three months, it is somewhat surprising that Maisel found the board action sudden and without proper foundation. He notes that the board's decision focused on three issues: the magnitude of the inflationary pressures, the question of coordination with other government agencies versus the independence of the Federal Reserve, and the money-tightening method to be used. The second factor produced the most dramatic split within the board. Maisel states that the majority preferred dramatic and independent action because if the Federal Reserve "did not occasionally demonstrate its powers by using them, it might lose them."[183] He reports that it was not until the week following the discount rate decision that he learned that the Treasury and CEA had offered to coordinate monetary and fiscal policies. These offers had not been reported to the board.[184]

What had become of the consensus to wait until the first of the year that had been contained in the Quadriad staff analysis in which Brill had participated? Okun reports that this analysis was never distributed to the members of the board:

Bill chose to sit on it. His own judgment was that financial markets just couldn't wait, and that there was a sufficient danger of a real mess that required the Fed to act at that time rather than waiting to make a coordinated budget decision.[185]

President Johnson's public reaction to the board's independent action was mild, more of disappointment than of anger. Expressing regret at the discount rate increase, the president explained that the administration's view was "that the decision on interest rates should be a coordinated policy decision in January, when the nature and impact of the administration's budgetary and Vietnam decisions were known."[186] The president later noted:

My argument with Martin was not over the rate increase but over its timing and the failure to coordinate the action with key fiscal policy decisions just ahead. When he announced the increase, Martin knew that three days later he was scheduled to come to the Ranch with the Director of the Budget, the Secretary of the Treasury, and the Chairman of the Council of Economic Advisers for a comprehensive review of the entire monetary and fiscal situation. I particularly regretted that he had acted before knowing the nature and likely impact of our budget and Vietnam decisions. But the Federal Reserve is an independent agency, and I accepted its action.[187]

Aftermath

On 4 December, the Troika informed President Johnson that while the Quadriad analysis of the previous month had indicated only a continuation, not an acceleration, of the pace of economic activity, "today, a significant and perhaps more troublesome acceleration in the pace of over-all economic activity must be recognized as a genuine possibility."[188] This memorandum was apparently written before the Troika learned of the action taken by the Board of Governors. However, it does provide some support for that action. Noting that increased pressures on prices are a likely result of a step-up in economic activity, the Troika advised the president:

This highlights the need for effective application of guidepost policy in assuring responsible action by business and labor. It seems probable also that the Government will be required to take the lead in moderating demand through firmer fiscal and monetary policies.

Considering the lead time required to implement fiscal decisions, the more likely response to the excess-demand pressures that were already being experienced would have been action to tighten monetary policy.

On 6 December, the Quadriad met with the president at the ranch. Gardner Ackley reports that the meeting led to a "reconciliation of sorts, on a personal basis, at least, between the administration and Bill Martin," but notes that "the discussion really didn't center on the Federal Reserve backing down, or changing its policy."[189] Arthur Okun has pointed out that, although at the time of the board's decision the administration economists believed that the time had not yet come to apply economic restraint, once the business plant and equipment survey (which provided information on plans for business investment) was available later in December, it was clear that the Federal Reserve had been right "on that score."[190]

Ackley reports that the members of the CEA were not entirely unsympathetic with the Federal Reserve's position:

We agreed that some kind of restraint was necessary. We would have preferred to see a tax increase rather than tighter money. But if there wasn't going to be any tax increase, we not only clearly predicted to the President that monetary policy would tighten considerably further, but I suppose in a sense we also had a certain amount of sympathy with what the Fed was doing, although we didn't always express that sympathy very strongly or clearly in the President's presence.[191]

Okun made the most persuasive case for delaying the decision on credit tightening until after the first of the year.[192] He noted that six weeks before the FY 1967 budget was to be submitted to Congress, the administration wanted to have all its options open. In that way, a program of fiscal constraint might have been presented to Congress and the nation as a means of avoiding monetary restraint. Once the decision was made to raise the discount rate, tight money appeared "inevitable and irreversible." Thus, to many in the Johnson administration it appeared that the Federal Reserve's action had impaired the chances of "rational and adequate" fiscal actions for the January 1966 budget program. However, he concludes, "In retrospect . . . overwhelming political pressures dominated the fiscal program and I cannot honestly claim that a different posture by the Federal Reserve would have made the difference."

In mid-January the president received from Governors Maisel and Brimmer an analysis of the impact of the discount rate hike which concluded that while it had driven interest rates up, it had failed to reduce credit expansion.[193] In an accompanying memorandum Ackley asserted, "Developments in money and credit markets since early December *reinforce our judgment that the discount rate hike was badly timed and poorly handled.*"[194] However, he noted that the rapid pace of economic activity in the latter part of 1965 made it clear that money should not be any easier and might have to become tighter "to keep things from boiling over." He concluded, *"We don't have to bless high interest* rates publicly, but we will have to live with them, at least for a while."

During 1966, as monetary restraint was applied to mitigate strong inflationary pressures, relations between the Federal Reserve and the Johnson administration moved closer. Okun suggests that in this period, the Federal Reserve's independence "proved to be a valuable national asset," permitting "the president and his administration to assume a passive role, tolerating an unpopular tight money policy silently without explicitly approving or endorsing it."[195] Thus, Federal Reserve independence was shown to cut both ways.

The Issue of Reform

There have been a number of proposals to "reform" the Federal Reserve System. In 1961, the bipartisan Commission on Money and Credit proposed a major restructuring of the system.[196] Its recommendations followed those made by George L. Bach to the Hoover Commission in the late 1940s. In order of importance, they included:

1. Centralizing responsibility for monetary policy (i.e., open-market operations, reserve requirements, and discount rates) in the Federal Reserve Board and abolishing the Federal Open Market Committee.

2. Reducing the Federal Reserve Board in size from seven to five members, with staggered ten-year (as opposed to the current fourteen-year) terms.

3. Making the Federal Reserve Board chairman's term coterminous with that of the president.

4. Eliminating special geographical and occupational qualifications for members of the Federal Reserve Board.

5. Eliminating technical ownership of the Federal Reserve Banks by member banks through retirement of the present capital stock.[197]

Reorganization of the Federal Reserve was considered during the Johnson presidency. In March 1965, Treasury Secretary Dillon wrote to the president concerning proposed changes in the Federal Reserve structure being urged by Representative Wright Patman:

> By raising the specter of radical changes in the Federal Reserve structure that are either unnecessary or unwise—and that would be unacceptable to virtually all segments of the business and financial community—he has increased resistance to an objective examination of any changes, including those that potentially have support both within the Federal Reserve itself and from less doctrinaire outsiders.[198]

In January 1966, Chairman Ackley asked the president if he would agree to the CEA testifying before the Joint Economic Committee in favor of a proposal made by President Kennedy in 1962 that the chairmanship of the Federal Reserve Board be made coterminous with the presidential term. Ackley told the president that the recommendation was favored by Chairman Martin and by the CEA. The president responded to the memorandum by writing, "Call Ackley and tell him 'Just to use his own good judgment' without having spoken to me about it. . . . I want him to do what he thinks is best."[199]

In the summer of 1967, the question of Federal Reserve organization was considered by the president's Task Force on Governmental Organization (the Heineman Commission).[200] Its final report, "Government Organization for Economic Policy Formulation and Administration," addressed not only the structural changes that had been proposed for the Federal Reserve, but also the issue of its independence and the coordination of monetary and fiscal policy. The commission observed that while it was neither endorsing or favoring the degree of independence that had existed since 1935, it did not think that the Federal Reserve's independence *"poses important current or foreseeable problems,"* nor did it believe it was *"at all imperative to incur the costs that would be required to make structural reform in this area at this time."*[201] The commission buttressed this pragmatic finding by recognizing the increased degree of communication and consultation between the Federal Reserve and the administration in the 1960s, observing that "the informal but effective consultative forms of recent years represent major progress and undoubtedly have contributed to the remarkable economic record of the decade."

The commission did suggest that "if it were feasible to make structural changes with less cost, . . . it would be desirable to reduce somewhat the independence of the Federal Reserve Board from the Executive." It associated itself with the "moderate" recommendations of the Commission on Money and Credit, that is, making the term of the chairman and vice chairman of the board coterminous with that of the president; reducing the size of the board from seven to five members and shortening the terms from fourteen to ten years; and vesting all monetary responsibilities in the board and abolishing the FOMC.

In its conclusion, the commission came down on the side of less independence for the Federal Reserve and for more coordination of monetary and fiscal policy:

> If implemented, *these three recommendations would retain the Board as a force for sound money but make it more responsible to the Chief Executive on matters of broad policy. And while we would not counsel subordination of monetary policy to the debt management requirements of the Treasury, we do believe the American Presidency can be trusted to reconcile the inevitable choices between growth, employment, and purchasing power. . . .* In the last analysis, we believe that an effective voice for the stable money point of view can best be assured if the makers of monetary policy participate in the total process of economic policy formulation as actively and continuously as pos-

sible. And the Administration's policy proposals will benefit from a clearer confrontation and Presidential reconciliation of the full range of economic policy goals.[202]

On 31 August 1968, Arthur Okun expressed concern to the president about the action of the District Federal Reserve Banks in moving to implement a board decision on lowering the discount rate. He observed that it had taken two weeks to get the discount rate lowered by all twelve district banks. "Some . . . were clearly dragging their heels. . . . Moreover, none of them was prepared to move more than a quarter of a point, even though the Fed Board had invited a decline of a half a point."[203] Calling the present attitude of the district banks "worrisome," Okun used this occasion to discuss possible reforms in the Federal Reserve structure, particularly centralizing all responsibility for monetary policy in the hands of the board, as suggested by the Heineman Commission. On 3 September, Okun wrote to presidential assistant Joseph Califano observing that Jim Jones had called him with the president's reaction to his memorandum. The president asked Okun to draft a proposal along these lines for possible inclusion in the State of the Union or Economic Message.[204] Neither message, however, contained the proposal.

Concluding Comments

Responsibility for managing monetary policy rests with the Federal Reserve System; more precisely, it rests with the Federal Reserve Board of Governors, supplemented by the Federal Reserve District Bank presidents through their participation on the FOMC. The Board and the FOMC jointly have responsibility for the formulation of monetary policy and its implementation, using the three basic tools of changes in reserve requirements, the buying and selling of securities for the system's account, and changes in the discount rate. The management problem faced by any president in formulating and implementing macroeconomic policy is to ensure that the actions taken by the structurally independent Federal Reserve are consistent with and supportive of the fiscal and debt management policies being pursued by the administration.

Strategic management by the president in the area of monetary policy involves the exercise of presidential leadership in establishing clear national economic objectives, as well as the design of a program of action to achieve these objectives. Operational management by the president in the field of monetary policy involves the establishment and maintenance of mechanisms for communicating his macroeconomic-policy objectives and planned program of action to the Federal Reserve. In addition, the president must develop mechanisms for ensuring participation by the Federal Reserve in the periodic assessment of the performance of the economy and its likely future performance under varying policy assumptions. Finally, he must seek to ensure coordinated application of monetary-policy instruments by the Federal Reserve with those of fiscal policy and debt management policy by the administration.

The latter task is made more difficult by the fact that the Federal Reserve is structurally independent of the president and the administration. Thus, the president must rely on methods of persuasion rather than direct mandate to accomplish the required coordination. In this aspect, the management of monetary policy is similar in nature to the management of fiscal policy: in the former, the president must persuade the Federal Reserve to take desired actions, while in the latter, the president must persuade Congress to act on his tax and expenditure proposals. The president's power to persuade in the area of monetary policy is enhanced by his power of appointment of members of the Federal Reserve Board and its chairman and vice chairman.

President Johnson established clear objectives for macroeconomic policy. He sought to achieve full employment and stable prices within an overall framework of economic growth. The Troika mechanism was the basic device used for the strategic management of macroeconomic policy; it also served as the operational management center.

To achieve operational management for monetary policy, President Johnson relied on the Quadriad, that is, the Troika plus the chairman of the Federal Reserve Board. The key difference between the Troika and the Quadriad was that the former was used both for strategic and for operational management, while the latter was used solely for operational management of monetary policy. Thus, with few exceptions, there was no staff work done exclusively for the Quadriad sessions. Their purpose was to ensure communication of the president's macroeconomic-policy objectives and program to the Federal Reserve, as well as to provide an opportunity for periodic reassessment of the performance of the economy and the need for changes in macroeconomic policy.

The Quadriad also provided the primary mechanism used by President Johnson for coordination of monetary and fiscal policy, and for presidential persuasion aimed at encouraging the Federal Reserve to take actions, or to refrain from taking actions, in accordance with the desires of the administration. However, the formal mechanism of the Quadriad was supplemented by a host of informal mechanisms designed to ensure frequent communication between the administration and the Federal Reserve, as well as occasional direct contacts by the president with the Federal Reserve chairman outside of the Quadriad format. President Johnson also used his opportunities for appointing board members to place on the board individuals who would support his economic philosophy and program.

The structural independence of the Federal Reserve serves primarily *to increase the uncertainty* surrounding the formulation and implementation of macroeconomic policy. One basic theme runs throughout the frequent communications between President Johnson and his chief economic advisers relating to monetary policy: What actions will be taken by the Federal Reserve? This uncertainty complicates the management of macroeconomic policy, and on rare occasions creates friction between the administration and the Federal Reserve.

However, there also are benefits from the structural independence of the Federal Reserve. The Federal Reserve can act without having to obtain the overt cooperation of political actors. (It would, however, have great difficulty acting over any substantial period of time in direct opposition to the wishes of Congress or the chief executive.) At times, this permits a president to achieve actions which would be difficult to obtain politically. It also ensures a strong and persistent voice for price stability at the highest level of macroeconomic-policy formulation.

The conclusions of the Heineman Commission with regard to the independence of the Federal Reserve are supported by the relationships that existed between the Federal Reserve and the administration during the Johnson presidency. The independence of the Federal Reserve System did not prevent it from working closely with the administration throughout the Johnson years. The unilateral decision in December 1965 by the Federal Reserve Board to increase the discount rate represents in retrospect not a breakdown of these close working relationships but an example of the practical value of a politically independent Federal Reserve that can act without first having to gain the approval of the president.

The Heineman Commission's recommendation to abolish the Open Market Committee would simply recognize formally what has already occurred in practice: a centralizing of responsibility for monetary policy in the hands of the presidentially appointed board members. It would, of course, remove the last vestiges of responsibility for monetary policy from the Federal Reserve District Banks—an action that, given the integration of the American economy today, appears long overdue. The proposed changes in the number and terms of board members and the terms of the chairman and vice chairman of the board would contribute to a strengthening of the board as a focus for monetary policy and to a closer coordination of that policy with the economic policies of the president.

Even in the absence of these changes, however, the record of monetary policy formulation and implementation during the Johnson presidency supports the view that sufficient mechanisms are already in place to ensure that an active president can achieve working coordination of monetary policy with the administration's fiscal and debt management policies.

5. The Management of Wage-Price Policy

Efforts to influence wage and price decisions by businesses and unions in order to lessen or eliminate their inflationary impact were another facet of the Johnson administration's macroeconomic policies. The wage-price guideposts, which were the primary policy instrument used by the Johnson administration during most of its tenure, were inherited from the Kennedy administration. Generally, the guidepost policy was regarded as a supplement to fiscal and monetary policies, as a way of dealing with "cost-push" inflationary pressures, especially when the economy was operating at less than a full employment level.

The wage-price guideposts received the explicit approval of President Johnson in his 1964 *Economic Report* (President Kennedy had never endorsed the guideposts as his own).[1] In 1964 and 1965 the administration focused its efforts primarily on wage and price increases in major industries. Some notable victories for the guideposts were won in the metals industries (steel, aluminum, copper), while the automobile industry in 1964 proved resistant to the administration's pressures.[2] In late 1965, as inflationary pressures in the economy intensified because of the Vietnam War spending, guidepost activity began to increase. The first two-thirds of 1966 constituted a period of intense guidepost activity. Price increases in a large range of industries were fought, often successfully, while the administration also labored to keep its own policies (such as public employee wage increases) in line with its anti-inflationary goals. Organized labor, however, was highly critical of the guideposts and, in some instances, achieved wage settlements in violation of the guideposts. Notably, the airline machinists' strike was finally settled with a 4.9 percent wage increase, which was considerably above the 3.2 percent guidepost principle. Some labor spokesmen and newspaper reports contended that this marked the end of the guideposts. Such claims, however, were inaccurate, at least for prices.

Guidepost activity continued throughout the remainder of 1966 and during 1967, though with somewhat lessened intensity and publicity. Throughout 1967 the administration struggled with the question of what sort of wage-price policy could replace the guideposts, which had proved to be of limited effectiveness in dealing with price increases fueled by the effects of the growing budget deficit. The result was that, early in 1968, President Johnson announced the establishment of the Cabinet Committee on Price Stability (CCPS), which was to analyze the causes of inflation and to make proposals for policies to counter inflation. However, little in the way of price- and wage-fighting activity occurred in 1968.

In its efforts to enforce the guideposts, the Johnson administration was confronted with a number of management problems. First was the need to develop reasonably clear, substantive standards of acceptable wage and price behavior to inform affected private parties and to guide the administration's intervention in wage-price matters. Such standards are necessary both in the interests of effectiveness and fairness.

Second, administrative arrangements and structures were needed to implement the wage-price guideposts. Should these be formal or informal, regularized or ad hoc? Who in the administration should be involved, and in what manner?

Third, although compliance with the guideposts was "voluntary," the administration did not want to depend only upon pronouncements and exhortations to secure cooperation. What sorts of additional pressures, or "levers," could be used to gain the consent of unions and businesses? What was the legal authority of the administration in this area?

Fourth, the government's actions in personnel and procurement matters had an impact upon wages and prices, both directly and by example. How then could the government manage its own affairs, hold down inflation, and contribute to guidepost compliance?

Fifth, if the guideposts did not prove economically workable or politically viable, what could replace them? Alternatives ranged from mandatory wage and price controls through study commissions to inaction.

In this chapter we will examine the Johnson administration's dealings with these problems. This treatment should provide a better analytical and managerial perspective on the administration's campaign to influence (or control) wage-price behavior than would a purely chronological one.[3] The discussion will illustrate in particular two tasks of presidential management. One is the need to build consent for presidential policies; this is especially important here because of the voluntary nature of the wage-price controls. The second is the need to develop implementation structures and arrangements; the wage-price controls discussed here involved the higher levels of the administration much more in administrative operations than did the other areas of macroeconomic policy.

The Wage-Price Guideposts

The wage-price guideposts used by the Johnson administration were fashioned by the Council of Economic Advisers (CEA) and first presented in their 1962 *Annual Report*. Underlying the guideposts was the notion that inflationary pressures in the economy would be mitigated if discretionary wage and price decisions were brought generally into accord with what would happen in competitive markets. (All prices and wages, in short, in the view of the CEA and various others, were not inexorably determined by the market.) The CEA outlined the guideposts as follows:

> The general guide for noninflationary wage behavior is that the rate of increase in wage rates (including fringe benefits) in each industry be equal to the trend rate of *over-all* productivity increase. General acceptance of this guide would maintain stability of labor cost per unit of output for the economy as a whole— though not of course for individual industries.
> The general guide for noninflationary price behavior calls for price reduction if the industry's rate of productivity increase exceeds the over-all rate—for this would mean declining labor costs; it calls for an appropriate increase in price if the opposite relationship prevails; and it calls for stable prices if the two rates of productivity increase are equal.[4]

Some modifications were also stated; for example, wage increases could exceed the general guidepost rate if they were necessary for an industry to attract an adequate supply of labor.

In late 1963 the CEA wrestled with the problem of how to strengthen the guidepost policy as price increases became more numerous. Gardner Ackley proposed retaining the guideposts and making them specific:

> This approach (a) would attempt to spell out the guideposts more fully than at present . . . in order to make them reasonably self-executing by anyone who *wanted* to respect them; (b) would not change their status as voluntary restraint and would not ordinarily involve the President's prestige in efforts to enforce

them; (c) would realistically (though not publicly) recognize that there would be many violations; (d) would warn in the most serious terms that wholesale violations will mean a revival of inflation; (e) would set up some reasonably low-level group of government technicians who would (if asked) freely interpret *ex post* whether, in their judgment, based on publicly available data, any important wage or price change was or was not consistent with the guideposts (frequently, the judgment would have to be "we can't tell," or "it looks a bit excessive, though our data are insufficient to be sure how much," or "it seems all right, but only the industry has enough data to be sure"). There would be *no moral judgments* expressed, simply factual statements. . . . [5]

For the wage guidepost, Ackley recommended that the CEA publish a figure for overall trend productivity and that it try to make the price guidepost more specific.

Neither of Ackley's ideas was embodied in the 1964 *Annual Report* of the CEA. A table in the report, however, did lead to the development of the 3.2 percent wage guideline. At a press conference preceding release of the annual report, the discussion turned to which of the figures in the table was the correct one for wage increases. Ackley recounts that "finally someone from the press said, 'well, the figure really ought to be 3.2 percent.' And I don't think Walter Heller said 'no'; so that's how 3.2 got its [designation]."[6] Thus, 3.2 percent, which was the average rate of productivity for the previous five years, became the standard for noninflationary wage increases.

Use of the 3.2 standard continued during 1965. Then in late 1965, the administration was confronted with the issue of what the wage guidepost number should be for 1966. It was anticipated that the productivity increase in 1966 would be less than 3 percent. However, the trend productivity increase for the previous five years was 3.6 percent. Ackley presented the situation to Johnson:

1. As indicated to you earlier, we expect to have a fight on our hands regarding the wage guidepost figure for 1966. The issue is important enough so that you should be aware of what we plan to do—and should stop us if we are making a mistake.

2. We plan to hold the wage guidepost at 3.2%. Labor will call it a betrayal if we don't go to 3.6%; and business will call it inflationary if we don't reduce the figure below 3.2%.

3. Secretaries Fowler, McNamara, Connor, and Wirtz, Director Shultze, Mr. Califano, and I have discussed the issue. All agree that we should not raise the guidepost figure. However, Secretary

Wirtz feels that we will have a great deal of trouble with labor unless this is part of a general "austerity" program. . . . We don't propose any change in the price guideposts, although, as you know, we do hope to apply them more vigorously.[7]

On the memorandum LBJ checked the line stating "Approve sticking to 3.2%." This decision, which severed the 3.2 figure from the CEA's computations and gave it a life of its own, was especially galling to organized labor.

In 1967 the administration stepped up its efforts to secure adherence to the guideposts, including the 3.2 percent wage increase standard. Most of the administration's actions were handled as quietly as possible. August 1966, however, was a big and bad month for the administration and the guideposts. Over the administration's protests, the steel industry increased its prices. The administration then suffered defeat in a dispute between the International Association of Machinists and several major airlines. Negotiations in this dispute dragged on from January until late July, when the president apparently gave in to the union. On 29 July, LBJ made a television statement that the dispute (and accompanying strike) had been settled by a new contract calling for a 4.3 percent annual increase in wages. The rank-and-file union members, however, rejected the settlement by a vote of 3 to 1. Negotiations resumed, and in the middle of August a settlement calling for a 4.9 percent increase was reached. Some observers proclaimed that this meant the end of wage and price guideposts. So far as the price guideposts were concerned, this view was premature, but the administration did no longer seem to have an operative wage guidepost. Secretary of Labor Wirtz informed the president that, on the basis of what went on at an AFL-CIO Executive Council meeting, "everybody is assuming 5% is the new guideline."[8]

The administration, although frustrated in its efforts to hold down wage increases, continued to be active on the price front. A section in a "Weekly Price Report" that Gardner Ackley sent to the president in December, for example, listed as having been taken in the previous week the following price actions:

1. Agriculture raised import allotments on sugar to contain further price increases.
2. The President of Texas Gulf Sulphur—who had promised to talk with me before raising prices—called me on Friday. I told him we hoped he would not move. But I think he will.
3. John Robson talked to the leading gypsum producer which

had not raised prices. There is some hope that he will not go along.

4. As we hoped, the chlorine increase announced last week was cut in half, perhaps partly reflecting our intervention. But instead most producers raised caustic soda prices (which is a by-product of chlorine manufacture).

5. Telegrams were sent to rubber sole and heel manufacturers urging the one which had raised prices to reconsider its increase and the others to make no increase.

6. Following a newspaper report that aluminum companies are planning to increase the price of aluminum ingot, John Robson called officials of the big 4 producers. They left the impression that no increase is imminent. They did not commit themselves not to increase the ingot price but promised to talk with us before taking any action.

7. Jim Duesenberry, Sandy Trowbridge, and John Robson met with machine tool producers to discuss prices.[9]

As this list illustrates, the administration's efforts were both extensive in scope and varied in nature.

The administration was aware that changes in the guideposts would be necessary for 1967. The CEA, Ackley informed the president, had "worked closely with Bill Wirtz, Jack Connor, and others to develop an approach which will retain the productivity principle, although sacrifice the rigidity of the 3.2%" standard.[10] No percentage figure for wage increases was included in the CEA's 1967 *Annual Report*; rather, the need for wage restraint was generally discussed. It was concluded that "if restraint cannot mean an average wage advance only equal to the rise in productivity, it surely must mean wage advances which are substantially less than the productivity trend plus the recent rise in consumer prices."[11] The abandonment of the guideposts was again reported by the press. However, the administration continued to be active in seeking to hold down prices during the first half of 1967.

An appraisal of the wage guidepost situation by CEA member James Duesenberry in the late summer of 1967 was pessimistic:

We are in bad shape. It was necessary to give up the 3.2% standard and we now have no real influence at all on wage settlements. If we have no *quid pro quo* to offer management, we cannot expect even verbal adherence to the voluntary restraint notion, unless we scare them with threats of *ad hoc* Government pressure or price control.

We have continued to send telegrams, hold meetings, and make speeches about price restraint but our effectiveness is diminishing. We are doing very little about wage settlements. It is clear that we need a new approach. An occasional confrontation will not be sufficient.[12]

Various administration officials had been concerned with developing a new approach to holding down prices and wages, and they continued to wrestle with this problem for the remainder of the year. Finally, the Cabinet Committee on Price Stability (CCPS), which will be considered in a later section, emerged from their labors. Whether a result of dissatisfaction with the guidepost approach, or of preoccupation with securing enactment of the administration's income tax increase proposal, or some other reason, guidepost activity tapered off during the last few months of 1967.

Yet the guideposts themselves were not to be scrapped. In December 1967, the CEA was again confronted with the question of how to treat the guideposts in its forthcoming annual report. According to Ackley, the CEA faced a dilemma: "If we establish a numerical wage guidepost, it will either have to be so high as to be merely placing a stamp of approval on continuing inflation, or too low to appear realistic given the inflationary forces already built into the economy." However, the only alternative to a numerical standard was "the kind of meaningless formulation used last year."[13] Ackley sought to include a fairly specific wage standard in the report. In January 1968, he reported to LBJ that the CEA, Secretary of Commerce Trowbridge, and Budget Director Schultze favored a statement that the economy would "make a 'decisive' turn back toward stability only if wage settlements should average about 4½ percent in 1968." Wirtz, he continued, said that this would be interpreted as a numerical standard and that labor would be "furious."[14] The CEA's *Annual Report* reaffirmed the validity of the productivity principle and discussed generally the need for price and wage restraint. The closest thing to a definite standard was a statement that the rate of inflation could be slowed only "if the average of new union settlements is appreciably lower than the 5½ percent average of 1967."[15]

Comparatively little fighting over wage and price increases was done in 1968 as the administration focused its efforts on fiscal restraint and the activities of the Cabinet Committee on Price Stability. Two notable exceptions were struggles involving the steel and automobile industries.[16]

Compliance with the wage-price guideposts was officially described by administration spokesmen as completely voluntary in nature. In point is the following statement by Ackley:

> The guideposts are *voluntary, require no reporting by business,* and are as far removed from public utility regulation and price controls as it is possible to get without doing nothing. They give a business or a union that wants to behave responsibly a definition of responsible behavior. They leave the Government a good deal of flexibility as to the frequency and depth of intervention. But they supply *a logic and a standard for intervention* when it becomes desirable to intervene.[17]

In somewhat similar fashion, Otto Eckstein described the guideposts to the American Economic Association as the "mildest and least bureaucratic form of intervention." They were, moreover, "informal, voluntary, capable of adaptation to the specifics of a situation, devoid of machinery and red tape." Intervention was limited by the guideposts "to those decisions which are so important that the national interest must be asserted."[18]

In such statements one finds an official ideology of the guideposts which emphasizes their voluntariness, flexibility, and limited nature. In actuality, however, there was some divergence between ideology and practice. Some who were subjected to guidepost activity would question their voluntariness, while others would contend that opportunism or arbitrariness, at least on occasion, characterized their use more than flexibility. There is no question, though, that the guideposts constituted a more limited form of intervention than mandatory price and wage controls would have.

Although the documentary record is fragmentary, it is clear that mandatory controls were sometimes comtemplated, particularly by President Johnson himself. Thus in December 1967, Ackley indicated that he was "troubled by the President's recent tendency to refer publicly to the possibility of price-wage controls," primarily because his reference to them was "a powerful force causing people to raise prices and wages. Rumors of such controls were circulating in the business community."[19] Most of the president's advisers were opposed to mandatory controls, although Okun believed that some of the president's "lawyer friends" were the source of his interest in them.[20] That there was some serious consideration of direct controls is evident from the fact that Stanford Ross explored the Truman administration's use of them during the Korean War and that Attorney General Ramsey Clark was queried concerning the president's legal authority to impose controls.[21] Clark's view was that the basic pow-ers of the president "would justify imposition of controls in a severe emergency pending action by the Congress." Califano has recounted that he did not know anyone who favored controls "except the Presi-dent . . . and he didn't decide to do that." But, he continues, "I do vividly remember sitting around the table [at a meeting] and every-body kind of agreeing in an informal, not firm way, that if we ever hit five percent [inflation] we'd have to slap them on."[22] Okun wrote to LBJ in May 1968 that for "the first time in modern history, we are engaged in active hostilities abroad without reliance on mandatory controls over prices and wages at home." Although controls were "surprisingly popular," Okun emphasized that there were many problems and limitations in their use.[23]

Had mandatory controls been imposed, their implementation would have required a vast administrative apparatus, as experience with them during World War II and the Korean War attests. A much, much more limited administrative apparatus (or structure) was used to manage the wage-price guideposts. We now focus our attention on this topic.

Administering the Guideposts: Organization

Because of their fluid, ad hoc quality, it is difficult to describe the administrative structures employed by the Johnson administration in implementing the guideposts. Between 1964 and 1967 various ar-rangements were made for handling guidepost activity. If one set-up did not prove satisfactory, it was quietly abandoned and another was devised to take its place. The problem of organization was never fully resolved.[24] There was one constant element in this administra-tive fluidity: the Council of Economic Advisers played the central, integrating role in guidepost activity throughout the Johnson admin-istration. Although this operational role was not consonant with its regular staff and advisory responsibilities, it fell to the CEA by de-fault. No other agency was available or (more accurately) willing to take on this responsibility. In the White House, Joseph Califano was the central figure involved in guidepost activity.

The informal, fluid, ad hoc administrative arrangements fit in with Johnson's preference that guidepost administration should be a "low visibility program." LBJ also preferred to keep his own role in guidepost activity out of public view, especially after he had gotten "burnt" in the airline machinists' strike. He also preferred to avoid direct confrontations with industry people. On the other hand, he took an active interest in guidepost activity, sometimes suggested "levers" that could be used, or made telephone calls and appeals to involved parties. The guideposts in a very real sense were the president's program. With these remarks as background, we will venture to describe the administrative structure for the guideposts.[25]

An early decision by the Johnson administration was to have a more activist guidepost policy. This in turn necessitated some administrative machinery. In early February 1964, Walter Heller informed the president that some "early-warning, screening, and evaluation machinery" (which he also referred to as "behind-the-scenes organization") had been set in motion. It consisted of:

—Early-warning procedures whereby industry specialists in Commerce and collective-bargaining specialists in Labor regularly feed us earliest possible across-the-board notification of new and impending price and wage changes;
—A technical "task force" set-up whereby working parties composed of Commerce, Labor and Council staff (possibly sometimes reinforced by other agencies) make intensive efforts to assemble and appraise comprehensive price, wage, other cost, profit, and productivity data on particular industries where trouble may be a-brewing. (In the past such compilations have been made for steel and aluminum. One is now underway for autos, and one is contemplated for construction.
—An interagency watch-dog committee at the Assistant Secretary level, chaired by a member of CEA, to ride herd on this fact-gathering analytical activity. This group should screen the tough cases, identify those that invite off-the-record jawbone action by the Administration, and suggest the lines such action should take along with supporting data.[26]

A "Cabinet-level group" (composed of Heller, Wirtz, McNamara, and some others) was established to review the recommendations of the watchdog committee, to decide whether and when there should be consultation with the parties to wage and price decisions, and to "determine whether it should (a) undertake some quiet consultation itself, or (b) recommend that Presidential influence be brought to bear directly on one or both of the parties."[27]

The CEA, aided by the Departments of Commerce and Labor, the Federal Trade Commission, and other agencies, now began following major price movements. Regular "early-warning reports" on prices were sent to the CEA by the Business and Defense Services Administration in the Department of Commerce. The cabinet-level group referred to in Heller's memorandum was involved in the 1964 automobile price dispute, but did little beyond that.

There was a tendency on the part of the administration to devise particular arrangements to deal with specific price or wage problems, especially major ones. A notable example is the effort begun in January 1965 to prevent an aluminum price increase, which culminated in a decision by the government to dispose of some of its aluminum stockpile. On 16 November, the day after the decision was made, Califano sent LBJ a "chronology of the highlights" on the aluminum stockpile situation. It included major meetings and contacts but not the "literally hundreds" of other calls and contacts; he and the president had themselves discussed the stockpiles in over twenty-five separate telephone calls. "Between the 1st and the 9th of November, Fowler, McNamara, Connor, Katzenbach, Knott, Ellington, and I met 8 times in the Cabinet Room. McNamara himself held a number of separate discussions with the aluminum industry. . . ." He continued: "Fowler had a series of discussions with aluminum executives on balance of payments and Knott and Ellington were in almost daily contact with industry representatives for the last several months."[28] Members of the CEA and a number of other top-level agency officials also took part in the episode. Much of the orchestration of the administration's activity was handled by Califano. Obviously, actions of this sort consumed a lot of administrative time and energy and could not be engaged in frequently.

Indeed, at a Quadriad meeting in late August 1965, the president had requested proposals to make the guideposts more effective. In a memorandum to the council on 9 September, Otto Eckstein commented on the need to strengthen the price- and wage-watching operations. Some "alternative institutional arrangements," such as a cabinet committee or a subcabinet committee, were discussed, along with some "wayout schemes" like prior notification of price increases and the use of a public review board to hold hearings on price and wage increases exceeding the guideposts. He concluded, however, that "in the present situation it would be politically impossible to do more than improve the present *ad hoc* procedures of the executive branch. . . . And in making these improvements it should be done in a way that does not run too great a risk of diluting the White House initiative and drive in support of price-cost stability."[29]

The "greatest weaknesses" of the guideposts, Ackley informed the president in November, were the "lack of consistent support for them within the Government itself, and the absence of effective procedures for securing coordinated Government appraisal and action in specific price and wage situations." He elaborated about the absence of "consistent support":

> In principle, the guideposts are the policy of the entire government. But in specific situations one Department or another often counsels against any effort to call the guideposts to the attention of those involved. The Mediation Service wishes the guideposts didn't exist. We were unable to get Defense to fight excessive wage settlements in the aerospace industry. We recently found that the Civil Service Commission hadn't figured out how to measure a guidepost raise for the Civil Service and so on.[30]

Commerce and Labor, because of their constituencies, were the major problems here. To deal with these and other problems, Ackley proposed creation of a cabinet committee on price-cost stability, composed of the secretaries of the treasury, defense, commerce, labor, and perhaps agriculture, the chairman of the CEA, the director of the Bureau of the Budget (BOB), and a White House representative. The committee would have responsibility for developing and assembling needed information, coordinating the strategy and tactics of guidepost implementation, and determining policy relating to the guideposts and more general price-stability issues. It would be assisted by a "technical committee of senior agency officials."[31]

A similar proposal for a "National Economic Council" had been sent to the president several days earlier by Commerce Secretary Connor. Connor was unhappy with guidepost matters in general and the aluminum stockpile situation in particular. (He believed that in the absence of legislation the administration lacked legal authority for the guidepost program.) His proposal was intended to lessen the influence of the CEA. For instance, he suggested that if the wage-price guidepost formula was to be reviewed, "others besides the Council should participate actively in the review, and not be brought in just to observe a 'crash landing' or help to pick up the pieces. You deserve the benefit of the *considered* judgment of *all* your advisors with something useful to contribute." He also suggested that LBJ ask Ackley, Fowler, Schultze, Wirtz, and himself to meet to discuss better organizational and procedural arrangements for handling domestic economic matters.[32]

Perhaps because of such recommendations, at a meeting at the White House on 18 November the president asked Fowler to convene a group consisting of McNamara, Connor, Wirtz, Ackley, Schultze, and Califano to discuss means for improving wage and price guidepost administration. After meeting informally several times, the group reached several conclusions, including: the group should continue to meet regularly; improved machinery for collecting data on prices, wages, and related matters was needed; the group should consider ways to mobilize public support for the guideposts; and there was a need for a small, informal staff located in the CEA to coordinate guidepost activities.[33] The generality of the report caused Califano to advise the president that "the group is not an effective apparatus for handling *specific* price situations at this time."[34]

A second report by the Fowler group on 7 January 1966 included a proposal that businesses and unions be requested to provide the government voluntarily with prior notification of major price and wage changes.[35] In a series of consultations and a large White House meeting, business and labor representatives would be informed of this proposal along with the need to avoid inflation during a time of enlarged hostilities in Vietnam. Johnson explicitly rejected the proposal for the White House meeting and any consultation with business and labor groups involving himself; the appeal for advance notification was made by others in the administration. The Fowler group made no further reports on guidepost matters.

We have already noted that the administration decided to stick with the 3.2 percent guidepost for wage increases in 1966. This occasioned another attempt by the administration to strengthen implementation of the guideposts. An "interagency technical committee," consisting of representatives from the CEA and the Departments of Labor, Commerce, Agriculture, and the Interior was organized to improve the reporting system for proposed wage and price changes. The committee was also to help provide the data needed for various guidepost application projects. A special three-member price staff was assembled by Ackley to work on price matters.[36] One of the members of this price staff, Saul Nelson (who had worked with Ackley on price controls during the Korean War), headed an Interagency Staff Price Committee which included representatives from the Departments of Labor, Agriculture, Commerce, and Defense. Its task was to provide more action-oriented groups with needed information.

The CEA also organized its staff internally to deal with pricing matters. Various staff members were assigned first- and second-line responsibilities for such areas as oil, steel, copper, aluminum, textiles, stockpiles, defense procurement, sulphur, food, and manpower shortages. Their duties included closely following the field day by day through trade journals and other sources, developing and maintaining statistical records, keeping up agency contacts, following government actions and devising new actions with respect to their industries, and being prepared for crises.[37] John Douglas, an assistant attorney general with the Justice Department's civil rights division, was brought on board to strengthen the CEA's legal and operational capacities.

Information flowed into this new setup from various agencies: the Bureau of Labor Statistics, Bureau of Mines, Business and Defense Services Administration, General Services Administration, and Department of Agriculture. The Nelson price committee met on Thursday afternoons to review and anticipate developing price problems and to consider appropriate actions thereon. It used information from the various agencies and followed an agenda prepared by the CEA. Ackley and Califano, and others as needed, met on Friday mornings "to discuss developments in the price situation."[38] Weekly price reports to the president were initiated to keep him informed of price and wage developments and of actions considered, proposed, or taken to deal with them. In the council itself James Duesenberry was assigned responsibility for guidepost matters, although Ackley indicated that he intended to keep an active role (this is borne out by the record).[39]

With this new administrative setup in place, the administration engaged in a high level of guidepost activity during the first half of 1966. By midyear, however, administrative problems had reappeared. The Nelson interagency committee ceased to meet. It had not been very successful because it lacked sufficient strength (because of the lower level, and status, of its administrative apparatus) to secure needed agency action. Bureaucratic resistance and inertia were problems that had to be overcome. To help invigorate the price-fighting campaign, Califano recruited John E. Robson, a former Harvard Law School classmate. The earlywarning reports on prices now went to Robson, who, with the assistance of Duesenberry, reviewed them to see what might be done to fend off or reduce proposed increases. Robson's time was spent seeking information, identifying "levers," proposing actions, attending the weekly price meetings, working on stockpile releases, and the like. He was assisted in his endeavors by an ad hoc "Price Policy" committee which included representatives from the Departments of Commerce, Labor, Treasury, Defense, and the BOB (Califano and Ackley, of course, continued to be deeply involved in the guidepost program). In mid-October, Robson informed Califano that he had been involved in seventeen "principal price actions" in such areas as eggs, copper, shoes, textiles, oil, furniture, farm machinery, and defense procurement.[40]

In early August 1966, a meeting of some of the president's advisers on how to strengthen the guideposts led to a proposal for a presidential wage-price review board. As presented by Ackley, the board would be tripartite, with members from labor, business, and the public sector. The agreement of labor and management to voluntarily submit important proposed wage and price increases to the board for review would be sought. The board, however, would not be bound by the guideposts and its recommendations would have no legal status.[41] A memorandum by Califano summarized the proposal for the board, and the arguments for and against it. It was supported by Fowler, Wirtz, Connor, Ackley, Clifford, and Fortas, who "basically feel that something must be done and that risks are not untakeable in view of benefits." Califano indicated that he and McNamara were opposed (and Katzenbach was inclined to agree with them) because the "risk of Presidential identification with almost certain failure of the proposals is great."[42] This proposal was abandoned. So too was a proposal by Ackley, in response to a Califano request, for a "commission to study how to achieve price stability in a full-employment economy."[43] The administration thus continued to avoid formalizing its wage-price administrative structure, preferring to rely on less visible, more informal arrangements.

A report prepared for the use of the president's Task Force on Government Reorganization (the Heineman Commission) contains a penetrating critique of the administration's handling of guidepost management:

> The experience of 1966 has confirmed once again the absence from the government of reliable machinery for monitoring and reporting private price and wage decisions and trends and of analyzing pros and cons of selective government intervention and pressure; of developing a strategy, in short, for government action to produce restraints. These tasks, in 1966, were handled by a variety of ad hoc crisis or emergency committees, depending on the issue. Late in the year, after some of the most important crises had passed, a more systematic ad hoc organizational arrangement, involving staff of the CEA, a consultant to BOB, and Califano's office was wheeled into place. Under the leadership of John Robson, the BOB consultant, . . . and with the support of Sandy Trowbridge of Commerce and Jim Duesenberry of the CEA, the government set up a price early warning system of sorts, evolved some interesting internal coordination arrangements as between Defense, Agriculture and GSA to reduce the inflationary impact of routine, large government procurement activities, and began to apply pressure for private pricing restraint

in a more orderly fashion. Still the arrangement was a jury-rig and is now being dismantled. It required too much time of CEA, BOB, and White House principals for price administration activities that should have been established elsewhere.[44]

The report went on to say it was "obvious" that those activities needed institutionalization. It was suggested that the proposed Department of Economic Affairs (which never was created) should include an "Office of Price-Wage Analysis and Administration" to handle them. If, however, the new department was not created, "it would seem necessary to create additional staff capacity for this work in the council or as part of an expanded Office of Fiscal Analysis in the Bureau of the Budget, unless it were possible to evolve a price-wage policy which both Labor and Commerce would accept and administer. Their record over the recent past is not reassuring."

During 1967 the administration was somewhat more restrained but by no means inactive in its efforts to hold down prices. Not much was done on the wage front because of opposition from organized labor and a lack of effective levers to use on wage increases. A central feature of the price program was a series of meetings between administration officials and executives from industries presenting price problems. Stanford Ross, an assistant to Califano who had taken over Robson's duties early in the year, and Alexander B. Trowbridge, who had replaced Connor as secretary of commerce, took on much of the responsibility for these meetings. Trowbridge was a more willing and supportive participant in price fighting than Connor had been. Duesenberry and Ackley were regular participants, while officials from other agencies were occasional participants as needed in these meetings. Topics covered at the industry meetings included the government's view of the economic situation and the need for wage and price restraint, the problems confronting the industry, and what the government might do to be of assistance. Price changes by individual companies were usually not discussed.[45] The administration also continued to take more particularized and focused actions against price increases.

In late June, in what he called a "hard look at our efforts on the wage-price front," Ross concluded there were two major problems, namely, "the policy that the Government follows" and "the agencies that pursue these policies." (This did not leave much outside the problem category.) The biggest difficulty with the guideposts themselves was that "they no longer carry the weight needed to accomplish very much in the way of actual restraint." Most of this attention, however, was given to guidepost administration (one can assume that here he drew on his experience with the guideposts in 1967):

> With respect to the agencies that pursue the Government's policy, the CEA has had to carry the heavy oar. Commerce, Labor, and Interior have helped to deliver some of the message. This activity is important and we have pushed it as much as possible. Commerce is holding meetings, Labor is talking to union leaders, and the CEA has been active in publicly stating the Government's position. However, what is going on increasingly amounts to the Government sermonizing on the need for restraint, and business and labor responding in argumentative fashion. *We might be able to accomplish more if there were a vehicle for getting business and labor people to sit down with Government people to work on particular wage-price problems.*[46]

The vehicle he recommended was a commission on stabilization policy, with its own staff, which would consult with business and labor and articulate the public interest in private price and wage decisions. It would have no enforcement powers.

Foreseeing the growth of inflationary pressures by the end of the year, it was Ross' view that unless some administrative mechanism like the commission was established, "we will be in no better shape institutionally to control price rises than we were the last time around in 1966 when only the fall off in the economy was able to calm inflationary pressures." The CEA, he thought, was more concerned with policy than with what agencies were used to administer it. "My own feeling is that policy is less important than having a governmental vehicle which works in sustained and direct fashion on the problems." Within that framework, the policy problems would probably sort themselves out "because we will learn a good deal more about what we can and cannot accomplish by encouraging voluntary actions in the private sector."[47] The Ross memorandum raises an important issue for those concerned with the administration of public policies. The Johnson administration, with its focus on immediate wage-price problems, never appeared to give much consideration to the longer-range adequacy of administrative arrangements. Would the guideposts have been more successful had a more carefully thought out and formal structure been developed for their administration?

Others in the Johnson administration in 1967 were also looking for alternatives to the guideposts. Prominent here, as always, was

Gardner Ackley. In June he drafted a proposal for an incomes policy which was designed to rely on voluntary cooperation, face up to the problem of income shares (especially between wages and profits), and seek to enlist voluntary cooperation by labor, business, and others in setting goals.[48] Essentially a form of indicative planning, it went nowhere in the administration. Ross thought the proposal went "too far, too fast to be an acceptable next step from the guideposts."[49]

In October, Ackley proposed the establishment of a task force on wage-price policy and organization. Because this was "a sensitive area with unions as well as of jurisdiction within the Government," Califano recommended that Ackley "put together a little group" to advise him rather than create a presidential task force. The president approved action of this sort, "quietly and off the record," to develop proposals for wage-price policy and organization in 1968 which would not require legislation.[50]

A few days after this action, Ackley submitted a paper that included proposals for change in the administration of wage-price policies.[51] The CEA, he said, should be moved out of its central role in wage-price policy administration because:

—It is too close to the President, and therefore involves him, at least by implication in whatever it does (or doesn't do);
—Its personnel is too "academic" to be effective in industry and labor contacts;
—Its small staff is overloaded, and should better be engaged in other priority activities.

He favored establishment of a "Cabinet Committee on Wage-Price Stability." It would have a small staff and perhaps a full-time "Executive Chairman," but the White House staff would be "conspicuously absent." The committee's responsibilities would include quarterly wage-price reviews, coordination of studies of rising costs and prices, and consideration of how other government policies could be used to support wage-price stability.

Ackley's statement was used as a discussion paper by the CEA's task force on wage-price policy and organization (a seven-member group chaired by Professor Robert Solow of MIT). The task force favored a permanent "wage-price productivity board, probably in the Executive Office of the President," to be composed of "three very hard-boiled and prestigious men, assisted by a small, permanent staff." This concept, they said, was not much different from the Price-Productivity-Income Office proposed earlier in 1967 by the majority of the Joint Economic Committee. They urged that the review board not be empowered to intervene in particular price and wage decisions.[52] The task force report and other materials were discussed at White House meetings in December and early January 1968.

A memorandum sent by Ackley to LBJ at his ranch in January summarized the thinking of a group which consisted of the CEA, Wirtz, Trowbridge, Califano, and Ross and which had been meeting for several months to discuss wage-price matters. By then it had become apparent that no really strong or innovative wage-price policy could win acceptance from the president, so the group decided to recommend a cabinet committee on price stability without any rule-making or enforcement powers. LBJ announced its formation a few weeks later.

The inception of the Cabinet Committee on Price Stability marked a major turning point in wage-price policy and administration. Except for a few final skirmishes, wage-price fighting of the sort that had occurred during 1964–67 was done with. Before we turn to the CCPS and its activities, then, let us consider the techniques and tactics used by the Johnson administration when price fighting was still in style.

Enforcement Techniques

Although the guideposts were often described by administrative spokesmen as voluntary in nature, they were not simply announced, publicized, and then left to the consciences of affected parties. Rather, the administration at various times devoted a lot of energy to their "enforcement." Lacking the sanction of law, the guideposts carried no legal rewards or penalties with which to induce or compel compliance. However, the administration did use other techniques, or "levers," to put some backbone into the guideposts. Some of this leverage involved simple exhortation; some of it went considerably beyond that. The various techniques can be classified into three categories: intangibles, tangibles, and governmental symbolism.[53] Intangible techniques included the use of discussion, publicity, and various official appeals to persuade parties to act as the administration preferred—to delay or reduce price increases, for instance. Tangible techniques or levers entailed the use or manipulation of other government policies and programs to bring more direct economic or governmental pressure to bear on those affected. These techniques involved actions having more concrete benefits or penalties, such as manipulation of the government's purchase of goods. Government symbolism encompassed government actions intended to demonstrate that the government itself was acting in accordance with the guideposts, that is, to influence others by example.

Intangible Techniques

Appeals to businesses to exercise restraint in pricing or other activities that might affect price levels were made by the president, the CEA, and other members of the administration. Presidential appeals of a general sort usually emphasized the burdens of the presidency, the need to prevent inflation while there was fighting in Vietnam, and the need for patriotic action by those to whom the appeal was made. In early January 1966, for example, LBJ sent the following telegram to the head of Bethlehem Steel, which had just announced a steel price increase:

> I am not announcing this wire so that you and your associates can consider the interests of your country and your company with complete freedom. The best economists of your Government say that your announced price increase—particularly at this critical time in our nation's life and in light of the fact that your after tax profits are eighty-three percent above 1963 and the industry's after tax profits are sixty-five percent above 1963—is not in the interest of your country, nor in the long-run interest of your company.
>
> Your President does not have any price or wage controls, but from where he sits, looking at the interest of all of the people and particularly the millions of our men in uniform, he appeals to you to put the interests of your country first.[54]

Johnson also sent telegrams to seven other steel companies asking them not to follow Bethlehem's lead.

Another Johnsonian appeal was made to a group of 150 businessmen following a dinner at the White House in 1966. The president, pacing up and down for more than an hour before the group, described the nation's economic problems. He focused particularly upon capital investment, a sector of the economy which showed strong signs of overheating. He then asked them to defer or curtail investment spending in 1966 wherever they could. Mrs. Johnson and he had planned an addition to their ranch house in Texas, he told them, but had now decided to delay it. During the next three weeks 42 of the dinner guests sent responses, most giving strong support to the president's efforts to dampen inflation by a voluntary reduction in capital spending. An oil company executive, for instance, reported plans to defer "certain sizeable investments that we had originally planned for 1966."[55]

The president's efforts to restrain capital investment also included use of a favorite Johnson instrument: the telephone. He made dozens of calls to corporate executives asking them to restrain plant expansion. A newspaper account tells this story:

> He began placing telephone calls to business executives, one of them an influential investment banker in New York. The President asked the banker, a friend of 15 years, how he felt about the economy—was it overheating and should there be a tax increase?
>
> As the two men chatted amiably, Mr. Johnson suggested that it would be helpful if business investment could be restrained somewhat.
>
> The call completed, Mr. Johnson rang up other executives around the country. Each conversation followed a similar pattern. The President sought information about what the executive and his friends thought about the economy. And, each time, Mr. Johnson gently dropped into the conversation the hope that business investment could be restrained.[56]

It was Johnson's view that much could be done to promote presidential purposes by using the power inherent in the office. As he confided to acquaintances, people just did not like to say no to a president.[57] Conventional wisdom has it people found it especially difficult to reject personal appeals from Johnson.

Appeals to businesses from the CEA and other government officials—whether made through speeches, letters, telegrams, telephone calls, meetings, or conferences—focused more directly and fully upon the economic conditions surrounding wage or price increases. Most appeals to labor unions were handled by the secretary of labor and his associates. On price matters, the CEA sometimes worked with the secretaries of commerce, the interior, agriculture, the treasury, and defense. Here as elsewhere in wage-price matters, though, the largest burden fell on the CEA. The secretaries of labor and commerce tended to be reluctant to offend their clienteles.

The CEA reported that during 1966 it had been involved in "perhaps 50 product lines" where price increases were imminent or announced. Letters or telegrams were sent to all the principal producers of a product, and telephone calls were placed if the matter was really urgent. Those who had raised prices were asked to reconsider and those who had not were requested to hold off if at all possible. In all cases invitations were extended to discuss the matter with the CEA. In the meetings that frequently followed, the representatives of the companies explained their reasons for price increases and the CEA presented its own relevant information, discussed price stability, and urged the companies to include the public interest in their considerations. These meetings were usually not publicly reported. "The outcome of these activities," the CEA states, "cannot be fully known. In a number of cases, it is clear that price increases which were announced or contemplated have been rescinded, reduced in amount or coverage, or delayed. Some companies have indicated that their subsequent price decisions were affected even where their decision in the immediate cases was not changed."[58]

A considerably different sort of intangible action is recounted by Joseph Califano. Concerned about rising food prices in 1966, LBJ had Califano direct Secretary of Agriculture Orville Freeman to hold a press conference and deplore the rising food prices. After checking with Califano a couple of times to be sure this was what the president really wanted, the reluctant Freeman held the conference. Califano explains Johnson's strategy and the ensuing events:

> Johnson thought such a statement by the secretary of agriculture would be unusual enough to attract wide attention. Coming from the secretary of agriculture, Johnson also thought it would make clear that he meant to jawbone farmers to hold down produce and meat prices. He was explosively correct on both counts. When farm interests came to the White House to demand Freeman's scalp, Johnson, of course, refused to give it. But he was not beyond deploring such a politically indiscrete statement by his secretary of agriculture, although he pointedly told one group, "Food prices sure must be out of sight if Orville Freeman is complaining publicly about them.[59]

Finally, the CEA sometimes issued formal public statements on particular wage or price decisions, such as the New York Transit Authority wage settlement (1965) or the aluminum (1965) and molybdenum (1966) price increases. These were obviously intended to help sway public opinion in support of the government's position.

Tangible Techniques

Tangible techniques, or levers, were fashioned from other government policies and programs and varied in availability and usefulness from one situation to another. Finding effective levers was a constant concern to those trying to fend off price increases, especially during 1966 and 1967. LBJ was reputed to be especially knowledgeable in this regard, undoubtedly because of his long experience in government.[60] Table 6 indicates some of the factors that were considered by the administration in fashioning its guidepost activity. We now turn our attention to some of the levers used to influence wages and prices.

1. Stockpiles. In the post–World War II years, large stockpiles of strategic materials were acquired and stored by the government. These included such materials as aluminum, copper, molybdenum, nickel, industrial diamonds, vanadium, lead, and zinc. The administration, with the aid of congressional authorization, disposed of many of these materials, usually in cooperation with producers and users so as to avoid disrupting markets. In the case of the 1965 aluminum price controversy, however, disposal of some of the aluminum stockpile was used as a lever to get the companies to rescind a price increase. The government then agreed to dispose of its excess aluminum on terms generally agreeable to the industry.

By early 1965 the government had in place a fairly systematic stockpile disposal operation. A stockpile committee concerned with disposal operations met weekly. Information of stockpile operations was included in the weekly price report sent to the president. And as Okun informed the president, "We are arranging for systematic weekly reporting of price movements and other developments in stockpile items in order to speed up stockpile sales and use stockpiles more effectively to influence prices."[61]

2. Procurement policies. As a large purchaser of various goods and commodities, the government could use its purchasing policies to influence prices. There are various illustrations of this. One of the levers applied to hold down a steel price increase in early 1966 was a decision by the Defense Department and other agencies not to buy steel from companies that had raised their prices. To combat rising butter prices the Department of Agriculture was persuaded to give up the inclusion of butter in the school lunch program, and the Department of Defense decided to buy oleomargarine rather than butter for the Army and Air Force. (It was required by law to purchase butter for the Navy and Marine Corps.)[62] A few months later, the Defense Department switched from large- to medium-sized eggs "with price depressing effect," and wholesale price index (WPI) relief, too, since only large eggs get into the WPI.[63] LBJ had been urging this action. It, however, received strong criticism from midwestern congressmen who represented areas where such eggs were produced.

3. Export controls. These were imposed on hides and copper to deal

Table 6. *Wage-Price Analysis and Action Checklist*

1. *Impact Measurement*
   a. Percent of production affected
   b. Effect on older commodities and services (e.g., steel price up
      $____(%) raises auto cost $____(%)
   c. Effect on WPI and CPI
   d. Timing of effect (when will indexes or other commodities and
      services respond)
   e. Balance of payments
   f. Procurement costs (DOD, etc.)
   g. Wage price pattern
   h. Other

2. *Justification Measurement*
   a. Cost justified?
   b. Economic position justified?
      Earnings
      Return on equity
      Cost flow
      Historical
      Stock prices
   c. Do they owe us one?
      Prior restraint record
      Have we helped them

3. *Action Analysis*
   a. Time
   b. Manageable? (Concentrated industry, etc.)
   c. Weigh against future action
   d. Available levers
      Export controls
      Import
      Stockpile
      Procurement (Timing-substitutes)
      Agricultural controls
      Freight and transport
      Renegotiation
      Set-aside
      Congressional or Agency investigations
      Pending matters (have they matters before the government:
         legislation, export-import, Anti Trust, Tax, SEC, etc.)
   e. Legal problems
   f. Labor-employment (negotiation coming up)
   g. Political Problems
   h. International ramifications
   i. Proposed action consistent with other programs and policies
   j. People analysis (who's the best one to see?)

Source: Attached to memo, John Robson to Joseph Califano, 27 October 1966, Robson-Ross Office Files, "Pricing Files: Guidelines," LBJ Library.

with price increases caused by shortages of these commodities. In early 1966 a shortage of hides was driving up the price of leather and shoes. To alleviate this situation the Department of Commerce was directed to work out a program of export controls on hides. The reduction of exports was expected to, and did, result in a substantial decline in hide prices. A meeting in March was held between Connor, Duesenberry, Ackley, and a number of shoe manufacturers at which the manufacturers expressed satisfaction with the action taken. According to Ackley, "the atmosphere of the meeting was very friendly, and I have the strong impression that the industry will be cooperative on the price front, at least partly because they know their own interests lie in that direction."[64] Soon afterward the leading shoe companies announced price increases of 2 to 7 percent on their fall 1966 lines, explaining that the increases would have been greater had not cost pressures been lessened by the export limitation.

4. *Import controls.* The quotas on residual oil imports were raised by 50 percent for the December 1965 through March 1966 period to help hold down oil and coal prices. It was Califano's view that by not completely removing the controls, the administration could "keep both the coal and New England people from becoming too unhappy."[65] In another instance, the Department of Agriculture acted to hold down the price of sugar by relaxing the import quotas on foreign sugar.

5. *Antitrust enforcement.* The use of the antitrust laws to break up concentrations of market power and to bring pressure to bear upon particular companies was sometimes mentioned or discussed by administration officials. For example, in a memorandum to LBJ concerning automobile price increases in 1966, Ackley discussed possible counteractions: "The automobile industry is a classic case for anti-trust action. . . . It is obviously a tough decision for any administration to make. It might be possible, however, to get some committee of distinguished private economists and lawyers to examine the facts and make a recommendation to the Anti-trust Division." Johnson checked the line on the memo approving discussion of this and other proposals by Ackley, Califano, and Katzenbach.[66] The files contain no further information on it, however.

Thoughts about antitrust action could also originate in the White House. Thus in October 1966, an "eyes only" memorandum to Joseph Califano informed him that Jake Jacobson had called from the president's bedroom concerning an article on rising food prices in the *Wall Street Journal*: "Jake wants you to call Ramsey Clark [the attorney general] first thing and get some Grand Juries to investigate food prices in about a half-dozen cities. Ramsey is going to be reluctant to do this and should be talked to 'sweetly.'"[67]

There is no evidence in the record, however, that antitrust activity was really used as a club against particular companies. Indeed, as measured by the number of cases started and completed, it actually declined during the Johnson years in comparison to the Eisenhower years.

6. *Regulatory policies.* Secretary of Transportation Alan Boyd was directed by LBJ to contact the transportation regulatory commissions and ask them to hold rate increases to a minimum. The results in this case were not especially pleasing to the administration:

Alan Boyd's letter to ICC [Interstate Commerce Commission], CAB [Civil Aeronautics Board], and FMC [Federal Maritime Commission] asking them to give heavy weight to the goal of over-all price stability in transport rate decisions produced generally disappointing replies. Assurances were given that the goal of price stability would be considered, along with other goals. But Murphy (CAB) defended the price record of the airline industry and Tucker (ICC) said that all ICC decisions are based on a formal record, and urged DOT to intervene directly in the scheduled investigation of proposed increases by the railroads.[68]

However, the ICC did respond to the administration's urgings when it issued emergency orders to speed up the return of boxcars to the western states to relieve a shortage of cars for lumber shipments, which was contributing to increases in lumber prices.

7. *Agricultural price supports.* Because of their visibility and broad impact, rising food prices greatly concerned the administration, especially in 1965–66. Agricultural price support operations were used and manipulated to hold them down. Illustrative is the following set of actions taken from "A List of Actions Taken to Stabilize Prices since October, 1965":

Food Prices
- Agriculture set a relatively low support price for feed grains.
- Agriculture released some high protein wheat to help stabilize the price of bread.
- Agriculture released other varieties of wheat to help stabilize grain prices.
- As of December 20. . . .

—Soybeans. Agriculture to defer CCC purchases for PL480 and to sell cottonseed oil.
—Dairy. Agriculture to substitute margerine for butter in domestic distribution program.
—Feed grain sales. Agriculture to offer feed grain stocks of CCC including corn, grain, sorghum, and barley for sale "to insure an orderly movement of supply into domestic use and export. . . . a further application of the ever-normal grainery principle of using reserve supplies when demand is strong after building up stocks to support prices in other years."[69]

Agricultural programs were not, however, always easy to manipulate. Milk price supports were usually lowered in the spring of each year because of increased production. In 1966, however, this was not done because of strong opposition from Congressmen Wilbur Mills and Carl Albert. In a meeting at the White House, Harry McPherson got the "distinct notion" that he should tell Orville Freeman that the administration should not be "messing" in that area.[70] The president apparently did not want to be messing in that area, either. On a memorandum on the matter he scrawled a note to McPherson: "Get Mills and Albert with Freeman and get Pres. out of this."[71]

8. *Labor programs.* Recommendations were made from time to time for the use of employment and job training programs to help eliminate labor bottlenecks in the economy. In November 1965, Ackley recommended several actions to help deal with labor shortages in particular industries, skills, or regional job markets. These included intensification of efforts to train and retrain workers, legislative action on the "portability" of pension rights, and better organization of the federal-state system of employment offices to speed the "redeployment" of workers. LBJ instructed Califano to "ask Wirtz do this."[72] One can only speculate on the effectiveness of this sort of activity.

9. *State agencies.* The possibility of a gasoline price increase in 1966 focused the administration's attention on the state production regulation agencies, especially in Texas. "At Joe Califano's request," Secretary of the Interior Stewart L. Udall wrote the president, "I touched base again today with Ben Ramsey of the Texas Railroad Commission to check on the slight decrease in [production] allowables. He explained this as a temporary adjustment to 'keep supply and demand in balance.' He and the Commissioners are most anxious to cooperate with us. They intend to follow a liberal policy to keep supplies adequate."[73] LBJ added his own touch to this effort by suggesting, "We need to get Bur. of Mines to give most generous esti-

mates of needs. . . ." (State production allowables were based on estimates of demand developed by the bureau.)

This list does not exhaust the range of intangible techniques or levers used or considered by the administration: the possibility of using dispute settlement procedures under the Taft-Hartley Act was raised in some labor negotiations and the halting of federal grants-in-aid for highway construction in New Jersey was considered but rejected during the 1966 construction labor dispute. However, the list should convey a notion of the scope and variety of the administration's efforts to combat wage and price increases. Following the discussion of government symbolism, two efforts to hold down prices will be examined to provide some additional detail and insight.

Governmental Symbolism

The best illustration of the use of symbolic action occurred in connection with the annual pay increase legislation for federal employees. As organized labor grew more hostile over the 3.2 percent wage guidepost, the administration felt it necessary, in order to maintain its credibility, to give the impression that it too was complying with the wage standard. The CEA was called upon to do the honors. In 1964 Walter Heller acknowledged that the federal pay bill did exceed the standard and contended that this was appropriate: "Indeed, by making Federal pay more comparable with private pay, this will help us *attract and retain the top level talent needed to make your government operate wisely, effectively, and frugally.*"[74] In 1965, Gardner Ackley's formal memorandum announced that "the present bill meets the guidepost criterion." A handwritten cover note, however, admitted that "this memo goes as far as possible. The *fact is that the bill really does exceed the guideposts a bit.*"[75] In 1966, Arthur Okun was able to deduce through creative arithmetic that the annual rate of increase was precisely 3.2 percent; the government would thus "once again be setting a good example for private wage settlements in giving full recognition to the importance of non-inflationary conduct."[76] Interestingly, a handwritten note on the CEA's file copy says, "Written at Joe Califano's orders." When he signed the 1966 pay bill into law, LBJ noted that "the Chairman of the Council of Economic Advisers has informed me that the percentage increase provided by the legislation is within the limits of the wage guidepost. In our own house therefore, we have set an example for labor and management throughout the country. I urge them to follow that example."[77]

Action was also sought in 1966 to keep the military pay bill and federal "wage board" settlements in line with the guideposts. Ackley, Schultze, and John W. Macy, Jr., chairman of the Civil Service Commission, developed a procedure to insure that pay increases for the employees of government contractors would also be within the guideposts. Thousands of contracts and billions of dollars were involved. Moreover, it was thought inequitable and politically unwise not to cover these employees. Secretary of Defense McNamara, whose department would have been extensively affected, was able to convince the others involved that the proposal should be abandoned because it was "administratively impossible of execution."[78] There was not a little truth to McNamara's argument, but this was also an area of low public visibility because of the nature, variety, and dispersion of government contracts.

Symbolism, to be reasonably effective, does not need to be fully pure in origin or complete in coverage. That the Johnson administration might engage in a little chicanery, as it did on the 1966 pay bill, will surprise very few people.

Two Cases of Inflation-Fighting

In this section we will briefly look at two instances of inflation-fighting. Both occurred in 1966. The first involves the molybdenum industry and is a somewhat typical example of price-fighting under the guideposts. In it we find the use of several levers. The second concerns the hardwood lumber industry, where there was no well-defined target, but rather a general economic situation in which excess demand was pushing up prices.

By July 1966, the administration's wage guidepost was under serious attack. A public price victory was needed to strengthen the government's hand. "To make our position on wages tenable, we must also say, loud and clear, that the price guideposts are still in effect. . . . If possible, public action should be taken to prevent or roll back some specific price increases. (The molybdenum case can be a starter.)"[79] This suggestion by Ackley to use the molybdenum industry as an example was agreeable to Califano who, as he put it, "was actively looking for somebody to knock off." The president was also sensitive to the need to do something.[80]

On 8 July 1966, American Metal Climax (AMAX) announced a 5 percent increase in the price of molybdenum, which is used as an alloy in high-strength steel. AMAX produced most of the United States' supply of molybdenum; Kennecott Copper and the Molybdenum Corporation of America were the other two major producers.

Prices had been constant since 1964 although there was a shortage of molybdenum.

The government had a variety of levers to use against AMAX: the company was being aided by the U.S. government in a number of mining ventures around the world; negotiations were in progress concerning the release of stockpiled molybdenum; AMAX, although worried about the imposition of export controls, favored retention of a tariff on imported molybdenum; and AMAX was under investigation by the Antitrust Division.[81] It was thus a rather vulnerable AMAX that was invited to meet with the CEA on 11 July. At that meeting AMAX officials argued that a price increase was justified because their level of productivity declined as output increased. Ackley responded that while the information that AMAX presented might be accurate, the administration's position was that "the price increase was badly timed."[82] On 13 July AMAX announced rescission of the price increase "at the specific request of the Government, which believes this will avoid inflationary pressures."[83] Preventing a price increase as an example to others rather than inducing compliance with the guideposts was the dominant motive of the administration in this case.

In the fall of 1966, following an earlier flurry in softwood lumber prices, the prices of hardwood lumber started to increase rapidly; this in turn pushed furniture prices upward. One action taken by the administration was a directive to the General Services Administration to stop buying high-grade hardwood lumber for governmental work. Next, an interagency group with representatives from the Appalachian Regional Commission, CEA, Economic Development Administration (EDA), Business and Defense Services Administration, Forest Service, and Department of Labor was set up to explore ways of increasing the hardwood supply, especially from the Appalachian area. EDA and the Small Business Administration (SBA), for example, provided financial and technical assistance to the many small sawmills in the area. A job training program handled by the Labor Department was intended to increase the availability of workers. "There is no clear evidence as to the success of these specific efforts, but the supply-demand balance for hardwood lumber did improve and prices did decline somewhat."[84] Unlike the molybdenum case, there was no obvious "culprit" here. The problem that captured the administration's attention was one of supply and demand producing rising prices; ameliorative action had little to do with the guideposts as such.

The Cabinet Committee on Price Stability

In his 1968 *Economic Report* President Johnson discussed the need for responsible wage and price behavior to restore price stability in the economy. "Existing Government organization," he said, "is not effectively suited to dealing with the full range and dimensions of the problem of prices."[85] Thus he announced he was establishing the Cabinet Committee on Price Stability to study and recommend ways to maintain price stability. To be served by a small professional staff, the committee would not become involved in "specific current wage or price problems."

Subsequently, in a memorandum appointing the secretaries of the treasury, labor, and commerce, the BOB director, and the CEA chairman to the CCPS, he outlined the various duties of the new agency. It would:

1. Prepare and publish from time to time studies in depth of economic conditions in those industries which are a persistent source of inflation.

2. Study intensively and make constructive recommendations concerning all aspects of Government policy that affect prices in particular sectors.

3. Work with representatives of business, labor, and the public to enlist cooperation toward responsible wage and price behavior and structural improvements that promote the achievement of overall price stability.

4. Hold a series of conferences both with representatives of business, labor, and the public interest at large, and with representatives of particular industries or particular segments of labor
—to attempt to reach some consensus or appropriate general standards to guide private price and wage decisions;
—to identify remedial problems that inhibit price stability in particular areas, and attempt to design cooperative programs for private and governmental action to deal with these problems.

5. Recommend suitable legislation which would advance the objective of price stability in a free market economy.[86]

The work of the committee was to be coordinated by the CEA chairman. Other departments and agencies were informed that the president assigned the "highest priority" to the work of the CCPS and were requested "to cooperate to the maximum extent possible" with its work.[87]

In mid-April Willard F. Mueller, formerly the chief economist at the Federal Trade Commission, was appointed executive director of CCPS. Several senior economists, a legal counsel, and a supporting staff were also hired. A deputies group of top-level officials was established to backstop the participation of the CCPS principal members. Several areas presenting price or wage problems were selected for study, including the construction industry, medical and health care, international trade, government procurement, regulated industries, and collective bargaining and manpower. The studies were undertaken by the CCPS staff and outside consultants. Staff members of other agencies were also utilized.

Although the CCPS was not supposed to become involved in specific wage or price problems, Okun secured permission from LBJ to have the CCPS issue a statement (a "blast" in CEA parlance) criticizing prospective inflationary wage agreements in the construction industry. In the first quarter of 1968, construction settlements had averaged 7.5 percent, whereas the average for all industries was 6 percent. This action, Okun informed the president, would not violate his instruction against specific involvements because "the wording of the statement focuses on an industrywide situation, not a specific negotiation. Of course, our timing is influenced by the fact that the Detroit [building trades union] contract expires May 1."[88] One sees here a certain amount of hair-splitting. Other than for an unsuccessful effort to hold down copper prices, this was the only specific wage-price action during the first half of 1968.

In July, while the CCPS staff was at work on its economic studies, Okun wrote to Califano concerning the wage-price situation. During the months of negotiation on the tax increase bill there had been a lull in the efforts to secure business and labor cooperation on wage-price restraint. "While the government was the main source of inflation," he said, "it was hard to ask business and labor to stem the tide."

> Now that the surcharge is law, the basic question is whether we should resume a more concerted and visible effort. In point of fact, matters are back in the lap of private decision-makers. The President has indicated his attitude by emphasizing the need for private restraint in his signing statement on the tax bill and his comments at the swearing in of Warren Smith. Unless we follow through these general statements with specific requests of restraint, we will be backing away from the past policy of activity. And we do not have a good economic rationale for inactivity.[89]

One idea that was acted on was the sending of letters by the CCPS (Okun called them "pre-sin sermons") to all unions and companies engaged in important wage negotiations. These letters discussed the inflationary threat confronting the nation and the national interest in responsible settlements (less than 5½ percent) and postsettlement price behavior. They would, in Okun's view, "remove ignorance as an excuse for irresponsible action. Despite clear statements to the contrary, many parties do—or choose to—interpret the 'abandonment' of a specific guidepost as a lack of interest by the Administration in the size of settlements and the subsequent price increases." Also, the letters might stiffen management's resolve in wage bargaining and make management more cautious in making price increases.[90] The administration also intervened in several price matters, notably for home-heating oil, steel, and automobiles, during the latter part of 1968.

In December the CCPS reported to the president on its activities during the past year. It also made a number of recommendations for future actions to achieve high employment and reasonable price stability. These included such things as greater antitrust enforcement to promote competition, improvement of federal procurement policies to reduce any inflationary impacts, and various actions to hold down the cost of medical care. Also proposed was an "equitable formula" for wage-price guideposts for 1969. New union settlements should average less than 5 percent (or halfway between the 1967 average of 6½ percent and the 3.2 percent productivity trend). Businesses "should absorb cost increases of 1% of unit costs without passing these on in higher prices, and should aim at profit margin targets no higher than the 1967–68 average."[91] This was the first time the administration had laid out a profit standard, which had been favored by labor and opposed by business. Within the CCPS the proposed guideposts were also a cause of controversy, which has been described by Willard Mueller:

In the many meetings with labor representatives it seemed clear to some of us the price and wage guideposts, alone, would not be sufficient. Before the final report was submitted to the President, the CCPS was faced with three separate versions of the guidepost section: (1) a Labor Department version, (2) a Commerce Department version, and (3) a CCPS staff version, which I believe also essentially reflected the views of CEA Chairman Okun and Budget Director Charles Zwick, and later of Secretary of Treasury Fowler. The Labor version provided for no wage and price guidelines, rather, it would have relied on extensive labor-management dialogue on the issue. The Commerce version provided for a weak form of price and wage guidelines. The CCPS staff version called for wage, price, and profit guidelines. After a somewhat heated debate among the Cabinet members, Secretary Fowler broke the deadlock by implying that if the Secretaries of Commerce and Labor felt constrained in accepting this position because they felt a special obligation to their constituencies, it would perhaps be in the public interest if they submitted dissenting statements. Secretary of Commerce C. R. Smith said, "hell no," he didn't object to a profit guideline. The deadlock was broken and the Committee unanimously agreed in principle to a profit guideline. Secretary Smith said, "just come up with the right number."[92]

This dispute over guideposts that were likely to have no effect, coming as they did at the end of the administration, is indicative of the different views which persisted to the end within the administration over price-fighting. Early actions of the Nixon administration included disavowal of the use of guidelines in fighting inflation and dismantlement of the Cabinet Committee on Price Stability. These actions led to a belief that "anything goes" and culminated in the imposition of formal wage-price controls by Nixon in 1971.

Of what value was the CCPS? Stanford Ross, who helped develop it, provides one perspective. It was, in his opinion, a "very useful structural innovation" which helped meet the need for continuous institutionalized action on some of the deeper, longer-term problems of inflation. The CCPS dealt with, and provided "public focus" on, some basic issues. It, in short, helped keep attention focused on the public interest in responsible wage and price behavior.[93] It also enabled the administration to at least appear to be dealing with inflationary wage and price actions.

Guidepost Management: An Appraisal

The application of the wage-price guideposts in the Johnson administration consumed a considerable portion of some top-level officials' time and energy, especially Joseph Califano and the members of the CEA. The president, too, invested quite a bit of time and energy in the guideposts. The burden that they placed on top-level officials would have been lessened had stable administrative arrangements and procedures been developed for their administration. Rather, ad hoc arrangements and actions were the order of the times.

To be effective, voluntary guideposts require support from the public and tolerance or acquiescence from the regulated. (This would also be true for compulsory standards in a large, complex economy).

The Johnsonian guideposts, however, do not appear to have ever had such public and group support. Gardner Ackley later attributed this to the manner in which the guideposts were developed:

To a considerable extent, the Kennedy-Johnson "guideposts" were simply dreamed up by economists and then promulgated. I have long considered the absence of any real participation by the interest groups in the origination and modification of the guideposts— and, as a consequence, the absence of any sense of responsibility on their part for the success or failure of the effort—to have been the greatest weakness of the guidepost system.[94]

One effort to build support for the guideposts, especially among organized labor, involved the revival in May 1966 of the Labor-Management Advisory Committee (LMAC). The LMAC had been initially established in 1961 to advise President Kennedy on various public policies and had been permitted to lapse early in the Johnson administration. Its revival did not prove very effective for guideline purposes, however, at least partly because the administration seemed disinclined to entrust it with much independence and responsibility. "The way to get the guidepost problem thought through on a long range basis," Califano told the president, "is not with this committee but with some good in-house staff work, which would then be blessed by this committee."[95] The administration sought support, not advice, from the LMAC. For a time at least the CEA viewed the committee as the "private property" of the secretaries of commerce and labor.[96]

Importantly, there was never unified support for the guideposts, within the ranks of the administration, where they tended to be viewed as the CEA's handiwork. "The guideposts were unilaterally developed in concept and in administration by the Council of Economic Advisers" was the view of the Department of Commerce.[97] Agency differences over the guideposts, illustrated elsewhere in the chapter, obviously complicated guidepost administration and reduced their effectiveness.

The actual application of the guideposts was characterized in large part by haphazard case-by-case activity. Robson has described guidepost activity as an "ad hoc, reactive, fire-fighting sort of operation." There was no systematic means for determining when action should or should not be taken.[98] Nor was there any effective way to determine in most instances whether a price increase was in accord with the guideposts. As one close observer noted:

It has become apparent that the cost data readily available to the Administration is not sufficient to make a tight guidepost case in controversial price situations. The hard fact is that the CEA is not in a position to make defensible independent cost and productivity calculations for most industries. The Administration's position on prices is, therefore, not likely to be based on whether or not a price increase is "warranted," but rather on efforts to have price changes re-examined in the light of their indirect or "ripple" effects on customers, suppliers, and the economy. The Council can often help even a large company develop a broader view of the implications of price decisions.[99]

Over time, the guideposts developed a momentum of their own and the focus of concern expanded. Attention was focused even on such items as men's underwear and women's hosiery. (One weekly price report stated that "the situation in men's underwear is tight"!) These areas can hardly be depicted as having major price implications for the economy, but attention to them did help satisfy the administration's urge to be doing something and LBJ's appetite for action. The guideposts, as developed, were to be applied to "major" wage and price decisions; this was largely true of the limited guidepost activity of 1968, but not of the rather frenetic price-fighting of 1966.

What wages and prices the administration could successfully hold down depended greatly upon voluntary compliance. The most widely used enforcement techniques—the most readily available and the least likely to generate political opposition—were the intangibles. Tangible techniques or levers were sometimes scarce; in the case of organized labor, they were essentially nonexistent. Moreover, their too frequent or heavy-handed use could have caused resentment and contentions about the abuse of power.[100] In short, guideposting was mostly jawboning.

Although some guidepost cases were much publicized, such as the 1965 aluminum and 1966 molybdenum cases, most of the activity was characterized by low visibility. This permitted the administration to proceed without endangering the government's or the president's prestige. However, "once it hit the White House, the rules were that we couldn't lose."[101] The point was made quite starkly by LBJ at the height of the 1965 aluminum imbroglio: "Somebody's going to eat crow and it isn't going to be the President of the United States."[102]

Questions of fairness, equity, and due process were sometimes raised about the guideposts as they were administered. The CEA, for instance, recognized that there would be violations, perhaps many, of the guideposts, and it was accepted that few, if any, penalties would befall the violators. In practice this put a burden on those who were compliant, or vulnerable, or both. As one critic put it:

> Moral suasion is inequitable in that it rewards noncompliance; it constitutes extra-legal coercion by government without judicial review; it is in violation of the "rule of law"; where promises, implicit or explicit, are involved, it entails the danger of an overly familiar relationship between regulator and regulatee; its ad hoc character adds an additional element of uncertainty to business decisions; and it may frequently be used in lieu of (i.e., as an excuse for) not implementing more effective legislation.[103]

In January 1966, at the time of the dispute with Bethlehem Steel, George Reedy sent LBJ a long and thoughtful memorandum on the guideposts. In his view the guideposts had really become wage-price control devices where "the Government sets a figure—without hearings and without an opportunity for the people who are affected to state their case—and then uses that figure as a ceiling beyond which industry and labor cannot go." He suggested that once the steel episode was over a study be made of the equities of using the guideposts "as a price control device without giving industry (and labor) an opportunity to state its case with at least some of the same safeguards that are accorded by regulatory agencies such as the ICC, the FCC and the FPC."[104] Reedy's memorandum was probably not warmly received in the White House. It does, however, raise an important point about the need for some regular procedures to ensure fair treatment of parties affected by government action. It was, however, LBJ's desire not to formalize the guideposts by setting up some regular administrative device, which might have in time produced more equitable procedures, for their implementation.

Now, questions of administration aside, what was accomplished with the guideposts? Robson takes a qualitative view, contending that guidepost activity created a degree of sensitivity on the part of the business community toward price changes and increases. Businesses had a desire to be viewed as responsible rather than be criticized for ignoring the public interest. Some companies modified their pricing behavior as a consequence. It was Robson's position that one could not quantify the effect of guidepost implementation. But read on.

A statistical study of guidepost activity between October 1965 and June 1967 found more than seventy instances of government contact with businesses involving several hundred companies. In forty-eight cases the government's concern was directed at actual or imminent price increases. Statistical analysis indicated that the administration was effective in eighteen cases and ineffective in twenty-eight cases (two were dropped for lack of data.) It was concluded that the eighteen cases of successful action "did have a small effect on the price level on the order of a few tenths of one percent."[105] The impact of the guideposts would assuredly have been greater had means been available to secure price *reductions* when these were called for by the guideposts.

Would prices have been stabilized had the Johnson administration resorted to mandatory price and wage controls? Perhaps, especially if adequate restraint had been applied to the economy through fiscal and monetary policy. In that case, though, the voluntary guideposts would probably have been adequate. More flexibility in the administration of the guideposts, particularly in 1966 when the decision was made to stay with the 3.2 percent standard, also might have made them more viable. As that decision amply demonstrates, managing the economy would be much simpler were it not a political as well as an administrative and economic task.

6. The Management of Foreign Economic Policy

The president's 1966 *Economic Report* summarized succinctly the objectives of the Johnson administration in the management of foreign economic policy:

>—to correct our remaining balance of payments deficit, so that the dollar will remain strong;
>—to improve the international monetary system, so that it will continue to facilitate sound and orderly growth of the world economy;
>—to work toward reduction of trade barriers, so that all nations may reap the benefits of freer trade; and
>—to press forward with other fortunate nations in the great international task of our age: helping those countries now economically less advantaged which are prepared to help themselves make rapid progress toward a better life in freedom.[1]

These objectives are closely interrelated and strongly linked to the administration of macroeconomic policy.

Attainment of equilibrium in the nation's balance of payments is commonly cited as one of the four goals of macroeconomic policy. In the Johnson years, continuing deficits in the U.S. balance of payments constrained the administration's freedom to pursue domestic policies aimed at achieving full employment, price stability, and economic growth.

The United States' payments deficits, coupled with the key role of the dollar in international trade and finance during the Johnson years, made domestic macroeconomic policy much more contingent upon the operation of the international monetary system than might have been the case. In conjunction with representatives of the nation's major trading partners, the Johnson administration made critical changes in the international monetary system, gold policy, and the provision of assistance to allies faced with international liquidity problems.

While trade policy traditionally has not been considered by economists to be macroeconomic in nature, decisions on *overall* policies affecting the level and composition of trade, as distinct from those relating to *specific* commodities or industries, have important impacts on employment, output, and prices at home. In the Johnson years, these decisions related to the management of the Export Expansion Act, the Kennedy Round of tariff negotiations, and the Export Control Act.

Assistance for foreign economic development is an important aspect of the nation's foreign policy. While it has little direct impact on the administration of macroeconomic policy, it is closely related to the nation's other foreign economic policies.

Taken as a whole, foreign economic policy is inextricably linked to domestic concerns. Often it involves substantial questions of internal U.S. economic policy; almost always, it is characterized by strong pressures from domestic economic interests. At the same time, foreign economic policy generally requires direct relations with other governments; thus, it forms an important component of American foreign policy. "The core of the problem of foreign economic policy is the need to balance domestic and international concerns."[2]

From an organizational viewpoint, issues of foreign economic policy almost inevitably are interdepartmental, requiring collaboration and cooperation among a number of line agencies. There are more than sixty agencies, departments, or other institutional mechanisms which have direct interests and decisionmaking powers in international economic issues.[3]

Foreign economic policy issues are also highly complicated and quite technical, requiring for their solution substantial economic and financial expertise. As I. M. Destler observes, "substantive complexity brings with it organizational complexity."[4]

The management of foreign economic policy is primarily a problem of coordination, involving both the resolution of disagreements among domestic interests and integration of separate policies and actions into a coherent, balanced, and consistent national program.[5] The president must give direction to this enterprise. Graham Allison and Peter Szanton note:

Only the President has the perspective to make the hard tradeoffs between foreign and domestic, regional and national, "economic" and "political" considerations, and only he can impose such decisions on his subordinates and lead their justification to Congress and to the public.[6]

But the president cannot perform this task alone. Reflecting on his eight years as secretary of state, Dean Rusk comments: "The real organization of government at higher echelons is not what you find in textbooks and organization charts. It is how confidence flows down from the President."[7] U.S. overseas commitments are so extended and complex, and reliance on lower-level decisions so necessary, that presidential lines of communication must extend down to the assistant secretary level if the president is to be effective in managing foreign economic policy.

Thus, the president must establish a coordination system which permits him to manage the decisionmaking process on foreign economic policy and to ensure that major high-level decisions in this area are implemented. The manner in which this coordination system actually operates depends not only—perhaps not even mainly—on its formal structures and procedures, but also on the "roles, informal styles, and working relations of the president and his senior officials."[8] Presidential decisions on the degree of centralization and the policy orientation of the coordinating structures and institutions are critical to the success of the outcome. For as Stephen Cohen states, "U.S. international economic policy is frequently a reflection of organizational dynamics . . . the procedures for reconciling values and goals . . . [and] the efficiency with which organizational processes reconcile competing intrabureaucratic concerns and perspectives."[9]

This chapter begins with an analysis of the organization and staffing for the management of foreign economic policy in the Johnson administration. It then turns to an examination of management efforts in two important areas of international monetary policy—balance of payments and international monetary reform—which are most closely related to the administration of macroeconomic policy. Because of space limitations, no similar effort is made to consider the Johnson administration's management of trade and aid policy.

Organization and Staffing

In the Johnson years, the central role in the operational management of foreign economic policy was played by the Treasury Department. However, the Department of State, Council of Economic Advisers (CEA), Bureau of the Budget (BOB), Federal Reserve System, Department of Commerce, Office of the Special Representative for Trade

Negotiations, Export-Import Bank, Departments of Labor, Agriculture, the Interior, and Defense, and the Agency for International Development (AID) also were involved significantly in one or more areas of foreign economic policy.

Lateral coordination among this diffuse set of departments and agencies generally was decentralized, that is, left to a combination of what I. M. Destler calls the "three C's" of coordination—committees, clearances, and compromises.[10] However, substantial day-to-day involvement of the White House and executive office staffs was required to provide coordination from above.

Formal Responsibility

In each major area of foreign economic policy, primary responsibility was assigned in the Johnson years either by legislation or by presidential mandate to a lead agency.

In *international monetary policy*, including both balance-of-payments issues and international monetary matters, the secretary of the treasury had clear primacy. He advised the president on the nation's overall policy stance in this area, and most of the supporting staff work and implementation efforts were carried out under his direction. The chief operating officer within the Treasury Department for international monetary policy was the undersecretary for monetary affairs, although others at the assistant secretary level and below were also involved.

In *trade negotiations*, the State Department was the lead agency until Congress created the position of the Special Representative for Trade Negotiations (STR) in the Executive Office of the President under the Trade Expansion Act of 1962. The supporting office was created the following year by executive order. The office was quite small, numbering about thirty-eight full-time employees, ten of whom were on loan from other agencies. The small size of the staff meant that the office could do little in the way of data collection. Most of the staff's efforts were directed toward the actual negotiation of reciprocal trade concessions with other countries. As a consequence, the office relied on data collected by the executive departments, in particular the Departments of Commerce and Agriculture. The STR divided his time between Geneva, where he resided and supervised the Kennedy Round trade negotiating team, and Washington, where he oversaw the interagency structure established to develop recommendations for the president on matters of trade policy.[11]

In *bilateral aid policy*, the secretary of state had formal line authority over the AID administrator. In practice though, the Office of the Secretary was not involved in economic aid questions in any substantial or consistent way. In *food aid*, the Department of Agriculture had long assumed major responsibility, with AID very actively involved. The BOB, Treasury Department, and White House staff reviewed aid agreements, and President Johnson ordered every food aid agreement and all development loans over $5 million to come to him personally for approval.[12]

In *multilateral aid policy*, AID represented the United States on the Development Assistance Committee and the United Nations Development Program. However, the secretary of the treasury appointed and instructed the U.S. representatives to the World Bank, the Inter-American Development Bank, and the Asian Development ment Bank.

Interagency Coordination

Interagency committees have been aptly described as the "crab grass" that proliferates in the gardens of governmental institutions.[13] In the area of foreign economic policy, a host of interagency structures were used to coordinate policy development and implementation. Among the more important of such groups were the Cabinet Committee on Balance of Payments, the National Advisory Council on International Monetary and Financial Problems, the Development Loan Committee, and the Trade Expansion Act Advisory Committee.

The interagency committees, with the notable exception of the Cabinet Committee on Balance of Payments, seldom met. Over time, they tended to develop, either formally or informally, a "three-tiered" structure: the principals, who set policy but met infrequently; the alternates (usually assistant secretaries), who sometimes met officially on key issues but conferred informally much more frequently; and the staff committees (middle management), which met frequently and had access to the agency resources needed to support policy formulation and implementation efforts.

For example, in the area of trade policy, the Trade Expansion Act Advisory Committee was chaired by the STR and included the secretaries of state, the treasury, commerce, agriculture, labor, the interior, and defense. In practice, trade policy recommendations were developed by an assistant secretary–level group, the Trade Expansion Act Executive Committee, which functioned to hammer out the basic compromises on interagency differences. It also oversaw the activities of the Trade Staff Committee, composed of middle-management representatives from each of the departments, which obtained information and advice from the agencies, reviewed summaries on specific trade issues, and recommended policies and alternatives to the Executive Committee.

Some of the interagency committees facilitated interdepartmental *operational* coordination at the staff level, particularly in the balance-of-payments and trade policy areas. In some cases, however, *policy* coordination took place through ad hoc groups, sometimes referred to as "clubs," which were created to deal with pressing problems and which operated at or around the assistant secretary level. During the Johnson years, these ad hoc groups were particularly in evidence and significant in dealing with the Kennedy Round of tariff negotiations and the reform of the international monetary system.

Finally, there were formal clearance procedures generally relating to aid agreements. These cumbersome processes involved review and comment on the staff level of the affected agencies and final approval of the president.

White House Involvement

Under President Eisenhower, formal responsibility for coordination of foreign economic policy was vested in the cabinet-level Council on Foreign Economic Policy located in the Executive Office of the President. In practice, however, the Treasury Department dominated international monetary issues, while leadership in other areas, particularly trade and aid, was exercised by Undersecretary of State C. Douglas Dillon.[14]

President Kennedy decentralized foreign economic policymaking, both in form and in practice. He abolished the Council on Foreign Economic Policy, formally transferring its functions to the State Department. But in fact, the influence of that department on aid and trade issues was reduced by the creation of the semiautonomous Agency for International Development in 1961 and the Office of the Special Representative for Trade Negotiations in the Executive Office of the President in 1963.

Under Kennedy and Johnson, the National Security Council (NSC) became the central policy-coordinating mechanism for foreign economic policy. The chief role in this regard was played by the deputy special assistant for national security affairs. In the Johnson years, this position was initially held by Francis Bator. In 1967, he was succeeded by Edward Fried, who assumed the role but not the title.[15]

Bator and Fried specialized in international economic issues and U.S.-European relations. They served as members of the interagency groups working on balance-of-payments and international monetary issues. Both were described as having had "intermittent" direct access to the president and were able to communicate with him through the special assistant for national security affairs, McGeorge Bundy, who was succeeded in 1966 by Walt Rostow. Bator and Fried had a very small staff, never exceeding two or three persons. However, they were able to secure staff support from their close working relationships with senior international affairs specialists in other units in the Executive Office of the President such as the CEA, the Office of the STR, and the Bureau of the Budget. It is important to add, however, that the NSC itself never acted as a central coordinating body for foreign economic policy. Bator and Fried served strictly as personal advisers to the president.

Foreign economic-policy coordination during the Johnson years was as highly decentralized as it was informal. In addition to Bator and Fried, White House officials whose primary responsibilities lay outside of this sphere participated as they saw fit. As with other issues, the involvement of the staff in foreign economic policy tended to wax and wane depending on the degree of presidential involvement and concern.

In 1965, President Johnson specifically delegated responsibility for trade matters to Harry C. McPherson, Jr. The deputy special counsel to the president, DeVier Pierson, also was extensively involved in trade issues. Ernest Goldstein was assigned specific responsibility for the balance-of-payments program in late 1967, and monitored the tourism and export promotion aspects of the program in 1968.

The role of a White House assistant to the president, whether he was a specialist like Bator and Fried, or a generalist like McPherson and Pierson, centered on the president's needs and desires. Fried observes that the White House staff performed four basic functions: (a) to see that the recommendations coming to the president were properly staffed out—that all of those interested or concerned had an opportunity to comment; (b) to ensure that the issues were properly developed—that the possibilities for action were identified; (c) to follow developments in the government in their general fields to see that emerging problems that eventually would require the president's attention got to him before the issues had been decided—before options had been closed off; and (d) to assist in settling disputes and in getting agreement among agencies where there were policy differences.[16]

Fried states that memorandums dealing with foreign economic policy addressed to the president from agency and department heads generally would be routed through Fried. He would send them to the president, often with his own analysis and summary of the issues, through the special assistant for national security, in this case Walt Rostow. Pierson indicates that a similar procedure was followed on trade issues:

> Ambassador Roth [STR] and the State Department and the Commerce Department, Labor, Treasury would all have views on a trade issue, and it would be a matter of getting together with them. Sometimes they'd all insist on sending their views to the president, so they'd send their views to the president. You'd collate them, put them together with a summary, and send them in. If he was enamored enough with the subject he might hold a meeting himself, but usually he wouldn't.[17]

In addition to screening communications to the president, the White House staff served as a source of information and advice on policy issues in their particular areas. Frequently, the president would pick up the phone and call them. Pierson notes, for example, that he "talked to him God knows how many times and at how many different hours."[18] White House staff members also participated actively on important study groups and interdepartmental committees wrestling with specific policy problems. In this role, they often acted as monitors, coordinators, mediators, advisors, and motivators. For example, on 23 May 1968, Goldstein reported to the president, "Yesterday we had a productive meeting concerning ways to improve both the commercial and agricultural export programs. . . . Weekly meetings, which should hopefully lead to action, will continue in my absence. Ed Fried and Bill Blackburn will be sharing responsibility for keeping things moving."[19]

An insightful report prepared for the presidential task force on governmental reorganization (the Heineman Commission) summarized the approach taken by the Johnson administration to the management of foreign economic policy:

> To sum up, our present approach to the "coordination" of [foreign] economic policies is essentially a set of recurrent adversary procedures among departments which may be relatively strong in one area and relatively weak in another. Decisions tend to turn on the relative balance of intelligent arguments, pressures, legal authorities and high officials which agencies can mobilize at particular times, with White House and EOP staffs struggling to maintain some kind of general control on the most important questions.[20]

We now turn to an examination of how this decentralized and informal coordination system worked during the Johnson years in the management of balance-of-payments policy and international monetary reform.

The Management of Balance-of-Payments Policy

When U.S. payments to foreigners, resulting from the free decisions of citizens, directly or through their government, regarding what to buy, where to travel, and how to invest their savings, exceed the payments received from abroad, the nation incurs a balance-of-payments deficit.[21] Payments deficits result in foreigners accumulating an increased stock of dollars. They can hold these dollars in bank deposits or in short-term investments in the United States, or they can seek to convert their dollar holdings into gold or other currencies. Thus, when the U.S. runs a deficit in its balance of payments, it either loses monetary reserves, that is, gold or foreign exchange, or it increases its demand liabilities to foreigners, that is, foreign-held dollar deposits in U.S. financial institutions and short-term government securities.

Prior to 15 August 1971, when the United States officially suspended the convertibility of the dollar into gold, the willingness of foreigners to hold dollars resulted from their confidence in the firm commitment of the U.S. government to redeem dollars on demand by selling gold at the then-fixed price of thirty-five dollars an ounce.[22] Obviously this confidence was affected by the size and duration of the U.S. payments deficits, as well as by the perceived health and strength of the U.S. domestic economy.

But if foreigners lost their confidence in the U.S. capacity and commitment to maintain the fixed price of gold, they would become unwilling to hold dollars, and the United States would suffer an outflow of monetary reserves. Since its reserves were finite, the United States could not afford to be complacent about such an eventuality. It had three options: it could act to eliminate the payments deficit; it could devalue the dollar by raising the price of gold; or it could let the dollar float, permitting market forces to set the price of gold.

Throughout the Kennedy and Johnson years, there was a firm commitment by the administration to eliminate the nation's payments deficit and a strong resistance to any suggestion of devaluing the dollar. The traditional policy prescription for balance-of-payments deficits was domestic deflation brought about through tight monetary and restrictive fiscal policies. This conflicted with the domestic objectives of full employment and economic growth. As a consequence, both presidents resorted to more direct efforts to stem the outflow of dollars through reducing government overseas expenditures, promoting exports, encouraging foreign travel and investment in the United States, and curtailing U.S. corporate investment and bank lending abroad.

An Overview of U.S. Balance-of-Payments Policy

For more than a decade following the end of World War II, the economic and financial policies of the United States in part were directed toward the reconstruction of the Free World economy. During this period, the U.S. ran an almost continual balance-of-payments deficit. However, because foreign monetary authorities were willing to hold these earnings as dollars or as claims on dollars, the payments deficits did not result in a net outflow of gold.

In 1958 and 1959, U.S. payments deficits increased sharply as a result of lagging exports and rising imports. Unlike in earlier years, however, the deficits resulted in large transfers of gold to foreign accounts. The International Monetary Fund began to characterize the U.S. balance-of-payments situation as a "problem."[23] In mid-November 1960, President Eisenhower announced a series of measures aimed at strengthening the balance of payments by reducing U.S. expenditures abroad. In the same month, the United States and seven other countries joined together to begin selling gold in London on an ad hoc basis to help stabilize the world price.

Because foreigners were less willing to hold dollars, President Kennedy upon taking office faced the prospect of large outflows of gold unless immediate steps were taken to eliminate the nation's payments deficit and to restore confidence in the dollar. On 6 February 1961, he transmitted to Congress his recommendations for a strengthened balance-of-payments program, affirming that the time had come to eliminate the deficit by "responsible, determined, and constructive measures."[24]

The U.S. recession bottomed out in the first quarter of the Kennedy presidency and the next two years were marked by economic recovery, stable prices, and over a 40 percent reduction in the nation's balance-of-payments deficit. By 1963, however, this progress was threatened by a massive outflow of long-term capital, primarily to borrowers from industrialized countries who were taking advantage of the relatively lower U.S. interest rates. On 18 July 1963, President Kennedy announced a new balance-of-payments program featuring a proposal for a "temporary" tax on purchases of foreign securities by

Americans—the Interest Equalization Tax—and intensification of policies already under way.[25]

President Kennedy had given Treasury Secretary C. Douglas Dillon primary responsibility for management of the balance-of-payments program. Shortly after assuming office, President Johnson received from Dillon a thorough summary of the status of the program. Dillon concluded that

> the balance of payments problem is many faceted and requires constant attention on many fronts. However, the combination of the 1961 and 1963 programs, plus such further savings as may prove possible in the defense area, now appear to be adequate to bring very substantial improvements over the course of the next year.[26]

In the early months of 1964, there were clear indications that the actions initiated by President Kennedy were leading to a reduction in the payments deficit. On 14 May 1964, President Johnson wrote to the heads of thirty-three departments and agencies reminding them of President Kennedy's July 1963 message and adding, "I have reaffirmed the July 18 message as the policy of this Administration."[27]

In early January 1965, it became apparent that the nation's balance-of-payments position was deteriorating. In the next few weeks, possible measures to reduce the deficit were actively debated within the administration. In a special message to Congress on 10 February 1965, President Johnson outlined a ten-point program to reduce the outflow of dollars, repatriate liquid funds from abroad, and attract foreign capital.[28] The most significant new aspect of the February 1965 balance-of-payments message was a voluntary restraint program to reduce capital outflow from corporate direct investment and bank and nonbank lending abroad.

Throughout 1965, the voluntary-controls programs acted to constrain foreign direct investment by U.S. corporations and lending abroad by U.S. financial institutions. After some deliberation, it was decided to maintain both programs for 1966, but to tighten the guidelines for the direct-investment program.

However, the balance-of-payments situation deteriorated in 1966, primarily due to U.S. commitments in Vietnam. Despite the worsening situation, the year-end review of the balance-of-payments program in the last months of 1966 led to a decision to continue the voluntary restraint program on the grounds that the 1966 deficit would be of a magnitude that foreigners would tolerate, recognizing its close association with the foreign-exchange costs of the Vietnam conflict.[29]

In his *Economic Report* transmitted to Congress on 10 January 1967, President Johnson recommended a number of additional actions to strengthen the nation's balance of payments.[30] During most of 1967, the administration focused on getting Congress to enact an income tax surcharge, an action that was expected not only to reduce domestic inflationary pressures, but also to improve the balance-of-payments situation, since lower domestic prices would encourage exports and discourage imports. However, the decision by the British to devalue the pound on 18 November led to a complete reexamination of the balance-of-payments program.

The last six weeks of 1967 saw a hectic effort on the part of the administration to develop a strengthened balance-of-payments program. The deliberations culminated in a meeting of the president's advisers at the Texas ranch on 30–31 December. Agreement was reached and the president held a press conference at the ranch on New Year's Day to announce the new program.[31]

The program contained a mixture of measures, some old and some new, some temporary and some long-term, some to put in place immediately and others to contemplate. Among the "temporary" measures, the president invoked his authority under the Banking Laws to establish a mandatory program to curtail direct investment abroad by American corporations. He also asked the American people to defer for the next two years "all unessential travel" outside the western hemisphere. Longer-term measures proposed by the president dealt with familiar areas—expansion of American exports and attraction of foreign investment and tourists to the United States.

In 1968, the nation's balance of payments showed considerable improvement. The year ended with a surplus for the first time since the 1940s.[32] The mandatory control program for direct investment abroad worked reasonably well.

Thus, it can be seen that balance-of-payments concerns occupied a good deal of the administration's attention during the Johnson presidency. From the outset, President Johnson accepted the policy objective that President Kennedy had articulated: to eliminate the deficit in the nation's balance of payments. He also adopted the administrative mechanism which had developed under President Kennedy for implementing this policy—the Cabinet Committee on Balance of Payments chaired by the secretary of the treasury.

From the beginning, the Johnson administration resisted pressures to impose mandatory controls and taxes to reduce the outflow of dollars, opting instead for a voluntary approach. The voluntary programs were combined with concerted ad hoc efforts to reduce overseas expenditures by the government, to encourage foreign investment and tourism in the United States, to promote expansion of U.S. exports, and to obtain from our allies contributions to the support of U.S. armed forces in Europe.

The combined pressures of the escalating Vietnam War and the British devaluation of the pound in 1967 led to the abandonment of the voluntary approach and to the imposition of mandatory controls in the last year of the Johnson presidency. Nonetheless, the improvement in the nation's balance-of-payments position in 1968 was due more to the passage of the income tax surcharge, the development of inflationary pressures in Europe, and the capital flight from France occasioned by the spring riots there than to the effects of the program announced by President Johnson on New Year's Day.

Management of the balance-of-payments program during the Johnson years involved a large number of separate actions coordinated by the Cabinet Committee on Balance of Payments. It also required continuous efforts on the part of the president to mobilize the cooperation and assistance of the departments and agencies within the government and the support and participation of the private sector. It is to these efforts that we now turn.

Implementation of the Voluntary Program

Treasury Secretary Dillon has observed that President Johnson did not initially exhibit a great deal of interest in balance-of-payments matters, but that the situation changed markedly after his reelection.

> I think he thought it was an esoteric thing that we should take care of. It had been a relatively calm period after he came in. . . . Then it began to get a lot worse after his reelection and in that late fall when he was working on it. Then he realized that this could be very difficult and devoted time to it, and was very interested in it.[33]

CEA Chairman Gardner Ackley offers an explanation for President Johnson's growing interest in the balance of payments: " . . . he had to get involved because a lot of things that needed to be done or that some people thought ought to be done were very controversial . . . pretty sensitive stuff, and he wasn't going to stay out of that."[34]

Having announced on 10 February 1965 his intention to institute a voluntary, rather than a mandatory, program to restrain capital outflows, the president was concerned with gaining acceptance and understanding of his policy, particularly among those whose voluntary compliance was needed for the program's success. On 18 February, he called together at the White House a stellar representation of the American business and banking community to be briefed by the president, Treasury Secretary Dillon, Secretary of State Rusk, Defense Secretary McNamara, Commerce Secretary Connor, AID Administrator Bell, and Federal Reserve Chairman Martin.

Lawrence McQuade, assistant secretary of commerce, recorded at the time his impressions of the meeting:

> I went to the White House to hear the president give a rousing pep talk to the three hundred odd first line business leaders. . . . Somehow Johnson really got to the assemblage . . . "If you guys don't help, Doug Dillon's going to make me do awful things. Save me and free enterprise from that." The sense of patriotism was high.[35]

It was recognized within the administration that the Federal Reserve would be greatly aided in implementing the program for limiting bank and nonbank lending abroad by its regulatory relationship to the financial institutions involved and by its close working relationship with them. On the other hand, the Commerce Department faced a much different institutional and political setting. Former CEA Chairman Walter Heller had cautioned the president that it was important that the voluntary program he perceived as being even-handed in its treatment of bank lending vis-à-vis corporate direct investment abroad.[36]

On 8 March, Ackley advised the president that the Federal Reserve *"seems to be doing a tough-minded and thorough job,"* but cautioned that *"the voluntary cooperation program for industrial firms is a difficult job."* He concluded: "While the banks are used to reporting requirements, businessmen emphasize the *free* in free enterprise. It is important that banks as a group don't get to feel that they are being asked to carry an undue share of the load."[37]

To assist him in formulating the voluntary program to limit direct investment abroad, Commerce Secretary Connor appointed a nine-member "blue chip" Balance of Payments Advisory Committee.[38] Reporting to the president at Jack Valenti's request on the first meeting of the Advisory Committee, Ackley voiced concern because the committee strongly opposed detailed reporting and advance notice of major new overseas investments, which Ackley "assumed were at the heart of the system for providing guidance and assuring cooperation."[39] Ackley pointed out that the administration faced a policy dilemma in that the program of moral suasion depended on voluntary compliance, which itself depended on businessmen believing that the failure of the program would bring about something worse (from their perspective). "Yet," he warned, "if they really think something worse might be coming, they are likely to take defensive actions which will defeat the objectives."

The program adopted by the Commerce Department did little to allay the fears of the skeptics. On 22 March, Secretary Connor wrote to the chief executive officers of 632 American corporations outlining the program of voluntary controls on direct investments abroad. He described his consultations with the Advisory Committee, which had "strongly urged that our program be set up on as informal and personal a basis as possible, with a minimum of formal reporting requirements and other 'red tape,'" and noted that the Advisory Committee "is particularly in favor of a flexible approach that enables each company head to work out his own program, based on the operating facts of his own business, rather than limit the means of meeting each company's objective by having the government prescribe some formula of general application."[40]

Ackley continued to express doubts about the Commerce Department program to the president. On 5 May, Ackley reported on a private conversation that he termed a "frank lecture" with Pierre-Paul Schweitzer, head of the International Monetary Fund, in which Schweitzer had expressed approval of the bank program but admitted that he had "very little confidence in the [voluntary] program for corporations, which he appears to regard as something of a sham."[41] Ackley noted that "this strengthens my conviction—expressed to you previously—that it is urgently necessary to have ready on a standby basis . . . a temporary system of direct controls on capital flows, and . . . a more permanent system based on tax incentives."

Responsibility for monitoring the balance-of-payments program was centered in the Cabinet Committee on Balance of Payments, chaired by the secretary of the treasury. Shortly after assuming office, President Johnson had been briefed by Secretary Dillon on the structure and role of the Cabinet Committee. Dillon noted that since its creation in June 1962, the committee had reported to the president two to three times a year on the nation's balance-of-payments and gold situation and on decisions taken, and that "where issues could not be resolved by the Committee, it had met with the President for his decision."[42]

Members of the Cabinet Committee included, in addition to the secretary of the treasury, the secretaries of defense and commerce, the undersecretary of state, the administrator of AID, the STR, the director of the BOB, and the chairman of the CEA. The White House was represented by the deputy special assistant for national security. Staff work for the committee generally was done by the Treasury Department. Dillon concluded:

> Since we wanted the Cabinet Committee . . . to operate informally, no executive order or other formal document was ever issued creating it. However, the Committee has been extremely useful in coordinating our efforts in this field and in reaching policy decisions necessary "to the defense of the strength and stability of the dollar." . . . As a result of our conversation Friday, it is my understanding that you wish the Cabinet Committee to continue as in the past.

The Cabinet Committee met approximately quarterly to review the balance-of-payments situation, and several times it met with the president. The most intense activity, however, occurred in the fall of 1965 and 1966, when the committee met frequently to develop recommendations for the following year's program to be submitted to the president.

For example, in the fall of 1965, the committtee met with the president on 20 September, and then by itself on 30 September, 18 October, 27 October, 3 November, and 16 November to formulate and discuss alternatives for the 1966 balance-of-payments program.[43] Following the 16 November meeting, Secretary Fowler provided the president with a four-page memorandum explaining that the committee would present its recommendations for the voluntary program for banks, nonbank financial institutions, and corporations during the week of 21 November, and that a full program incorporating decisions on the other aspects of the 1966 program—government expenditures abroad (military, aid, and civilian), tourism, factors affecting the trade balance, foreign investment in the United States, etc.—would be presented to the president by 1 December.[44] The promised report from the Committee reached President Johnson on 26 November. It appraised the balance-of-payments outlook for 1966 and recommended that the "lion's share" of the 1966 improvement in the deficit come from a reinforced Commerce Department program.

Bator sent his own candid assessment of the effectiveness of the proposed program for 1966 directly to the president:

> . . . the Cabinet Committee proposals represent our best move *for now.* I think it is a fair three-to-one bet that most of Connor's clients will play ball—for a while. . . . In the end, I suspect that

we will have to go further and impose a tax on virtually all capital outflow. But there is a good case for moving one step at a time. If Connor's people do not play ball, we will be in a stronger position to impose a tax after having given the voluntary route a real try. If they do go along for a while—as I think likely—you have more time to consider asking Congress for a standby tax, with a variable rate, which is what we really need for the long pull.[45]

President Johnson accepted the recommendations of the Cabinet Committee and made them public on 2 December by a Fowler-Connor-Martin-McNamara-Bell press conference at the White House, followed by the release of a letter from the president to Secretary Fowler.

The Cabinet Committee met on 25 March 1966 to review the payments situation, and Secretary Fowler reported the results of this meeting to the president.[46] While there was no detailed forecast available, some key changes had occurred in the assumptions used in the previous November 1965 projection. The committee initiated an extensive review of the situation in order to find ways to cut the prospective deficit by $1.5 billion. There was general consensus that by intensifying existing efforts, about half of the desired level of savings could be obtained. Secretary Fowler believed that any savings beyond this amount would have to come from taking some type of firm action on travel abroad by U.S. citizens. However, as he reported to the president on 23 April, there was general opposition within the committee, with the exception of the Treasury and Defense departments, to a proposed travel tax.

On 10 May, Secretary Fowler indicated to the president that important decisions needed to be made on the balance-of-payments program:

Literally, I have gone as far as I can go in taking decisions, i.e., "coordinating." Much as I would like to avoid it in view of the consequences of the alternatives at hand, further decision making must involve you now. Otherwise, events may overtake us rather than our controlling events.[47]

Fowler recommended an ad hoc meeting with the president to include Secretary McNamara, Federal Reserve Board Chairman Martin, CEA Chairman Ackley, Undersecretary of State Ball, Undersecretary of the Treasury Deming, Bator, and Deputy Undersecretary of the Treasury Knowlton. There is no record of the president's response to this request, and no decision was made at this time to impose a program of restraint on American tourism abroad.

The balance-of-payments position of the United States continued to deteriorate during the summer of 1966, largely due to the foreign-exchange costs of the Vietnam War.[48] The closing months of the year saw intensified discussions within the administration of possible measures which might be taken to reduce or eliminate the payments deficit.

Action was initiated to determine the extent of presidential authority to stem the outflow of dollars under existing laws. On 20 September, John Robson, an assistant to presidential aide Joseph Califano, reported to him that the Justice Department and counsel for the Treasury Department had, at the president's request, investigated whether the Trading with the Enemy Act could be used to limit the outflow of funds from the United States.[49] Robson concluded that the act could be used to limit or prohibit capital investment abroad, to restrict the amount of money U.S. travelers could take or spend abroad, and to impose interest rate ceilings.

On 28 September, the president received a formal opinion on this issue written by Assistant Attorney General Frank Wozencraft and approved by Attorney General Nicholas Katzenbach.[50] The opinion expressed was identical to that contained in the Robson memorandum, which Califano also had submitted to the president. Califano cautioned that "historically, the use of Section 5(b) [of the act] for economic controls reveals such a complicated interplay of executive and congressional action that in our view it would be desirable to obtain the approval and confirmation of Congress following the issuance of any Executive Order establishing such controls."[51]

On 6 December, Secretary Fowler submitted to President Johnson the year-end review by the Cabinet Committee on Balance of Payments of the voluntary restraint programs for direct investment and bank and nonbank lending abroad. Noting that the payments deficit for 1967 would likely be about the same as for 1966 if the voluntary programs were continued, the committee cautioned that in its judgment, "based on past painful experience," there likely would be "slippage in elements of this forecast, and the deficit could easily run much higher."[52] While reporting that Commerce Secretary Connor was proposing targets for the direct investment program that would reduce the combination of direct investment ouflows and overseas retained earnings by $100 million from their 1966 level, the committee expressed the view that "additional savings of $300 million should be sought by further tightening of the guidelines." It noted that "Secretary Connor dissents from this recommendation on the ground that it is an unreasonable expectation." In his forwarding memorandum to the president, Secretary Fowler added, "We must submit this issue to you for resolution."[53]

A week prior to receiving the Cabinet Committee report, the president had been informed by Califano that among the items that CEA Chairman Ackley wanted to review with him at a meeting scheduled for 30 November was "Balance of Payments prospects and programs—mainly to urge the need for a more rigorous Commerce program."[54] On 1 December, Ackley followed up with a memorandum expressing to the president his belief that "on any reasonable set of assumptions, *we have to expect significant problems next year,*" and "*the Commerce program offers prospects for considerable further savings.*"[55] Ackley cautioned that if the voluntary program could not do the job, the administration would have to face up to designing tax or other legislative means to limit direct investment abroad.

On 7 December, Bator advised the president of the existence of a split within the Cabinet Committee, noting that "this is a tough decision. . . . On the merits, my vote is strongly with Fowler and the rest of the Committee."[56] Califano forwarded to the president the Cabinet Committee report along with memorandums from Fowler, Ackley, and Bator, advising that "because the issues are tough and because there is a split among your advisers, I recommend that we at least take a last crack at a compromise to split the difference."[57]

The effort to seek a compromise was not successful, however. On 9 December, Bator told the president that he understood that Fowler had recommended against another meeting of the Cabinet Committee and instead had suggested that President Johnson phone Connor to probe "his mind and mood." In seconding Fowler's recommendation, Bator observed that "Jack is dug in up to his ears vis-a-vis the rest of us—this tug of war has been going on for weeks—and a private conversation with the President is the only graceful way to extricate him."[58] However, Johnson, pushed by the need for an early public announcement of the program targets to permit planning by affected companies, resolved the issue on 10 December in favor of a tightened program.[59]

On 27 January 1967, Ackley responded to the president's request for his views on a possible shift of responsibility from Commerce to the Treasury for the voluntary program to constrain direct investment abroad. This request appears to have been prompted, at least in part, by the resignation of Connor and the pending appointment as acting secretary of commerce of Alexander (Sandy) Trowbridge, whom Ackley described as "a career bureaucrat, young, handsome, and intelligent."[60] Given Trowbridge's youth and lack of business experience, it was feared that he might be unable to make the voluntary restraint program work effectively.

Ackley observed that Secretary Connor had "played his cards very close to his vest and we don't know just how much of the activity he handled himself." Nonetheless, Ackley expressed doubts that Trowbridge could have as much success as Connor in getting businessmen to cooperate. However, he argued, a formal transfer of the program to the Treasury would create "public relations" problems, and might be taken as an indication that the program was failing and that the administration was applying a new hard line to business. Ackley recommended instead a "low key" method to get Secretary Fowler and his staff more deeply involved through the creation of a steering committee for both voluntary programs (i.e., the program for corporations and that for banks and nonbank financial institutions) with Fowler as chairman. Joseph Califano could then make clear to Trowbridge that "he should count on Fowler's help in dealing with problem children and with the businessmen's advisory committee for the program."[61] This action was not taken, however, and Trowbridge subsequently gained the confidence of the president, who in August appointed him secretary of commerce.

Move to a Mandatory Program

Although planning for the 1968 balance-of-payments program actually began in March 1967, it was the British devaluation of the pound on 18 November that gave rise to significant changes in the balance-of-payments program and the move from a voluntary to a mandatory system of controls on capital outflow.[62]

Fried relates that in early November there was a repetition of the previous debates within the Cabinet Committee on Balance of Payments over how tight the controls on direct investment abroad should be, with Treasury arguing for stiffer controls and Commerce resisting. The president met with Trowbridge, Fowler, and Fried and the issues were presented and resolved in favor of an additional reduction of $200 million in capital outflows. Fried observes, "It wasn't hard—they weren't that far apart. . . . It gave us a chance to brief the President on the issues."[63] In a move designed to give the private sector time to plan its investment program for 1968, the guidelines for the 1968 voluntary programs were announced on 16 November 1967.[64]

The British devaluation of the pound two days later and the "gold rush" that followed brought the international monetary situation and the United States balance-of-payments problem to the acute stage. The crisis environment precipitated by the sterling devaluation, the delay in getting the administration's income tax surcharge bill through Congress, clear indications of a significant deterioration in the payments deficit in the fourth quarter of 1967, the pressure on the gold market, and the demand by European monetary authorities for strong action led Fowler to ask the president for a complete review of the country's balance-of-payments program.

Fried reports:

> Secretary Fowler felt that he had to have a dramatic program to sort of show that it was a bad performance and we were going to get our house in order. He prepared a memo, almost on his own—the only copies he sent was one to me and one to the president. Then he arranged a meeting . . . with the president (in a small office off the main office), and he outlined to him how bad the situation could be and that we had to have a greatly tightened program.[65]

The president, according to Fried, was concerned and recognized the seriousness of the situation. He told Fowler and Fried, "All right, step it up." Thus, Secretary Fowler got a commitment that everything would be reexamined, and proposals for action which had previously been considered and rejected would be reconsidered in light of the new situation.

Having received permission from the president to instigate a complete overhaul of the administration's balance-of-payments program, Fowler and Fried had to tackle the implementation problem: while it was clear that the decisions on recommended changes would be made by the principals through the Cabinet Committee on Balance of Payments, how was the staff work to be accomplished in the brief time available and how was the process to be kept secret? Fried states that he and Fowler agreed to staff the reconsideration procedure through what was then known as the Deming Group.[66]

The Deming Group had been established in June 1965 as a small, high-level study group on international monetary problems with particular emphasis on forward planning.[67] It was chaired by Under Secretary of the Treasury for Monetary Affairs Frederick L. Deming, and its membership included assistant secretary–level representatives from the Federal Reserve Board, the CEA, the Department of State, and the White House staff, and the U.S. Executive Director of the International Monetary Fund Board.

Fried reports that Secretary Fowler took personal charge of the reconsideration effort and the Deming Group became, in effect, the Fowler Group, spinning off small study groups when necessary: ". . . Secretary Fowler had a number of meetings, usually sort of separate circles with each of the people. . . . But the central corp [*sic*] group was in all of them, and that was essentially the Deming Group throughout."[68]

There were constant meetings over the course of the next month and a half; most of those who were intimately involved spent half to three-quarters of their time on these sessions. At the White House, President Johnson requested that Ernest Goldstein, a newly appointed special assistant, become involved in the balance-of-payments deliberations.[69]

One of the principal tasks in the review was to establish an overall goal for projected savings. Commerce Secretary Trowbridge reports that the goal of $3 billion was adopted and approved by the president on 20 December.[70] The savings were to be obtained through a comprehensive program that was described as a "four-legged stool," involving trade, tourism, investment, and government expenditure savings. As it eventually emerged, the 1968 balance-of-payments program drew on considerations that had arisen in the Cabinet Committee on Balance of Payments during the previous four years.

The genesis of the mandatory program to control direct investment abroad is somewhat obscure. For some time, it had been believed at the Commerce Department that there were those within the administration who favored mandatory controls because they did not trust businessmen to comply with a voluntary program. Secretary Trowbridge observes:

> There were a number of people within the White House and the Bureau of the Budget, particularly, and the State Department, who just felt that you couldn't trust the business community to really do it, you had to have mandatory control. Every time you got that kind of statement made our hackles would go up, and we'd fight like hell, and we'd try and get Treasury to support us and generally they would. You could never tell about Secretary McNamara. He would and he wouldn't, depending on what the issue was. But it was a matter of trying to get support prior to the meeting so that you didn't get attacked and you knew generally what the line of attack was going to be, so you had your ducks in a row and you had others primed to help argue it out.[71]

Lawrence McQuade, then assistant secretary of commerce, expresses a similar view: "There's a forest full of people who don't believe that the system's going to work unless everything is done under their control . . . and I used to get very deeply angry at them because they felt that unless they personally made these decisions, that you couldn't really trust this decentralized system to work."[72] Mandatory controls over direct investment abroad had, of course, been considered at the time of the adoption of the voluntary program in February 1965. As early as September 1966, the president had inquired and been informed that mandatory controls on capital outflow could be established by presidential authority granted in the Trading with the Enemy Act.[73] McQuade states that he believed that as long as John Connor was secretary of commerce, mandatory controls could be defeated.[74]

Goldstein reports that he suggested a mandatory program for direct investment abroad in one of the early scheduled meetings following Secretary Fowler's conversation with the president in mid-November 1967, and that Fowler reacted negatively, saying "My God, don't even mention it, because this begins to smell of exchange controls. . . . And as soon as you start getting into the exchange control game, then the run on the dollar will be tremendous, and this should not be mentioned."[75]

Goldstein states that he talked with Fred Smith, the general counsel of the treasury, and asked him to find out if the president had the power to impose controls on direct investment without legislation. Smith produced a two-page memorandum which Goldstein then distributed at a meeting of the Cabinet Committee, chaired by Joe Califano. This meeting was held in the Cabinet Room some three weeks after the balance-of-payments revision exercise had begun. Goldstein reports that after some "kicking and screaming," the principle of mandatory controls on capital outflow under presidential mandate was established.[76]

McQuade, who was present at the Cabinet Committee meetings, provides a somewhat different version of these events, observing that Fowler knew for some time that mandatory controls on capital outflow could be imposed without legislative action, but that at one meeting of the committee, someone inadvertently mentioned that the president had the power and Goldstein "perked up his ears." McQuade believes that Fowler had not intended for this to get out, but "once at the White House, Tony Solomon [assistant secretary of state for economic affairs] and gung-ho people for direct controls heard that, I think the die was basically cast."[77]

McQuade complains that the committee staff was intentionally left out of meetings at which the foundation for the imposition of mandatory controls was prepared, noting that he felt "as if these guys would have meetings without inviting us, because they knew we would oppose and were afraid we might be successful." He attributes the failure of the Commerce Department to prevent the imposition of mandatory controls to the fact that they "had so few chips—not really enough in the poker game of making policy. . . . The rest of the agencies and the White House assistants really had the power, not Commerce."

The decision to adopt mandatory controls, however, appears to have been dictated more by the demands of the task than by a conspiracy of White House assistants. Trowbridge observes that a few days before Christmas, it had become clear that of the $3 billion target for overall savings, the private investment portion would be $1 billion. The issue then became, can the voluntary program be expanded to produce $800 million in additional savings in 1968?

Trowbridge met with his Advisory Committee and put this question to them. They answered, "It has gone about as far as it can go."[78] He also consulted with former Commerce Secretary Connor, who advised that Trowbridge didn't have any choice: " . . . 'this clearly requires mandatory controls because you're essentially getting into an area where, without a sense of voluntary cooperation, you're going to get everybody grabbing for what they can if you don't have rules which apply to everybody.'" On Christmas Day, believing that it would not be possible to save a billion dollars with a voluntary program and concerned about the inequity of attempting to do so, Trowbridge agreed to the mandatory program.[79]

Fried reports that after agreement was reached on a large direct investment program, it was easier to obtain agreement on a large bank-lending program that was simpler, "not technically but in policy terms."[80] Because the banks were more "disciplined," the Federal Reserve program did not have to be mandatory. Banks would cooperate. In the end, the Federal Reserve was given a goal and left to work out the technical details of the program.

Obtaining additional savings in government overseas expenditures was primarily a task of accelerating the already agreed upon schedule for military offsets and carefully reviewing all possible ways of identifying savings and cuts in overseas personnel. The two most difficult and controversial issues within the administration were the proposals for improving the trade and tourism balances. In both areas, concerns were raised about the efficacy of the proposals, as well as about the political feasibility of taking action.

To improve the trade balance, Secretary Fowler favored the enactment of a border tax, which he termed a "trade adjustment" tax, of 2 or 4 percent, imposed as an import surcharge and an export subsidy.[81] The justification of the tax would be to adjust import and export prices to reflect indirect taxes existing in the United States. The STR and the State Department objected to the imposition of a border tax on grounds that it might lead to retaliation by the Europeans and to a dismantling of the General Agreement on Tariffs and Trade. Alternative approaches to improving the trade balance focused on export stimulation. Consideration was given to providing a tax incentive to promote exports, but this was rejected by the Cabinet Committee before mid-December.[82] Agreement eventually was reached on an expansion of the Export-Import Bank rediscount facility and the amendment of the bank's statute to create an export expansion facility.[83] The former would encourage commercial banks to lend to exporters, while the latter would finance high-risk loans that the Export-Import Bank and commercial banks would otherwise be unwilling to make.

Numerous actions to increase foreign travel to the United States and to reduce expenditures by American tourists overseas had been considered by the Cabinet Committee. In November 1967, the president had announced the formation of a Special Travel Task Force, formed with industry participation and chaired by Robert McKinney, former U.S. ambassador to Switzerland, to recommend specific measures for increasing foreign travel to the United States.[84] To reduce the outflow from Americans traveling abroad, the Cabinet Committee recommended the imposition of a travel tax.

Fried reports that the president was kept closely informed about the deliberations of the Cabinet Committee on the 1968 balance-of-payments program:

> I would say the president's contacts with this program were just
> about as full as they could be. Throughout, as the program itself
> was developed, he was kept informed. At one point he was kept
> informed through a whole series of communications with Air
> Force One while he was on his way to Australia on an around the
> world flight. We were getting constant communications back
> and forth telling him about the program. By this time, Califano
> was in it. When he came back . . . on Christmas Day . . . his
> reaction was, "I will do anything that we can do without legis-
> lation. I don't like the trade proposals, and I don't like the tour-
> ism proposals."[85]

The president believed that the proposal for a tax on tourist expenditures would not pass the Congress, while the trade proposals might lead Congress to impose a number of restrictions on imports. Fried states that on Christmas morning, at 7 AM, Walt Rostow told him, "Ed, the president wants you to rewrite the program, leaving out these two items [trade and tourism], rewrite the whole program, and then we'll have a meeting on this basis." [86]

Thus, on Christmas Day, Fried joined Deming and Rostow in redrafting the proposals. Fowler was away for the day visiting his family in New Jersey. The following day, there was a meeting in the White House with Fried, Rostow, Califano, Fowler, and the president. Fried reports that the newly reworked proposal, which by happenstance had been written on Treasury stationery, was passed around, and when it came to Fowler, he said, "I disown this!" The president then told Fowler, in effect, that if he felt so strongly about a border tax, he could "go and see what assurances you can get from Congress, from Mills and some of the others, that if we put something through in the trade bill that [it] will be contained." [87]

The week between Christmas and New Year's Day was spent in a frantic effort to reach agreement on a final set of proposals. Califano's report to the president on individual assignments made following the White House meeting on 26 December gives some indication of the administrative complexity of the policy-formulation process:

Details of mandatory controls, including an Executive Order and proposed lists of a three-man board. To be worked out under the leadership of Treasury, with Commerce, Justice, CEA, and Goldstein.
Scenario for a negotiating team [on trade] *to leave promptly, including draft letters from the president to Chiefs of State.* To be worked out under the leadership of State with Treasury and Ed Fried.
Federal Reserve Credit Controls. To be worked out by Bill Martin.
Tax incentives. Ed Fried is working with Stan Ross and Treasury.
Congressional Contacts. These are being made by Fowler, Rusk, Trowbridge, and Barr, with a list of Congressmen that has been cleared by Manatos and Sprague (both O'Brien and Barefoot are out of town). [88]

The procedure called for Rostow to collect all the reports as they came in and to send a summary memorandum with appropriate back-up papers to the ranch on the morning of 28 December. The president then could decide whether to make the final decision on the basis of that memorandum or to see Fowler or anyone else he deemed appropriate.

During the week, an issue arose concerning where to place the responsibility for administering the mandatory-control program for direct investment. Commerce wanted the program to be managed by Treasury, and Treasury was anxious that the assignment be given to Commerce. Goldstein reports:

> Fowler, myself, Trowbridge . . . we weren't getting anywhere with it. I advised the president what was going on, that this was the hang-up; and he suggested that Charlie Schultze, . . . Nick Katzenbach, and I get together with the two Secretaries—and I think with Frank Wozencraft. . . . So we had a meeting up here and in effect, Schultze and I were to sit as a court of inquiry and see who got the black bean . . . and the answer came out that it was going to be Commerce, and Treasury would lend the money and lend the personnel. . . . [89]

Trowbridge recalls that on 30 December he flew to the Texas ranch with Fowler, Rusk, Ackley, and Roth. Also flying to the ranch that morning were Representatives Mills (Dem. Ark.) and Boggs (Dem. La.) and Senators Long (Dem. La.) and Mansfield (Dem. Mont.). The group gathered with the president, Califano, and Jim Jones in the ranch guest house, and went through the entire balance-of-payments program. Fowler led the discussion and everyone added their rationale to it. Trowbridge states that the president felt that the toughest part of the proposal would be the tourist tax, which he believed would not pass Congress. The congressmen present agreed with this judgment. The border tax proposal was not very well received by Representative Boggs. However, in the end, everyone agreed that a strong program was required and the president gave his final approval to it late in the afternoon. [90]

Fried, who had remained in Washington, recalls that he received a phone call from Califano giving him the particular language to use on the trade and tourism proposals:

> In effect, the compromise was that on trade we would go and consult with the Europeans immediately, and then on the basis of those consultations see whether we would propose legislation; and similarly, a voluntary appeal on tourism, and then consult

with Congress on legislation. But the rest of the program went pretty much as it had been worked out, and the message went through a number of versions.[91]

The final message was hammered out on the night of 30 December and early in the morning of the next day it was teletyped to the ranch, where it was edited.

At about 11:00 AM on New Year's Day, the president held a press conference at the ranch to announce the new program. Califano has a vivid recollection of the briefing he had to give to the hastily assembled reporters:

> I'll never forget New Year's Day. He decided on New Year's Eve we'd brief on the most complicated program he announced in his whole presidency . . . and he called those reporters from Austin. . . . I'll never forget that audience. I looked out at that audience and thought, "Jesus Christ. They are all hungover, some of them are still a bit tight, and this is the most complicated program they have ever seen." They also landed in a terrible rain storm. . . . As I was briefing, Johnson kept walking up and down in front of me and in the back. He would occasionally walk on the stage and elaborate on an answer.[92]

Back in Washington, Rusk, Fowler, Trowbridge, Ackley, and Martin met in the Cabinet Room at noon to hear the president's briefing at the ranch. At 2:30 PM, they held a briefing for the press at the Treasury Department.

Implementation of the 1968 Balance-of-Payments Program

Initial implementation of the 1968 balance-of-payments program was closely orchestrated from the White House. Immediate efforts were begun to inform key members of Congress and to solicit statements of support for the president's program.[93] Califano and Rostow took the lead in coordinating a host of activities by interagency groups. While the Cabinet Committee on Balance of Payments continued to serve as a policy forum, its activities were supplemented by a number of ad hoc efforts directed from the White House.

On 9 January, Califano reported to the president in a seven-page memorandum on the status of all parts of the program and on deadlines which had been established for additional actions to be taken.[94] On 18 January, Califano sent the president a memorandum outlining discussions among seventeen advisers concerning the trade, travel, and capital outflow issues; the advisers met with the president on the following day.

On 18 January, the president directed Rusk and Budget Director Schultze to undertake a program to reduce U.S. personnel overseas, including a mandated reduction of 10 percent in such personnel by 1 April and a special review of activities and staffing of overseas missions—starting with the countries having the largest missions and proceeding as rapidly as possible to other countries.[95] On the same date, the president also requested all department and agency heads to reduce official travel outside of the United States to a minimum consistent with the "orderly conduct" of the government's business, and asked them to notify Schultze by 15 March of the actions taken, the expected results, and recommendations for additional measures.[96]

Presidential zeal in curbing travel abroad by U.S. government personnel threatened at one point to get out of hand. William Hopkins, who served as secretary to the cabinet, reports that on 26 January he was informed by presidential aide Marvin Watson that the president wanted Hopkins to call each cabinet officer and tell him that he should provide Hopkins with a written notice of any person in his department who was going to travel abroad attending conferences or on other official travel, including when the travel was to occur, the length of stay, and the destination. Cabinet officers were to make certain that Hopkins confirmed that he had received this information before the travel commenced.[97] Hopkins dutifully complied by notifying each of the departments.

As might be expected, the request created a potential administrative nightmare. The Department of Defense notified Hopkins that about 100,000 individual overseas trips are made each year by Defense civilian and military personnel, not including permanent changes of station and troop deployments.[98] Hopkins eventually kicked the matter back to Watson, noting that while a tough program to reduce overseas travel by government personnel was undoubtedly needed, "I am convinced that from a practical standpoint, this cannot be controlled effectively on a *case by case* basis from the White House."[99]

Hopkins recommended that the oral instructions given earlier be rescinded and the president agreed. However, on 14 February, Budget Director Zwick issued a bulletin to the heads of all departments and establishments setting forth in some detail requirements for reducing official travel overseas.[100] Each agency was asked to seek a 25 percent reduction in overseas official travel and to submit revised travel plans and quarterly progress reports to the president through the Bureau of the Budget. The agencies evidently cooperated in this effort, for on 25 October, Zwick notified the president that in the second half of FY 1968, agencies had reduced their overseas travel by 33.5 percent, or $16.2 million.[101]

Presidential aide Goldstein took the lead in developing a draft executive order limiting tourist expenditures abroad. Although there was general consensus within the administration that a voluntary appeal would not do the job, there was substantial disagreement over the wisdom of attempting to limit foreign travel by executive action.[102] Treasury Undersecretary Joseph Barr was given the task of drafting legislation to impose a tax on expenditures of U.S. citizens overseas. Eventually it was decided to opt for the travel tax alternative and the proposed legislation was carried to the Hill by Secretary Fowler. However, House Ways and Means Committee Chairman Mills refused to act on the travel tax until the administration reached a decision on the imposition of a border tax.[103] In the end, the border-tax proposal was dropped and the administration reconsidered the feasibility of mounting a voluntary campaign to limit tourist expenditures abroad and concluded that the effort might be counter-productive: "We might cut too deeply while at the same time creating a fear of eventual harsh controls. This was the history of the voluntary direct investment program."[104]

Goldstein also was given responsibility for working with the McKinney Travel Task Force to increase foreign tourism in the United States. Throughout 1968, the president received frequent detailed reports from him on a host of activities related to this objective. These included: negotiating differential round-trip fares with domestic and foreign airlines for inbound tourists; increasing public and private expenditures aimed at attracting foreign tourists; negotiating discounts for foreign tourists with domestic hotel and car rental concerns; and working with customs, immigration, public health, and agricultural personnel to develop a one-step entry inspection for those entering the United States from abroad.[105] The administration tried, but failed, to get Congress to appropriate funds for an expansion of the U.S. Travel Service in the Department of Commerce.

To implement the mandatory control program for direct investment abroad, an Office of Foreign Direct Investment (OFDI) was created within the Commerce Department. Efforts to recruit a permanent director for the OFDI began shortly after the president's announcement of the program. Efforts to recruit Robert Anderson, who had served as secretary of the treasury under President Eisenhower, to become permanent director failed.[106] In late January, Trowbridge resigned due to ill health and was replaced by a close friend of the president, C. R. Smith. Joseph Bartlett, general counsel of the Commerce Department, continued to serve as acting director of the OFDI until May, when Charles Fiero, a New York City attorney, was recruited to head the office.

From the outset, however, the mandatory-control program was overseen by an interagency group. Thus, on 4 January, Goldstein reported to the president on the first of what was billed as a series of weekly meetings to review developments and current and emerging problems in the capital outflow program, noting that the "primary function of these meetings is to facilitate coordination and exchange of views."[107] Attending the first meeting, held in the White House, were representatives from the CEA, the Departments of Commerce, State, and the Treasury, the Attorney General's Office, the Federal Reserve Board, the Agency for International Development, and the White House staff.

Goldstein notes: "I advised the president that I thought it would be desirable if we kept up an informal arrangement which we started off as once a week and then gradually went to twice a month, and petered out to maybe once a month or whenever a big policy change came. . . . the White House was in it from the beginning to the end."[108] The president received reports from Goldstein, and in Goldstein's absence, from White House aide DeVier Pierson, on the meetings of this interagency group. After reporting on one such meeting, Goldstein informed the president, "The value of these meetings in providing a forum for interdepartmental consultation is continually demonstrated. For some reason, communication does not take place during the rest of the week to the degree possible in these meetings."[109]

On 25 April, Goldstein briefed the president on the status of the program to control foreign direct investment. The president's January 1 Balance of Payments Message had set a target of $1 billion in savings from the then-unknown 1967 level of foreign direct investment. Goldstein indicated that, based on preliminary data showing a 1967 outflow of $3.5 billion, theoretically the potential savings from the program might total $1.6 billion. However, the president's message had contained a loophole in the form of an exemption from control of prior commitments to less-developed countries (LDCs). Goldstein pointed out that "no one knew on January 1, 1968, how big a backlog of pre-January 1 commitments existed" and that "mining and petroleum contracts in the LDC's exceeded expectations."[110] As a consequence, about 800 special authorizations had been filed for prior commitments, which amounted to a potential outflow of $1.67 billion. However, it was uncertain how much of this allowance would actually be spent.

On 12 June, Goldstein forwarded to the president a progress report on the mandatory-control program from Secretary Smith, noting that, while present statistics indicated that the targeted savings of $1 billion might be missed by several hundred million dollars, "Secretary Smith promises to keep a tight rein, and as earlier reported, we are trying over here to make sure that Commerce does so."[111] The Smith memorandum stated that the OFDI had compiled data on over 2,800 organizations and individuals and analyzed over 400 specific authorizations granted under the prior commitment criteria established in the president's January 1 message. Smith concluded that "it is clear that there is no *leeway* and that it will be necessary to adopt an increasingly uncompromising position in the administration of the program."[112]

There appears to have been strong disagreement within the administration on the desirability of maintaining the mandatory-controls program. Thus, on 5 August, Secretary Smith wrote the president to urge, "You want to have done with this restriction as soon as the balance of payments situation will permit."[113] Goldstein, however, clearly envisioned that the mandatory program would be continued into the coming year. On 4 September, he urged the president to announce the 1969 balance-of-payments program as soon as possible, and concluded: "In the meantime a very small group is reviewing possible long range alternatives to the present controls. . . . The idea is to leave behind the benefits of experience and thought that have gone into these problems."[114]

In early October, Secretary Smith again made known to the president his views on the foreign direct investment program:

In principle, foreign investments should not be controlled by the Federal Government. Decisions in that area should be made by investors. I agreed 100% with the need for such controls at the time they were instituted, on the basis that they would be temporary. Such controls should not become embedded in the government structure. As soon as the balance of payments situation will permit, they should be removed.[115]

However, he added that at the present time there was no basis for a forecast about the date on which such controls could be eliminated. Smith enclosed a letter from Albert Nickerson, chairman of the Commerce Balance of Payments Advisory Committee, expressing concern on the subject.

On 12 November, Goldstein informed the president that all concerned departments and agencies had approved the 1969 OFDI program and asked the president to approve its announcement on 15 November.[116] Attached to the Goldstein memorandum was a memorandum from Secretary Fowler that indicated that at least some of those concerned with the program expected a more permanent place for it:

> In short, we will pass along to the incoming Administration a viable and much improved Foreign Direct Investment Program. Although the program was designed to be temporary it has been modified to minimize any adverse long-term effects. It has also been supplemented to facilitate an orderly transition to a more permanent system to restrain direct investment outflows should future circumstances require.[117]

The year closed with Goldstein and Secretary Smith informing the president that the foreign direct investment outflow savings target of $1 billion for 1968 would be realized and might be exceeded by several hundred million dollars, due to the fact that businesses had not utilized their allowances and had financed foreign ventures through borrowing abroad.[118]

Reform of the International Monetary System

From the outset of the Johnson administration, it was recognized that the elimination of the U.S. balance-of-payments deficit would remove the primary source of world liquidity for the finance of trade and development. This would place severe pressures on the international monetary system—a system that was already beginning to show signs of inadequacy. Thus, a major effort was initiated to bring about reform of the international monetary system to provide for an additional source of liquidity through the International Monetary Fund (IMF).

Briefing the President

On 5 June 1964, CEA Chairman Heller sent President Johnson the first in a series of three background memorandums explaining the operation of the international monetary system and its problems. The concise and lucid explanations contained in these memorandums are models of how to describe extremely complex issues to a busy executive. Referring to them, Ackley observes that the president "just loved our memoranda because we were willing to try and make things clear and understandable."[119]

In the first memorandum, Heller explained that "the dollar occupies a special position which gives the United States both benefits and headaches."[120] The benefits derived from the fact that the United States could run a balance-of-payments deficit as long as other countries were willing to hold additional dollars as reserves. The headaches resulted from the fact that the willingness of countries to hold dollars depended on their confidence that the United States would not change the dollar price of gold and would continue to let countries holding dollars use them as they wish. Obviously, this confidence was affected by the size and duration of the U.S. payments deficits, as well as by the perceived health and strength of the U.S. domestic economy.

In the second memorandum, sent on 22 July 1964, Heller observed, "Almost everyone thinks our international monetary system has a 'liquidity problem'—that there's either too little, or too much, or the wrong places have it."[121] Heller summarized three basic criticisms of the system: that it lacked a systematic method of creating the right amount of new monetary reserves; that it had a built-in tendency toward instability, and that the United States had created too much liquidity and forced other nations to hold it. While admitting that the first two criticisms had some merit, Heller stated that the third criticism, which came primarily from the European countries, was *"largely wrong."* He concluded that as the United States moved to eliminate its payments deficits, thus ceasing to provide dollar reserves, "they [the Europeans] won't like that any better."[122]

In the final memorandum in the series, dated 5 August 1964, Heller discussed "solutions and remaining issues," pointing out that "there are almost as many international monetary proposals as there are international monetary experts."[123] Efforts to expand short-term credit availability dated to 1961–62 when the General Arrangements to Borrow under the IMF were agreed upon, in which nine advanced countries joined with the United States to provide standby credit facilities of up to $6 billion to the IMF. The participants became known as the Group of Ten. They included Belgium, Canada, France, Germany, Italy, Japan, the Netherlands, Sweden, the United Kingdom, and the United States.

During 1962 and 1963, with the short-term credit facilities in place, the Group of Ten had turned its attention to the longer-run consequences of the resurgent financial strength of Western Europe and Japan, the large cumulative payments deficits of the United States, and the periodic difficulties of the pound sterling. Heller reported to the president that after "nine months of pulling and hauling," the Group of Ten had agreed to support a modest (i.e., 25 percent) increase in IMF quotas—as favored by the United States, and to establish a system of "multilateral surveillance" under which countries would watch over each others' practices in financing payments deficits—as favored by the French and other European countries.

The Group of Ten had also agreed to two important procedural steps. Regarding international balance, it called upon Working Party 3 of the Organization for Economic Cooperation and Development (OECD) to undertake a thorough study of the "measures and instruments best suited for achieving this purpose compatibly with the pursuit of essential internal objectives."[124] A second study was commissioned that would examine the various proposals for the creation of additional reserve assets either through the IMF or other channels. The latter effort was to be under the chairmanship of Mr. Rinaldo Ossola of the Bank of Italy.

The president earlier had been notified of the Group of Ten's recommendations by Treasury Secretary Dillon, who noted that he had briefed the Senate Foreign Relations Committee and the House Banking and Currency Committee on the results of the Group of Ten Study and the prospects for an IMF quota increase.[125] In forwarding the Dillon memorandum to the president, Bator and Bundy noted that "the overall outcome of this year-long exercise, though we should put a good face on it, is more mouse than elephant," adding:

> We shall have thought to the reforms we might attempt in two or three years, by when, more likely than not, the Europeans will be plagued by balance of payments troubles and we'll have the whip hand. We must not then be as myopic as the Europeans have been. The Foreign Economic Policy Task Force will be taking a hard look at the problem.[126]

The President Acts

In his Balance of Payments Message to Congress on 10 February 1965, President Johnson took note of the studies being made by the Ossola Group and indicated, "We must press forward with our studies and beyond, to action—evolving arrangements which will continue to meet the needs of a fast growing world economy."[127] The president's remarks, coming closely on the heels of a widely publicized press conference by General Charles de Gaulle in which the French president had lauded the pure gold standard and made critical remarks about the gold exchange standard, set the stage for action on reform of the international monetary system.

The initiative for the February message appears to have come from

Bator. A comparison of the Treasury Department's draft proposal of the President's message—submitted for interagency review on 4 February 1965—and the final statement, reveals an important difference. While the Treasury draft spoke of the "possible" need for man-made reserve assets at some indefinite point in the future, the final statement argued for immediate consideration of reserve assets. This position was suggested by Bator in the form of a revised draft of the presidential message.[128]

In the spring of 1965, concern continued to focus on the international monetary system, spurred by a speculative attack on the British pound, which many attributed to the French government.[129] Jacques Rueff, an influential French economist and close adviser to General de Gaulle, publicly attacked the gold exchange standard and called on the United States to double the price of gold. Rueff's views were widely discussed within the administration, although CEA Chairman Ackley reported to the president "there is no disagreement in the U.S. Government that Rueff is a nut, and that his ideas are mistaken and dangerous."[130]

In early May 1965, the CEA provided the president with a series of brief papers on "dominant economic problems" facing the United States over the next two to three years; the papers were described as providing their "preliminary thinking" and "tentative proposals."[131] One paper dealt with international monetary reform. The council observed that "reform of the international monetary system may well turn out to be the *major economic challenge of the decade of the 1960s*," but cautioned that in dealing with this issue, "Secretary Fowler will need strong support from outside of his Department to overcome the inevitable bias of the conservative Treasury machine, often reinforced by the Federal Reserve."

The Johnson administration's organization and staffing for international monetary affairs had its roots in the Kennedy administration. Beginning in 1961, Undersecretary of the Treasury for Monetary Affairs Robert Roosa directed the Treasury's activities in the international monetary field. Due in part to his previous association with the Federal Reserve System, Roosa maintained a very close and effective personal liaison with the Board of Governors and the New York Federal Reserve Bank, which acted as the operating agency both in the government bond market and in the New York foreign-exchange market.

When the Group of Ten was created, the U.S. representatives were Treasury Secretary Fowler and Federal Reserve Chairman Martin. The U.S. representatives to the Deputies of the Group of Ten were Roosa and a member of the Federal Reserve Board of Governors,

Dewey Daane. Thus, in the international monetary sphere, the two principal operating agencies, the Treasury and the Federal Reserve, became the most active team in establishing and carrying out U.S. policy.

However, the Treasury maintained close contact with the CEA and with the White House through the deputy special assistant for national security affairs. Major decisions generally were discussed with the president by the secretary of the treasury and his undersecretary for monetary affairs. The Treasury also continued the well-established practice of consultation with the National Advisory Council on International Monetary and Financial Problems (NAC), which had been created to coordinate U.S. policy toward the IMF and the World Bank and to coordinate the financial policies of the Export-Import Bank and the U.S. AID program. The NAC was chaired by the secretary of the treasury and its members included the secretary of state, the Federal Reserve chairman, the president of the Export-Import Bank, and the secretary of commerce.[132]

To give further emphasis to internal coordination, and to recognize the importance of the new era of long-range planning in the field of international monetary affairs, in August 1962 President Kennedy had established the Long Range International Payments Committee (LRIPC). This group included representatives from the Treasury Department, State Department, CEA, Federal Reserve, and White House staff. At the end of 1965, the Commerce Department requested that it be represented, and the request was approved. The LRIPC met approximately biweekly from October 1962 through April 1966, under the chairmanship of the undersecretary of the treasury for monetary affairs. In 1965 and 1966, this group focused on the study of the balance-of-payments adjustment process being made by Working Party 3 of the OECD. The LRIPC became inactive following the submission by Working Party 3 of its final report.[133]

Arthur Okun, who represented the CEA on international monetary matters, notes that in the spring of 1965, Bator "felt that there was a strong need for some kind of more formal and still informal interagency group that would report to the president on these issues."[134] On 2 June, Bator drafted a proposal for creating such a group. Undersecretary of the Treasury for Monetary Affairs Frederick L. Deming (who had succeeded Roosa) redrafted the proposal, establishing the committee as a Treasury group, and returned it to Bator on 4 June. Bator then produced a second draft—with the support of Secretary Fowler—which left the group interagency in nature but to be chaired by Deming. The intent clearly was to establish responsibility for the group's direction with the participating White House officer, Bator.[135] This provides the background for an important memorandum from the president to Secretary Fowler on 16 June 1965 on "Forward Planning in International Finance."[136]

The memo began by observing that there was a need to develop policies relating to the improvement of the international monetary and payments system and the role of the United States in the system. As the United States moved to eliminate its payments deficits, and thus to stop providing reserves in the form of dollars, the world economy would require some means of systematically producing the additional liquidity needed to support continued growth in trade and development. Additional sources of liquidity, in turn, could only be generated through international agreements among the nations that were the primary sources of liquidity. The president affirmed, "I believe that it would now be desirable to push forward with more intensive effort, so as to be fully prepared for full scale negotiations when the time is ripe and right."

The president asked Fowler "to organize a small high-level study group to develop and recommend to me—through you, and the other principals directly concerned—a comprehensive U.S. position and negotiating strategy designed to achieve substantial improvement in international monetary arrangements." The study group was to include senior officials from the Departments of the Treasury and State, the CEA, the Federal Reserve, and White House staff, and the president noted that "I understand that you would have in mind that it would be chaired by the Under Secretary of the Treasury for Monetary Affairs."

The president specified that the study group should be small and should work in utmost secrecy, with knowledge of its existence and access to its work available on a strict need-to-know basis. The study group, the president indicated, was not intended to substitute for the continuing work of the Cabinet Committee on Balance of Payments, NAC, or LRIPC.

The president also asked Fowler to establish "a panel of consultants, consisting of people outside of Government with broad knowledge in this field, who would be available to you for counsel." The consulting group should be small in number, and should include people from the academic, banking, and business communities. The president suggested that former government officials such as Douglas Dillon, Robert Roosa, and former Budget Director Kermit Gordon would be appropriate members.

In response to the president's request for the creation of an internal study group, the Deming Group was formed. In accordance with the president's instructions, in addition to Deming, its initial membership also included Bator, Daane, the U.S. IMF Executive Director William B. Dale, Okun, Assistant Secretary of State for Economic Affairs Anthony Solomon, and Assistant Secretary of the Treasury for International Monetary Affairs Merlyn N. Trued. George H. Willis, deputy to Trued, served as its secretary. Subsequently, Bator was replaced by Fried, Okun by James Duesenberry and then by Warren L. Smith, and Trued by Winthrop Knowlton and later by John R. Petty. Deputy Undersecretary of the Treasury for Monetary Affairs Frank W. Schiff also later joined the group.[137]

Okun provides an excellent description of the operation of the Deming Group:

> We met regularly, a primarily principals-only kind of session in Deming's office, not the big staff meeting type arrangement. It got to be a very good group, I think, because we worked through the issues, and we did them when they weren't crises. We did a lot of contingency planning. We developed a very close personal relationship which transcended agency positions. We didn't report regularly to the principals or ask for authorization.[138]

Solomon shares Okun's favorable assessment of the Deming Group: "I think that was a leading example of an effective and successful interagency mechanism. . . . We seemed to have the right mix."[139]

The Deming Group met quite frequently, several times a week if needed, and became the focal point within the administration for formulating policy related to gold and international monetary reform. Deming estimates that he spent about 70 percent of his time on the international side.[140] Solomon observes that "a tremendous amount of personal time is given by the members of the Group. We would spend hour-after-hour, Sundays, well into the night working on these problems."[141]

The outside consulting group requested by the president was formed in July 1965. Called the Advisory Committee on International Monetary Arrangements, it was chaired by former Treasury Secretary Dillon. Its prestigious membership included the individuals indentified in the president's memorandum as well as other international financial experts.[142] The Advisory Committee met forty times between its establishment in July 1965 and the end of 1968.[143] Secretary Fowler observes:

> It was a very high-level, very experienced group. They came down faithfully for meetings which would usually last from around

nine-thirty to four-thirty or five in the afternoon every month or
every six weeks for the entire three-year period of operation. . . .
we would present them, in the early part of the day, through Mr.
George Willis . . . a review of developments since the previous
meeting and the specific questions and topics on which we wanted
to have their advice. . . . They would . . . exchange views together in the course of the morning. Then around twelve o'clock
they would be joined by the Treasury staff people concerned, Mr.
Deming, Under Secretary Barr, others on the Treasury team, plus
the Chairman of the Council of Economic Advisers, the Chairman of the Federal Reserve Board, Governor Daane, plus the
Under Secretary of State for Political Affairs, Mr. Eugene Rostow,
plus Mr. Bator or Mr. Fried. . . . We would all sit around the table
and discuss what was the appropriate position for the United
States negotiating team to take on these questions, what the
strategy and tactics of negotiation should be.[144]

The operation and membership of the Deming Group and the Advisory Committee were well suited to the tasks assigned to them.
Having worked out the organizational backup arrangements, the
president next turned his attention to initiating the formal process
of negotiations on international monetary reform.

The U.S. Takes the Initiative

In July 1965, the United States took decisive steps in making the deliberate creation of a supplementary reserve asset the central feature
of international monetary negotiations for the next two and a half
years. The result was the first major change in restructuring the international monetary system since the Bretton Woods Agreement.
With the approval of President Johnson, Treasury Secretary Fowler
determined to take a bold initiative by proposing multilateral negotiations on international monetary arrangements.

On 10 July 1965, in a speech to the Virginia State Bar Association
at its meeting in Hot Springs, Virginia, Fowler announced:

I am privileged to tell you this evening that the President has
authorized me to announce that the United States now stands
prepared to attend and participate in an international monetary
conference that would consider what steps we might jointly take
to secure substantial improvements in international monetary
arrangements.[145]

Since this proposal advanced the U.S. position beyond the area that had been fully explored and tested by international contacts and technical studies, the secretary undertook to follow up the initiative with personal visits with each of his counterparts in the Group of Ten.

Supporting the timing of the decision to move forward with active negotiations was the release at the end of August 1965 of a very important congressional report, *Guidelines for Improving the International Monetary System*, by the Subcommittee on International Exchange and Payments of the Joint Economic Committee, under the chairmanship of Representative Henry S. Reuss (Dem. Wisc.).[146] This report laid down twelve basic guidelines covering the future roles of gold and the dollar, new reserve assets, conditional credit facilities of the type long provided by the IMF, bilateral financial arrangements, and the payments adjustment process. It supported the creation of new reserves in the IMF and recommended that the newly created reserves be distributed to all IMF members who qualified under criteria applicable equally to all countries. Fowler observes that "this was a tremendous value to us because it did crystallize the position of the most informed men on Capitol Hill on the subject."[147]

During 1965–66, the deputies at the direction of the Group of Ten succeeded in reducing the number of potential approaches to reserve asset creation to five schemes. At the ministerial meeting of the Group of Ten in the Hague in July 1966, at the urging of the United States, it was agreed that negotiations should be expanded to include the full membership of the IMF, as well as the Group of Ten. The method chosen for carrying out the broader negotiations was to have joint meetings between the Deputies of the Group of Ten and the twenty executive directors of the IMF. This decision was approved by the ministers in Washington and endorsed by the IMF at its annual meeting in September 1966.[148]

The following two years were marked by intense negotiating activity. A consensus gradually developed over this period for creation of a uniform type of supplementary reserve asset—called Special Drawing Rights (SDRs)—in the IMF. Following two ministerial meetings in the summer of 1967, the plan prepared by the Group of Ten deputies and the IMF executive directors was approved and made public on 11 September 1967 by the IMF. It was approved by the Board of Governors of the IMF, by formal resolution, in Rio de Janeiro later in September. The resolution directed the executive directors of the IMF to put the plan into legal form as an amendment to the Articles of Agreement of the IMF by 31 March 1968. A final ministerial meeting in Stockholm on 30 March 1968 led to the adoption of a final plan.[149]

Legislation authorizing U.S. participation in the SDRs plan and acceptance of the various amendments to the IMF's Articles of Agreement was approved by the House of Representatives, with bipartisan support, on 10 May 1968. The Senate approved the legislation without dissent on 6 June 1968, and President Johnson signed Public Law 90-349, formalizing U.S. approval, on 19 June 1968.[150]

The adoption of the SDRs plan represented a major victory for the administration. The final agreement closely conformed to the initial proposal put forward by the American negotiating team. President Johnson, through the Deming committee and the deputy to the special assistant for national security affairs, was actively involved in the development of the U.S. negotiating position and in the working out of the tactics and strategy to secure approval of this position. Fried observes, "In each of the key critical points in the SDR negotiation, the president was informed of what the issues would be and what we proposed to do, not the general negotiating range."[151] As a consequence of his organization and staffing decisions, President Johnson was able to gain sufficient understanding of the highly technical and complex details to manage the negotiating process. Deming states that the president was "absolutely first-rate" in his understanding of the SDRs negotiations.[152]

Concluding Comments

In the best of times, the management of foreign economic policy is a difficult and demanding task. It requires a delicate balancing of domestic and foreign, economic and political interests. Only the president can provide the perspective needed for this balancing of conflicting forces. But presidential leadership in and of itself is insufficient. It must be matched by presidential direction of the foreign economic-policy process. This involves *operational management* through systems of coordination reaching beyond the White House to the upper levels of the myriad of affected agencies and departments, as well as *strategic management* at the highest levels of government of the formulation and implementation of foreign economic policy.

It is inevitable and desirable that most day-to-day operations of foreign economic policy be carried out by a host of departments and agencies. Lateral coordination of this decentralized system can be assured through interagency groups on the working level. However, as has been pointed out, "the real dilemma is posed by the manner in which the various microissues are to be coordinated at the senior policy levels in an effort to assure good macropolicies."[153]

In a cogent analysis of the management of foreign economic policy, Francis Bator observes that operational management can best be accomplished by a standing committee at the undersecretary level charged with identifying issues before technical moves by the various departments constrain presidential choices. This means identification and early warning of situations where decentralization is likely to create problems or lead to forfeiture of major opportunities. Such a committee should have the active participation of a first-rate White House staff officer, who "has his fingers in every important pie in every department, who has a well-developed spy system throughout the bureaucracy and is constantly on the lookout for clusters of cross-cutting issues and in a position to bring them forcibly to the president's attention."[154]

Regarding strategic management, Bator points out that if the president wishes to keep his options open, and most presidents do, he will not be agreeable to signing off on a strategy that locks him in. The solution is the timely establishment of ad hoc subcabinet task groups of often overlapping membership, each charged with forward planning and management of some specific cluster of issues. In short, the creation of a Deming Group for each cluster of foreign economic-policy issues.

Bator provides a succinct explanation of why large, formal committees are incapable of providing strategic management:

> Serious work just does not happen in a crowd. Blue chips are not played if marginal people are present, records kept and the like. Also they do not get played for subordinates representing their superiors. Anyone who has served time in the inner circles of Government is familiar with what happens to the quality of discussion when participants are wrapped in their institutional roles and surrounded by a bevy of committed and watchful .retainers.[155]

Open options require contact and collegial interaction among the members of the management team. This makes limited and highly knowledgeable membership a requirement. In explaining why this is so, Bator provides an excellent insight into how the Deming Group operated:

Especially in situations where the President wishes to maintain strategic control, effective management requires frank and full discussion of the long-term context and background of any immediate policy choice. I would assert that this kind of running conversation among the men charged with managing a problem—conversation that embeds the tactical choices in their full strategic and long-term context—is by far the best form of forward planning. . . . It is the essence of the "open options" rule that this kind of thinking can rarely be fully captured in written documents. There is an enormous premium on open, hard, challenging discussion. Anything that inhibits people from really arguing things out, and giving the real reasons for their positions, is deadly.[156]

Let us now turn to an appraisal of the performance of the Johnson administration in managing foreign economic policy. The discussion will focus on presidential leadership, operational management, and strategic management.

It has been alleged that President Johnson's strength was in the field of domestic affairs and that he was less experienced and knowledgeable in foreign affairs.[157] However, in the Eisenhower years, in his capacity as Senate majority leader, Johnson had actively consulted with the president on foreign-policy issues. His extensive travels around the world as vice president, combined with his participation in foreign-policy briefings and deliberations under President Kennedy, served to reinforce his knowledge and understanding of international affairs.

His exercise of presidential leadership in the field of foreign economic policy testifies to Johnson's understanding of foreign affairs. Thus, Walt Rostow notes:

No one who observed Johnson making the sequence of decisions he did during the Kennedy Round negotiations and the monetary crises of 1967–68 . . . was ever likely to take seriously the notion that he was either unsophisticated or unsubtle in foreign affairs. His command of the technical issues, combined with a sure-footed sense of direction, took the West forward at a time when progress was by no means inevitable.[158]

The goals of foreign economic policy were clearly defined and enunciated by the Johnson administration. The president was deeply committed to restoring balance-of-payments equilibrium, reforming the international monetary system, reducing trade restrictions, and providing assistance to less-developed countries.

Perhaps nowhere was President Johnson's commitment to a goal more clearly evidenced than in the area of trade policy. Fried observes that "the president was consistent throughout in taking essentially a free trade position. I think he felt this very strongly. . . . it was sort of bred into him. . . . he seems to have grown up with it in his period in the Congress."[159]

Johnson's commitment to free trade led him to take actions which were politically risky. Trowbridge observes, for example:

> In spite of some real pressures, particularly in the Northeast on shoes; Southeast on textiles; I. W. Abel and the steelworkers plus the steel companies on steel; he was very consistent, very very strong in saying, "Look, I'm not going to lead this country into a trade war. I'm proud of the Kennedy Round; I'm proud of the general objectives, and I just think there are other ways and you guys are going to have to figure out where they are, of doing this job without getting us into a stroke and counterstroke trade war."[160]

At times this commitment to free trade hindered Johnson in taking actions to achieve other foreign economic-policy objectives. For example, it was his fear of stirring up the always-latent protectionist sentiment in Congress which led him to be skeptical of the proposal for a border tax—even though this measure was believed by Secretary Fowler to be necessary to restore equilibrium to the nation's balance of payments.

President Johnson's dedication to the development of the Third World was equally as strong as his espousal of free trade. This led him to take personal command of the provision of the development loans and food aid. His commitments to restoration of the balance-of-payments equilibrium and to reform of the international monetary system were less visceral, and resulted from his acceptance of the arguments made by his principal advisers on these issues. But once convinced, he was determined in his efforts to achieve these objectives.

While the nation's foreign economic-policy goals were relatively straightforward, organization and staffing to attain them in the Johnson years was quite complex. The president's management of this process is well illustrated by events and actions in the balance-of-payments area.

First, Johnson exercised *presidential leadership* by establishing a clear policy—to eliminate the payments deficit—and a program of specific actions to achieve this objective, as well as by enunciating this policy to departments and agencies within the government, the Congress, and the general public. He actively sought to build support for this policy within each of these constituencies.

Second, he established a *system of coordination* for implementing his balance-of-payments program and for monitoring its impact in terms of his stated objective. By the nature of the task, responsibility for actions essential to the attainment of balance-of-payments equilibrium was decentralized among a number of departments and agencies. Lateral coordination among them was achieved via an interagency structure—in this case, the Cabinet Committee on Balance of Payments. But central direction from the presidential perspective was given to the committee through its chairman, the secretary of the treasury, and by the active participation in its deliberations of the deputy to the special assistant for national security affairs. Operational responsibility for monitoring the government's overseas expenditures was assigned to the BOB, while the CEA provided the president with weekly reports on balance-of-payments developments. President Johnson facilitated multiple lines of communication which were routed through the deputy special assistant, who played a key coordinating role in balancing the often-conflicting interests and views of the departmental and agency participants, identifying issues that should come to the attention of the president, and ensuring that the president was well briefed on these issues. Through these presidential agents, Johnson directed the *operational management* of balance-of-payments policy.

Third, when the operational management system identified problems or opportunities that indicated a need for reassessment of the balance-of-payments program, Johnson set in motion its reappraisal and provided for *strategic management* of the policy decision process. While primary responsibility for coordination rested with the secretary of the treasury, this was augmented by presidential meetings with all or subgroups of his advisers to thresh out policy alternatives, assess their implications, and make critical interim decisions, for example, setting the target for balance-of-payments savings in the 1968 program. As the policy decision process moved toward closure, the president's chief White House aide increasingly became involved in orchestrating the forging of a concensus. Thus, a new balance-of-payments program would emerge and the management process would begin anew.

A similar management process existed in the area of trade policy. The STR served as the agent bringing a presidential perspective to the development and implementation of trade policies, while the Trade Expansion Act Advisory Committee and its assistant secretary–level and middle management counterparts served as the interagency forum for lateral coordination. In addition, presidential assistants were assigned specific responsibility for monitoring trade policy issues and bringing them to the attention of the president for resolution.

In the area of international monetary reform, the need for operational management was not as great as in other areas. Since the primary responsibility for action rested with the Treasury Department and the Federal Reserve, lateral coordination was not a problem. The NAC served to coordinate U.S. policy toward the IMF and the World Bank, but it has been aptly described as playing only a "perfunctory role."[161] Similarly, the LRIPC served as a study committee bringing together the views of the Departments of the Treasury, State, and Commerce, the CEA, the Federal Reserve, and the White House on the balance-of-payments adjustment process; however, it played a limited coordinating role.

When President Johnson exercised presidential leadership in deciding to move forward with multinational negotiations to create a supplementary reserve asset in the IMF, his problem was to establish a strategic management system to provide guidance and direction to the process. The Deming Group was created to take the lead in formulating U.S. policy positions, while the Advisory Committee on International Monetary Arrangements provided external advice and counsel not only on proposed policy positions but also on negotiating strategy and tactics. These two bodies represented organizational responses to the unique management problems created by a presidential decision to commit the nation to a long series of negotiations on a complex, technical, and highly sensitive issue. There was a need for sophisticated policy analysis, forward planning, prompt responses to changing circumstances, and strict secrecy. The Deming Group and the Advisory Committee were quite successful in carrying out their assigned roles and in providing the president with a strategic management system to guide the negotiations while keeping his options open.

If there was one area of foreign economic policy in the Johnson years in which the presidential management system tended to break down, it was the area of aid policy. Operational management of aid policies occurred through several interagency coordinating committees that operated at the staff level. In addition, there were cumbersome clearance procedures that called for reviews by the secretary of state, the director of the BOB, the secretary of the treasury, and the

White House staff. However, there was no mechanism to provide coordination at the upper levels of the administration.

In practice, President Johnson directed aid policy from the Oval Office, personally approving development loans over $5 million and all food aid agreements. As might be expected, this degree of presidential involvement centralized policy direction, and Johnson was able to secure more cooperation and support for his aid policy from his secretary of agriculture and other cabinet officials than might normally have been the case had the president not been so directly involved. But aid policy in the Johnson years was never very well integrated with overall domestic and foreign policy. This breakdown was due primarily to the absence of a system for strategic management of development assistance.

The primary benefit of a decentralized management system for foreign economic policy, particularly given the informal and open nature of the system in the Johnson years, is that it provides great flexibility to the administration in responding to changing circumstances. The primary costs, on the other hand, relate to the system's structural ambiguity and to the high demands it places on the president's time and attention.

The ambiguous nature of decentralized management in the Johnson years sometimes caused resentment among those who perceived that important issues would disappear into the upper reaches of the administration only to emerge as presidential decisions without their having had the benefit of full participation. Such was the feeling of a number of top officials in the Commerce Department, for example. The high demands on the president's time and attention required by a decentralized, often informal, and substantially open management system can only be met by an active president, one who is capable and willing to master complex issues and provide personal guidance and direction to the decisionmaking process. Fortunately, Lyndon Johnson was such a president.

While organizational structure plays an important role in determining the success of presidential management of policy processes, an equally important role is played by staffing decisions. A successful president will manage to have the right people in the right places at the right times. In this respect, President Johnson has to be given high marks in the area of foreign economic policy. The major actors were individuals of unusual competence who had the experience, tact, grace, and self-confidence to operate effectively within a highly fluid system requiring frequent and close cooperation and coordination with their peers.

It has been asserted that "the U.S. government has never found a

way to manage its own international economic policy effectively."[162]
Certainly in the 1970s, there was much dissatisfaction with the
presidential management of foreign economic policy and many recommendations for change.[163] It is instructive that many of these recommendations called for greater use of interagency mechanisms of
coordination and for the re-establishment of the position of presidential assistant for foreign economic affairs.

Francis Bator has provided an excellent description of the operational criteria for assessing effective presidential management:

> The main test of organization is whether, in a strategic situation,
> the President is given a full and fair crack, in time, at the choices
> the way they really are. Does the Government confront him with
> a good map of reality; a hard specification of the choices open to
> him, and the contingent consequences and uncertainties, long
> and short term, of deciding in favor of option 1 or option 2 or
> option X? And does the execution truly reflect the President's
> will and intention after he has been confronted by such a map of
> reality and after he has been exposed, face-to-face on important
> matters, to the sharply stated views of his own principal barons
> within the executive branch and appropriate barons from the Hill
> and otherwise?[164]

Judged in these terms, the Johnson administration succeeded in
effectively managing the decision making process in foreign economic policy for completing the Kennedy Round negotiations, the
negotiations over reform of the international monetary system, and
the efforts to restore balance-of-payments equilibrium.

7. Conclusions

The purpose of our study has not been to analyze the Johnson administration's macroeconomic policy record. Rather, it has been to discuss and analyze the administration's management of macroeconomic institutions and policy development. That this task was performed in such manner as to yield reasonably good economic results can be viewed as a broad measure of successful management.[1] We do not contend, however, that this supports either the propriety or effectiveness of all the Johnson administration's policy actions, or that there are not other ways to successfully manage macroeconomic institutions or to measure the success of such management.

With this as preface, what were the distinguishing characteristics of presidential management of macroeconomic institutions during the Johnson years? In providing an answer we shall proceed along three different paths: a characterization of Johnson as economic manager, a discussion of the operation of the macroeconomic subpresidency, and a brief review of the character of presidential responsibility in the various macroeconomic policy areas.

Johnson as Economic Manager

In his role as economic manager, Johnson was personally much interested in and actively involved with the formation of macroeconomic policy. Activist in inclination and possessed of a set of populist economic values, he was neither theoretically inclined nor technically well informed. He knew, however, what he wanted in economic policy: economic growth, a high rate of employment, low interest rates, and stable prices. He made full use of the presidency in pursuit of his policy goals and exercised continuing leadership in the development and management of macroeconomic policies.

Johnson wanted, got, and consumed large amounts of economic information. Adept at using others' expertise, he tended to seek second, third, and fourth opinions and to test ideas and recommendations against their likely opponents. He wanted to know the shades of differences in the opinions of his various economic advisers. He placed considerable weight on the advice of those he trusted, and yet in his use of advice he was always somewhat skeptical. As Henry Fowler put it, Johnson was not a person who was easily "snowed." He relied substantially upon himself for judgments on the political feasibility of his advisers' recommendations. His decision not to seek a general tax increase in early 1966, for example, was a political judgment based on his own appraisal of the possibility of securing congressional action, and the likely political consequences thereof.

In making economic decisions Johnson preferred face-to-face meetings with groups of his advisers in which differences could be worked out and resolved. This contrasts with Richard Nixon, who preferred to make decisions alone on the basis of memorandums, and Jimmy Carter, who held lots of meetings, and then made decisions on the basis of memorandums. The advisers Johnson met with varied from time to time, depending upon such factors as the problem being addressed and his own notion of who could usefully be included. Individuals who participated in the group process were free to send the president their independent assessments. Normally, once a presidential decision was made all participants were expected to support the decision, at least publicly. At times, though (for example, after his decision not to seek a general tax increase in 1966), he permitted some of his advisers to continue to advocate to him the need for alternate action. Johnson's concern for loyalty on policy matters from his advisers and appointees seems to have been focused most strongly on his Vietnam policies.[2]

In policy development, Johnson preferred informal organizational structures and arrangements—task forces and ad hoc committees. These provided flexibility and adaptability in the development of policy proposals. Notable examples of more structured management devices were the Troika, the Quadriad, and the Cabinet Committee on Balance of Payments. Such arrangements on the whole also served him well, although it will be recalled that he lost interest in the use of the Quadriad, at least partly because the need for it diminished.

In policy implementation, for example, in the administration of the wage-price guideposts, he also favored the use of loose, informal arrangements. He rejected all recommendations for regularized (but not necessarily legally mandated) structures and procedures to implement the guideposts. Had such arrangements been made, they might have contributed to more coherence, consistency, and fairness in the enforcement of the guideposts. However, they might also have attracted undesired public attention and controversy, which might have complicated implementation of the guideposts.

Johnson was better served by informality in the development of policy proposals than in their implementation. Effective policy implementation usually requires (among other things) consistent and sustained effort and a clear location of administrative responsibility. When the Carter administration decided in 1978 to employ wage-price standards, the Council on Wage and Price Stability was assigned responsibility for them. This did not ensure the success of the Carter standards, however, partly because of a lack of adequate presidential support and the complex nature of the standards.

Under Johnson's leadership, his administration intervened extensively in the economy, as exemplified by some of his activist discretionary fiscal policies, wage-price activities, and balance-of-payments policies. Some actions had major positive consequences. But many, at least in retrospect, appear to have been trivial in terms of their likely impact on the problem at hand. One can point to such examples as the familiar story of Johnson's turning off the White House lights to reduce government expenditures, instructing the Department of Defense to buy medium rather than large eggs to reduce this miniscule portion of the price index, and demanding written prior notification of all overseas travel to control the outflow of American dollars.

The more trivial actions may be viewed as symbolic gestures, designed to indicate presidential concern and place the institution of the presidency behind established policy. President Johnson was well aware of the political value of symbolism. He lost no opportunity to demonstrate to the bureaucracy his firm commitment to specific goals. He also demonstrated considerable concern for and adeptness at building public support for his economic policies. He was highly conscious of the need for consent to help ensure the effectiveness of presidential policies.

Finally, Johnson demonstrated a preference for voluntary rather than mandated programs. In some areas, he lacked authority to mandate and was reluctant to seek it from Congress. In other areas, he simply preferred the voluntary approach, although he did not hesitate to use the full powers of his office to persuade others to cooperate.

The Macroeconomic Subpresidency

For the management of macroeconomic policy there exists a distinguishable subpresidency, the various components of which were discussed in Chapter 2. Here we will focus on some of its operating characteristics during the Johnson years.

First, only a small number of agencies and officials were centrally involved in the management of macroeconomic policy. Most of the more technical economic data and information that Johnson received came from the Troika agencies and the Troika operation. The Troika operation also was the primary mechanism for the development of basic policy recommendations. Other administrative units—the Departments of Agriculture, Commerce, and Labor, for example—were called upon only on an occasional basis.

The individuals who met with Johnson on macroeconomic matters can be characterized as belonging to inner and outer circles. In the inner circle and most influential were the chairman of the Council of Economic Advisers (CEA), the director of the Bureau of the Budget (BOB), the secretary of the treasury, Secretary of Defense Robert McNamara, the White House assistants for domestic affairs (Bill Moyers and Joseph Califano), and, on international economic policy matters, the special and deputy special assistants for national security affairs. Private citizens who regularly provided economic advice were David Ginsburg, Abe Fortas, and Clark Clifford (who replaced McNamara in early 1968). In the outer circle were such officials as the secretaries of commerce and labor, the attorney general, three or four White House officials, a couple of top-level officials in the BOB, some advisers from the business community, and a few others. In all, there were only a dozen or two persons from whom Johnson regularly drew economic advice.

All participants in the macroeconomic subpresidency were not, of course, equally concerned with all of the subareas (fiscal, monetary, and so on) of macroeconomic policy. While some, such as the CEA and Califano, were involved in some manner in all of the areas, others, such as the secretary of labor and some White House officials, for example, Harry McPherson, Ernest Goldstein, and Francis Bator, were involved in only one or two areas. In this light, the macroeconomic subpresidency can also be viewed as a series of overlapping circles. This reflects some specialization of concern on the one hand and the potential for some integrating and coordinating activity on the other. However, because no one else really possessed such authority, much of the burden for coordinating macroeconomic-policy actions fell upon the president himself. In the Ford administration, in contrast, and by design, the Economic Policy Board played an important coordinating role.[3]

Second, the macroeconomic subpresidency in general operated harmoniously. There were few sharp conflicts or disagreements among its members. Probably most dissatisfied with its operations were Secretary of Commerce John Connor and Secretary of Labor Willard Wirtz, who were relegated to the outer circle. Contributing to sub-presidency harmony were the general belief of its members in the ac-tivist economic policy favored by Johnson, the bond created by the fact that several members were professional economists, and the pressure exerted by Johnson for consensus among his advisers on fiscal-policy recommendations. Remarkably, almost all of the Troika reports sent to Johnson were endorsed by all three members; dis-sents were rare. In one instance, when Califano reported to Johnson the lack of agreement among his advisers on the timing of an eco-nomic proposal, the president enjoined Califano, "For God's sake, get agreement."

Moreover, Johnson clearly served as his own economic spokes-man, thereby eliminating the possibility of struggles among his advisers over who would serve as the administration's economic spokesman. Such conflicts did occur during subsequent administra-tions (e.g., the Carter and Reagan administrations). There was also a notable lack of public bickering among Johnson's economic advisers, in contrast to that which occurred in the first term of the Reagan administration.

Third, although one cannot find concrete evidence of any sort of "Executive Office Alliance," it seems clear that agencies within the Executive Office of the President were generally the dominant actors in developing policy proposals. The major exception appears to have been in the balance-of-payments area, where the Treasury Depart-ment dominated policymaking. This was an area long within the purview of the Treasury, which did most of the staff work for the Cabinet Committee on Balance of Payments and thus was in a strong position to shape the actions of the committee. The CEA, which might possibly have challenged the Treasury Department, concen-trated its efforts on fiscal policy and wage-price matters. The prox-imity of Executive Office agencies and officials to the president clearly contributed to their greater influence. Also, it should be ob-served that they had better staff resources for generating economic data and recommendations than did the cabinet departments during this time. This situation changed in later administrations, as the departments strengthened their internal capacities for economic analysis.[4]

Fourth, the macroeconomic subpresidency provided Johnson with an adequate supply of timely and usually accurate information in various areas of macroeconomic policy. (Here we separate informa-tion from policy recommendations and advice.) Notable especially was the three-level Troika operation, which provided the president with quarterly economic forecasts. The information received was focused almost entirely on present and near-future problems. Little attention was given to longer-range economic planning. The CEA, which would have been a logical agency to handle such planning activity, was occupied with short-range tasks. Moreover, presidential perspectives tend to be truncated, focused on the current problem or, at most, the next election. Also, economic forecasting was not an exact science (it still is not), and the further into the future it sought to look the more inexact it became. Such factors explain but do not necessarily justify a lack of longer-range planning. Even the short-run forecasts of the Johnson administration, and actions based thereon, encountered resistance from those who preferred to act on "facts" rather than forecasts, such as certain members of Congress.

Fifth, Johnson used officials from Executive Office agencies as personal advisers on economic matters, notably the BOB director and the CEA chairman. There was no professional economic adviser or assistant in the White House office during the Johnson administration, nor was there an organized domestic- or economic-policy unit such as has existed in subsequent administrations, for example, the Economic Policy Staff in the Carter administration. The only White House people who dealt generally with macroeconomic policy were Bill Moyers and his successor, Joseph Califano, and they acted largely as catalysts and coordinators rather than as providers of substantive advice. An exception was Califano's involvement in wage-price guidepost administration. Although some have argued that the BOB suffered internally because the director did not devote enough attention to day-to-day management problems, this seems to us a judgment lacking a solid factual basis.[5]

Indeed, it is difficult to understand how Executive Office agencies and officials can in practice avoid acting directly for the president in office rather than for "the presidency," as is sometimes suggested to be more appropriate, if this is what the president desires. And Johnson did. The Executive Office of the President exists, after all, because (in the words of the President's Committee on Administrative Management) "the president needs help." Had the BOB director or the CEA chairman not responded to the president's needs, they would have undoubtedly declined in influence and effectiveness, and others would have been sought out to take up the slack.

Sixth, although the White House staff usually was not an important source of substantive economic advice, it did perform some vital management functions in the area of macroeconomic management. First, it provided linkages between the president, the other

Executive Office units, and the various departments and agencies. In so doing it helped to bind together the macroeconomic subpresidency and to meld it into a workable, coordinated advisory system. Thus, most economic-policy communications flowed through Califano's office. He acted to secure and assemble the technical information, advice, and political judgments helpful to presidential decisionmaking. Presidential requests and decisions were usually transmitted through him to the relevant parties. Next, the White House staff was also concerned with the implementation of presidential decisions, seeking to ensure that the departments and agencies carried out assignments. In some instances this involved the coordination of interagency action. In addition, the White House staff on occasion became directly involved in program operations, most notably in the cases of the wage-price guideposts and balance-of-payments issues. Here the staff was useful because it was readily available, unencumbered with clientele ties, and committed to the attainment of presidential goals. In all of this the staff acted with fidelity to protect presidential interests and to advance the attainment of presidential purposes, even though they did not always agree personally with the president's decisions.

The Tasks of Macroeconomic Management

In the first chapter we indicated that there were four interrelated tasks involved in the management of macroeconomic institutions: developing an information-gathering and decisionmaking system, coordinating actions, securing consent from other participants and affected parties, and supplying administrative leadership. What the president specifically does as manager of macroeconomic institutions and how he handles the various management tasks are matters on which it is somewhat difficult to generalize. This is a consequence of such factors as variations in his legal and constitutional authority, in the number and variety of participants, in the problems confronted, and in the sources of needed consent among the various subareas of macroeconomic policy. Many more White House and executive branch officials were involved with development of international economic policy than with fiscal policy, for example, which made achieving consensus more difficult in the former area. Again, consent-building in the fiscal-policy area was focused on Congress, while in wage-price controls it was directed at business and unions in the private sector.

In this section we will take a summary look at the tasks of macroeconomic management from two perspectives. First, we will discuss the tasks that are particular to the various subareas of macro-economic policy. Second, we will take a broad but brief look at the four general tasks of macroeconomic management. This second perspective will help convey further understanding of Johnson's management style. We turn now to the policy subareas.

The Subarea Perspective

In fiscal policymaking, the president shares authority to act with Congress, and during the 1960s Congress continued to be quite protective of its authority relating to taxing and spending. Given a particular policy problem, such as the need to reduce aggregate demand, the major management tasks confronting the president were essentially two. The first was to develop a policy proposal which would satisfactorily deal with the problem. This could be handled within the executive branch and required adequate definition of the problem, the acquisition of adequate information and advice, formulation of an appropriate alternative, and creation of support for it within the administration.

Once a policy proposal was developed, the task then confronting the president and his people was to secure its adoption by Congress. If a decision was made that the appropriate proposal would be unable to win congressional approval, recourse to a second-best alternative was necessary: this is what Johnson did early in 1966 when he decided to request the "bits-and-pieces" tax program. The political nature of presidential management becomes fully clear when attention is on the adoption of fiscal-policy proposals. Securing consent then becomes a crucial task of presidential management and involves the president in the legislative-policy process.

Monetary policy has been assigned by Congress to the formally independent Federal Reserve Board (FRB). In comparison to fiscal policy, in which action requires concurrence of the president and majorities in Congress, monetary-policy decisions are made by a majority of the seven members of the FRB (or the Open Market Committee). "All" the president has to do, then, to achieve his monetary-policy preferences, is favorably influence a majority of the FRB. There are, however, no formal channels of communication between the White House and the FRB, and no formal sanctions that the president can use to shape its actions. To influence the FRB and to coordinate monetary policy with other economic policies, the president must rely on public pressure and persuasion, informal relationships, shared purpose, and, when it is available, the power of appointment. These were sufficient to permit the Johnson administration to maintain a satisfactory relationship with the FRB during most of its tenure. Monetary policy was generally in accord with administration preferences, the major exception being the flap over the discount rate increase in December 1965. However, that was more a dispute over the timing of the action than a major policy conflict.

Wage-price policy—the guideposts—was an administration construct based on presidential preference and decision rather than congressional authorization. The task confronting the administration was that of developing a viable policy within the bounds of permissible authority. To be "viable," a policy had to be able to restrain price and wage increases by securing the voluntary compliance of labor and management. The guideposts, geared to the trend increase in industrial productivity, were the heart of the wage-price policy developed by the administration.

While fully endorsed by the president, the guidepost program suffered from such problems as lack of regularized enforcement, insufficient support from the Departments of Labor and Commerce, and strong opposition from organized labor. Those businesses that were "vulnerable," who were open to presidential pressure, were most affected by the policy. This is not an adequate basis for a really effective and consistent (or fair) policy. The guideposts eventually disappeared, but wage-price policy was never formally abandoned by the administration. Its last effort, the Cabinet Committee on Price Stability, which was mostly devoted to fact-finding, was largely symbolic.

In many respects, the international economic-policy area presented the administration with its most complex problems. A large number of national administrative agencies had some sort of interest in or managed programs with an impact on international economic policy (including the FRB). This compounded the tasks of policy development and implementation. A fairly complex set of interagency committees was evolved for these purposes. The effectiveness of its balance-of-payments policies depended upon the capacity of the administration to secure the cooperation of both the public and private sectors and also of foreign governments. Even when, in 1968, the Johnson administration shifted to a mandatory control program, the need for much voluntary cooperation continued, and a new dimension was added to the management problem, namely, the need to secure congressional support. Overlaying all of this activity was the need to bring about reform of the international monetary system; this melded diplomacy into the management task. Johnson's management skills were fully tested, and proven adequate, in international economic policy.

The Management Tasks Perspective

The loose collection of agencies, officials, and individuals that we have designated as the macroeconomic subpresidency constituted Johnson's information system. As we have already noted, it provided the president with an adequate and timely supply of economic data, policy alternatives, and advice. Not deliberately created by Johnson, it was rather the product partly of inheritance from the Kennedy administration (e.g., the Troika), partly of necessity (e.g., the inclusion of the Federal Reserve Board because of its monetary role), and partly of presidential preference (e.g., the reliance upon Robert McNamara and private advisers like Abe Fortas and Clark Clifford). It reflected Johnson's preferences for loosely structured administrative arrangements, multiple sources of advice and information, and personal contact with his advisers.

The task of policy coordination essentially was handled in two ways. Much of the responsibility for the overall coordination of action among the four policy subareas rested with the president himself, and was largely a product of the presidential decisionmaking process. (The exceptional case of monetary policy has already been noted.) Johnson chose not to use a top-level coordinating body, such as the Ford administration's Economic Policy Board or the Carter administration's Economic Policy Group.

Some lower-level coordinating mechanisms also existed. One was the Cabinet Committee on Balance of Payments, which included representatives of the major departments and agencies involved in that area. Another was the set of informal relationships that helped the Council of Economic Advisers and the Federal Reserve Board exchange information and reduce friction. The role of the deputy assistant for national security affairs in the international economic area also should be noted. Such mechanisms helped provide *operational* coordination. *Strategic* coordination was largely a presidential preserve.

A lack of strong formal authority or, to put it another way, the fact that much ultimate power in the macroeconomic policy area rests outside the presidency, means that the president will have to rely heavily upon persuasion and bargaining to gain approval for his policies. Consent was needed from the departments and agencies, Congress, the general public, and special segments of the public. The persuasional skills of Johnson have been widely commented upon. In 1967–68, however, the administration had to engage in extensive bargaining with leaders of Congress to secure enactment of its proposed income tax increase.

Presidents, however, are not limited to persuasion and bargaining techniques in their quest for consent. Johnson was well aware of the power (or influence, if one prefers) that rested with the presidential office. The status and prestige of the office, especially when coupled with Johnson's strong personality, made it difficult for many persons to reject presidential requests or appeals. Johnson consequently made considerable use of the power inherent in the office, as in his appeals to business executives to comply with the wage-price guideposts. Leverage obtained through the manipulation of other governmental policies (e.g., import controls and procurement policies) was also used to gain cooperation in the wage-price area. Such actions add an element of command to the powers of the presidency and, when skillfully exercised, strengthen the capacity of the president to build consent.

Johnson provided strong administrative leadership in the macroeconomic area. Unlike Richard Nixon, who assigned much responsibility for economic policy first to Treasury Secretary John Connally and then to George Schultz, Connally's successor, Johnson maintained full control over macroeconomic policy. He was deeply interested in it and he had economic goals that were clearly defined and strongly articulated. Moreover, he reserved the power of decision on all important matters, and many not-so-important matters, for himself. However else the economic problems of the Johnson administration might be defined, they could not be viewed as the products of presidential indifference or omission. Unlike Jimmy Carter, Lyndon Johnson was never charged with indecisiveness in the macroeconomic-policy area. His delay in seeking a general tax increase was a matter of calculation and timing rather than uncertainty and hesitation.

Final Comments

The president, as we stated earlier in this volume, has more responsibility in the macroeconomic area than he has authority. Presidential responsibility for economic stability is a product of statutory obligations, public expectations, convenience, and necessity. The last three are probably most important in the development of this role. That is, the public (including government officials) has come to expect the president to develop macroeconomic programs, both because of the desirability of the goal of economic stability and because there is really no good alternative to presidential leadership and management in this policy area. To put it somewhat differently, public expectations and congressional incapacity have created a policy area into which the executive has moved, or probably more accurately, has been impelled to move.

The president, however, is not well equipped with formal authority to meet this responsibility. Article II, with its vesting of the "executive powers" in the president and its direction that he "take care that the laws be faithfully executed" is an uncertain source of authority. Congressional assignments of power, as in the Budget and Accounting Act and the Employment Act, provide some authority, but mostly for policy recommendations. In all, presidential macroeconomic authority is limited. However, presidential *capability* does not depend upon legal authority alone. The president's leadership skills, his will to act, his political support, and his general constitutional position can all help to increase or enhance his capability as macroeconomic manager. Such was the case with Lyndon Johnson until political support for him waned because of opposition to his Vietnam War policies. More recently, Ronald Reagan has demonstrated that a popular and determined president can be an effective economic manager.

There was a strong tendency on the part of many persons within the Johnson administration to think of macroeconomic management as primarily an administrative or even a technical task.[6] Economists were quite influential within the administration and had the notion, which was shared by many noneconomists, that they understood how the economy worked and that, based on Keynesian economics, they had the skills and techniques to effectively manage it. By taking action to stimulate or restrain the pace of economic growth, maximum employment and price stability could be achieved. They saw the politics of economic management as creating sufficient political support within Congress, the administration, and the community to enable the government to do the right things. The economists, of course, were overly optimistic concerning their ability to "fine-tune" the economy, especially considering the bluntness of the instruments of macroeconomic policy.

It has become clear in recent years, however, that macroeconomic management is foremost a political task, in that agreement must be reached on the more specific, if not the broader, goals (e.g., preventing inflation) of macroeconomic policy. The determination of these more specific goals (e.g., reducing inflationary pressure generated by business expansion), helps determine the economic strategies that can be effectively pursued. To put it another way, agreement is often lacking on the more specific policy goals that should guide macroeconomic management. Johnson recognized this more fully than did some of his advisers and, we should add, some of his critics. His refusal for a year and a half to seek a general tax increase was predicated on his belief that it could not be obtained from Congress: he perceived a clear lack of agreement on specific policy goals (which was compounded by other factors, especially the Vietnam War) such as reducing inflationary pressures by an income tax increase. In all, the struggle over the tax surcharge illustrated the importance of politics in macroeconomic policy management.

Whether a macroeconomic policy can be judged "successful" depends on whether it ameliorates the policy problem at which it is aimed. In this sense, successful policies do not just appear; they must be sought. Advisory agencies and personnel must be directed and coordinated to produce data, advice, and policy options. The appropriate policies must then be adopted by whatever authorities can best put them into effect. This requires the type of management activity outlined in this book.

Good management processes, however, do not guarantee that good policy decisions will always be made. The decisionmaking process depends also on the political factors—presidential values and intentions, the nature of the problems themselves, partisan considerations—that characterize the management of democratic public affairs.

Notes

All subject file citations from the LBJ Library are from the Executive Files unless otherwise noted.

1. The President as Economic Manager

1. Quoted in Robert Aaron Gordon, *Economic Instability and Growth: The American Record* (New York: Harper and Row, 1974), p. 22.

2. See, for example Paul R. Abramson, John H. Aldrich, and David W. Rohde, *Change and Continuity in the 1980 Election* (Washington, D.C.: Congressional Quarterly Press, 1982).

3. Clinton Rossiter, *The American Presidency*, rev. ed. (New York: Harcourt, Brace and World, 1959), pp. 36–37.

4. Cf. E. Cary Brown, "Fiscal Policy in the Thirties: A Reappraisal," *American Economic Review* 46 (December 1956): 868ff.

5. The legislative history of the act is well told by Stephen K. Bailey, *Congress Makes a Law* (New York: Columbia University Press, 1950).

6. Herbert Stein, *The Fiscal Revolution in America* (Chicago: University of Chicago Press, 1969), p. 204.

7. For extended discussion of the CEA, see Edward S. Flash, Jr., *Economic Advice and Presidential Leadership* (New York: Columbia University Press, 1965), and Hugh A. Norton, *The Employment Act and the Council of Economic Advisors, 1946–1976* (Columbia: University of South Carolina Press, 1977).

8. Memo, Robson to Califano, 30 August 1966, Robson-Ross Office Files, LBJ Library.

9. James Tobin, *The New Economics One Decade Older* (Princeton: Princeton University Press, 1974), p. 7.

10. Arthur W. Okun, *The Political Economy of Prosperity* (New York: Norton, 1970), p. 37.

11. Ibid.

12. Walter W. Heller, *New Dimensions of Political Economy* (Cambridge: Harvard University Press, 1966), p. 59.

13. See, for example, memo, Califano to the president, 16 March 1966, BE 5, WHCF, LBJ Library.

14. Cf. Richard E. Neustadt, *Presidential Power: The Politics of Leadership from FDR to Carter* (New York: John Wiley and Sons, 1980).

15. On the use of case studies for presidential research, see Norman C. Thomas, "Case Studies," in *Studying the Presidency*, ed. George C. Edwards III and Stephen J. Wayne (Knoxville: University of Tennessee Press, 1983), Ch. 2.

2. The Johnson Administration: Structure and Policy

1. Richard E. Neustadt, *Presidential Power: The Politics of Leadership from FDR to Carter* (New York: John Wiley and Sons, 1980).

2. Walter W. Heller, manuscript, BE 5, WHCF, LBJ Library. Heller's estimate is probably low.

3. Gardner Ackley, interview transcript, Vanderbilt Institute for Public Policy Studies, p. 5. An edited version of this interview transcript can be found in *The President and the Council of Economic Advisers*, ed. Erwin C. Hargrove and Samuel A. Morley (Boulder, Colo.: Westview Press, 1984), pp. 217–266. This volume contains highly useful interviews with all of the CEA chairmen who served during 1949–1981. The interviews were held at the Vanderbilt Institute for Public Policy Studies.

4. This point is made by George Reedy, *Twilight of the Presidency* (New York: New American Library, 1970), Ch. 2.

5. Emmette S. Redford and Marlan Blissett, manuscript, LBJ School of Public Affairs, Austin, Texas.

6. Harry McPherson, interview, 27 June 1979.

7. Arthur M. Okun, Oral History Interview, tape 1, p. 13, LBJ Library.

8. Stanford Ross, interview, 25 June 1979.

9. Joseph A. Califano, Jr., interview, 28 June 1968. Quoted in Lawrence C. Pierce, *The Politics of Fiscal Policy Formation* (Pacific Palisades, Calif.: Goodyear Publishing Company, 1971), p. 99.

10. Joseph A. Califano, Jr., interview, 17 May 1980.

11. Memo, to the president, 2 January 1966, BE 41 / Steel, WHCF, LBJ Library.

12. Joseph A. Califano, Jr., interview, 17 May 1980.

13. Arthur M. Okun, interview transcript, Vanderbilt Institute for Public Policy Studies, p. 15.

14. Walter W. Heller, *New Dimensions of Political Economy* (Cambridge: Harvard University Press, 1966), p. 2.

15. Arthur M. Okun, interview, 29 June 1979.

16. Administrative History of the Council of Economic Advisors (hereafter CEA), Vol. I, Ch. 1, p. 2, LBJ Library.

17. Ibid., pp. 2–3.

18. Memo, Ackley to the president, 27 July 1967, FG 11-3, WHCF, LBJ Library.

19. William Chartener, Assistant Secretary of Commerce for Economic Affairs, quoted in the *Washington Post*, 27 September 1968, p. D 6.

20. Gardner Ackley, Oral History Interview I, p. 15, LBJ Library.

21. Memo, CEA to the President's Task Force on Government Reorganization, "Economic Policy Formation" folder, Files of James Gaither, LBJ Library.

22. Memo, Heller to Moyers, 15 October 1964, FG 11-3, WHCF, LBJ Library.

23. Heller, *New Dimensions of Political Economy*, p. 52.

24. Gardner Ackley, Oral History Interview I, pp. 12–13, LBJ Library.

25. Gardner Ackley, "The Contribution of Economists to Policy Formation," *Journal of Finance* 21 (May 1966): 176.

26. Memo, Heller to the president, 5 June 1964, FG 11-3, WHCF, LBJ Library.

27. Memo, Heller to Valenti, 7 August 1964, FG 11-3, WHCF, LBJ Library.

28. Memo, Dryden to the president, 21 January 1966, C.F., LBJ Library.

29. Memo, Ackley to Califano, 27 January 1966, FG 10, WHCF, LBJ Library.

30. Memo, Director, Bureau of the Budget, Chairman, CEA, and Director, Office of Emergency Planning to Califano, 21 April 1966, C.F., FG 11-1, WHCF, LBJ Library.

31. Quoted in Roger B. Porter, "The President and Economic Policy: Problems, Patterns, and Alternatives," in *The Illusion of Presidential Government*, ed. Hugh Heclo and Lester M. Salamon (Boulder, Colo.: Westview Press, 1981), p. 215.

32. Memo, Gordon to the president, 23 November 1963, FI 4, WHCF, LBJ Library.

33. Quoted in Larry Berman, *The Office of Management and Budget and the Presidency, 1921–1979* (Princeton, N.J.: Princeton University Press, 1979), pp. 69–70.

34. Gardner Ackley, interview, 15 August 1979.

35. Memo, Martin to the president, 28 April 1966, BE, WHCF, LBJ Library.

36. Gardner Ackley, interview transcript, Vanderbilt Institute for Public Policy Studies, p. 20.

37. Harry McPherson, Oral History Interview, tape 8, p. 19, LBJ Library.

38. Alexander B. Trowbridge, Oral History Interview, tape 1, p. 23, LBJ Library.

39. Joseph A. Califano, Jr., *A Presidential Nation* (New York: W. W. Norton Co., 1975), p. 223.

40. Ibid., p. 217.

41. Cf. *Administrative History of the CEA*, Vol. I, Ch. 2, LBJ Library, and Heller, *New Dimensions of Political Economy*, pp. 58–73.

42. Cf. James Tobin, *The New Economics One Decade Older* (Princeton: Princeton University Press, 1974), pp. 6–18.

43. Heller, *New Dimensions of Political Economy*, pp. 65–66.

44. Arthur W. Okun, *The Political Economy of Prosperity* (New York: Norton, 1969), pp. 47–48. See also Rudiger Dornbusch and Stanley Fisher, *Macroeconomics* (New York: McGraw-Hill, 1970), pp. 304–316.

45. CEA, *Annual Report of the Council of Economic Advisers, 1965* (Washington, D.C.: Government Printing Office, 1965), pp. 99–100.

46. See memos, Ackley to the president, 11 March 1965 (FG 11-3), and 10 July 1965 (FG 11-3), WHCF, LBJ Library.

47. Memo, Ackley to the president, 17 December 1965, FI 4, WHCF, LBJ Library.

48. Memo, Ackley to the president, C.F. FI 4, WHCF, LBJ Library.

49. *Public Papers of the Presidents of the United States: Lyndon B. Johnson, 1966,* Vol. I (Washington, D.C.: Government Printing Office, 1967). Hereafter *LBJ Public Papers.*

50. *LBJ Public Papers, 1966,* I, 326.

51. Memo, Schultze to the president, 11 May 1966, FI 11, WHCF, LBJ Library. See also Ackley's memo to the president, 10 May 1966, FI 11, WHCF.

52. *LBJ Public Papers, 1966,* II, 985–991.

53. Ibid., 1355–1356.

54. Memo, Troika to the president, 30 December 1966, C.F. BE 5, WHCF, LBJ Library.

55. Memo, McNamara and others to the president, 9 January 1967, FI 4, WHCF, LBJ Library.

56. *LBJ Public Papers, 1967,* I, 301–303.

57. U.S., Congress, Senate, Committee on Finance, *Restoration of the Investment Tax Credit,* 90th Cong., 1st sess., S. Rept. 79, 1967.

58. Memo, Troika to the president, 19 June 1967, BE 5, WHCF, LBJ Library.

59. Memo, Fowler and others to the president, 22 July 1967, FI 11, WHCF, LBJ Library.

60. Okun, *The Political Economy of Prosperity,* p. 88.

61. *Washington Post,* 18 October 1968.

62. Memo, Troika to the president, 5 August 1968, BE 5, WHCF, LBJ Library.

63. Okun, *The Political Economy of Prosperity,* pp. 93–94.

3. The Management of Fiscal Policy

1. Walter W. Heller, Oral History Interview II, p. 78, LBJ Library.

2. Arthur M. Okun, interview transcript, Vanderbilt Institute for Public Policy Studies, p. 3.

3. Walter H. Heller, interview transcript, Vanderbilt Institute for Public Policy Studies, p. 41.

4. Robert A. Wallace, interview, 13 August 1979.

5. This discussion of the Troika operation draws generally upon Lawrence C. Pierce, *The Politics of Fiscal Policy Formation* (Pacific Palisades, Calif.: Goodyear Publishing Company, 1971), esp. Chs. 3, 6.

6. Charles Zwick, interview with Brooks Myers, 21 April 1978.

7. Robert A. Wallace, interview, 13 August 1979.

8. "How Washington Makes Its Forecasts," *Business Week,* 30 December 1967, p. 82.

9. Arthur M. Okun, interview transcript, Vanderbilt Institute for Public Policy Studies, p. 35.

10. Arthur M. Okun, Oral History Interview I, p. 26, LBJ Library.

11. Gardner Ackley, Oral History Interview I, p. 14, LBJ Library.

12. Pierce, *Politics of Fiscal Policy Formation,* p. 56.

13. Memo, Ackley to Califano, 9 December 1966, FG 11-3, WHCF, LBJ Library.

14. Letter, Ackley to Wirtz, 10 December 1966, CEA Microfilm, roll 69, LBJ Library.

15. Memo, McNamara, Fowler, Wirtz, Connor, Schultze, Ackley, Clifford, and Califano to president, 9 January 1966 FI 4, WHCF, LBJ Library; memo, Troika to the president, 30 December 1966, C.F., BE 5, WHCF, LBJ Library.

16. CEA member quoted in Pierce, *Politics of Fiscal Policy Formation*, p. 82.

17. Gardner Ackley, interview transcript, Vanderbilt Institute for Public Policy Studies, pp. 16–17.

18. Arthur M. Okun, interview transcript, Vanderbilt Institute for Public Policy Studies, p. 64.

19. Charles Zwick, interview with Brooks Myers, 21 April 1978.

20. Gardner Ackley, interview, 15 August 1979.

21. Arthur M. Okun, *The Political Economy of Prosperity* (New York: W. W. Norton and Company, 1970), pp. 62–69.

22. Memo, Ackley to the president, 17 December 1965, FI 4, WHCF, LBJ Library (emphases in original).

23. Memo, Ackley to the president, 26 December 1965, C.F. FI 4, WHCF, LBJ Library (emphases in original).

24. Memo, McNamara to the president, 9 December 1965, C.F. FI 4 / FG, WHCF, LBJ Library. The memorandum was marked "secret."

25. Memo, Califano to the president, 23 December 1965, FG 110, WHCF, LBJ Library.

26. Memo, Fowler to the president, 29 December 1965, C.F. FI 4, WHCF, LBJ Library.

27. Memo, Schultze to the president, 27 December 1965, C.F. FI 4, WHCF, LBJ Library.

28. For example, David Halberstam, "How the Economy Went Haywire," *Atlantic Monthly* 227 (September 1972): 56–60.

29. Gardner Ackley, "LBJ's Game Plan," *Atlantic Monthly* 230 (December 1972): 46–47.

30. Gardner Ackley, interview transcript, Vanderbilt Institute for Public Policy Studies, p. 46.

31. Walter W. Heller, interview transcript, Vanderbilt Institute for Public Policy Studies, p. 122. This story is corroborated by Dewey Daane, who was then a member of the Federal Reserve Board.

32. Lyndon Baines Johnson, *The Vantage Point* (New York: Holt, Rinehart, and Winston, 1971), pp. 444–445.

33. U.S., Congress, Joint Economic Committee, *Economic Prospects and Politics*, 92nd Cong., 1st sess., 1971, p. 421.

34. Memo, Eckstein to the president, 29 April 1966, BE 5-4, WHCF, LBJ Library.

35. Edwin L. Dale, Jr., "The Inflation Goof," *New Republic* 160 (4 January 1969): 16–17.

36. Charles L. Schultze, interview, 28 June 1979. This view is generally shared by Gardner Ackley.

37. Gardner Ackley, interview, 15 August 1979.

38. Arthur M. Okun, interview transcript, Vanderbilt Institute for Policy Studies, p. 62.

39. "Special Message to the Congress on Fiscal Policy, 8 September 1966," *Public Papers of the Presidents of the United States: Lyndon B. Johnson, 1966,* Vol. II (Washington, D.C.: Government Printing Office, 1967), pp. 986–991. Hereafter *LBJ Public Papers.*

40. Memo, Schultze to the president, 10 June 1966, C.F. FI 4, WHCF, LBJ Library.

41. Memo, Schultze to the president, 24 January 1966, FI 4, WHCF, LBJ Library.

42. Memo, Hughes to Califano, 22 March 1966, FI 4, WHCF, LBJ Library.

43. Memo, Califano to the president, 24 March 1966, FI 4, WHCF, LBJ Library. The attorney general's study is attached thereto.

44. Memo, Schultze to the president, 10 June 1966, C.F. FI 4, WHCF, LBJ Library.

45. Ibid.

46. Memo and attachments, Cohn to Califano, 23 June 1966, FI 1-2, WHCF, LBJ Library.

47. Memo, Califano to the president, 25 June 1966, FI 4, WHCF, LBJ Library.

48. Memo and attachment, Califano to the president, 7 July 1966, C.F. FI 1-2, WHCF, LBJ Library.

49. Memo and attachment, Califano to the president, 15 July 1966, C.F. FI 1-2, WHCF, LBJ Library.

50. Memo, Califano to the president, 18 July 1966, FI 4, WHCF, LBJ Library.

51. Memo and attachment, Califano to the president, 20 July 1966, C.F. FI 1-2, WHCF, LBJ Library (emphases in original).

52. Memo, Troika to the president, 22 August 1966, FI 4, WHCF, LBJ Library.

53. Memo, Fowler, McNamara, Katzenback, O'Brien, Schultze, Ackley, Ginsburg, and Califano to the president, 2 September 1966, BE 5, WHCF, LBJ Library.

54. Memo, Schultze to the president, 15 September 1966, FI 4, WHCF, LBJ Library.

55. Memo, Schultze to the president, 28 October 1966, FI 4, WHCF, LBJ Library.

56. Memo, Schultze to the president, 22 November 1966, FI 4, WHCF, LBJ Library.

57. Barr's report is summarized in a memo by Califano to the president, 23 November 1966, C.F. FI 4, WHCF, LBJ Library.

58. Memo, Schultze to the president, 28 October 1966, FI 4, WHCF, LBJ Library.

59. "The President's News Conference of 29 November 1966," *LBJ Public Papers, 1966,* II, pp. 1406–1410.

60. Schultze to the president, 8 December 1966, FI 4, WHCF, LBJ Library.

61. Memo, Troika to the president, 30 December 1966, C.F. BE 5, WHCF, LBJ Library.

62. "Statement by the President Announcing the Release of Deferred Funds for Federal Programs," 17 March 1967. *LBJ Public Papers, 1967*, I, p. 357. This statement pertained to the release of $791 million in funds for housing, highways, flood control projects, and other purposes.

63. Memo, Hughes to the president, 15 March 1967, "Release of 1967 Cutbacks (OBR)," loose folder, 7006-12,8(4)4, Bureau of the Budget Records, Office of Administration, Washington, D.C. A variety of material relating to the release of cutback funds can be found in this folder.

64. U.S., Congress, House, Committee on Ways and Means, *Hearings on the President's 1967 Tax Proposal*, 90th Cong., 1st sess., 1967, I, pp. 41–42.

65. Memo, Council of Economic Advisers (hereafter CEA) to the president, 12 March 1966, C.F. FI 4, WHCF, LBJ Library; memo, Martin to the president, 8 April 1966, BE 5, WHCF, LBJ Library.

66. Memo, Califano to the president, 7 May 1966, C.F. BE 5, WHCF, LBJ Library. Included in the memo was this sentence: "If you decide to go for a tax increase, Fowler thinks we should make a deal with Martin to roll back 5% on Regulation Q and ease the money situation." Regulation Q imposes ceilings on interest rates for bank time deposits. Rolling back the rate would ease monetary policy which had been tightened by the "go it alone" tight monetary policy of the Federal Reserve Board at this time.

67. Gardner Ackley, interview, 15 August 1979.

68. Memo, Califano to the president, 16 August 1966, BE 5, WHCF, LBJ Library.

69. Joseph A. Califano, Jr., interview, 17 May 1980.

70. Memo, Ackley to Califano, 29 August 1966, C.F. BE 5, WHCF, LBJ Library.

71. Memo, Califano to the president, 1 December 1966, C.F. FI 11, WHCF, LBJ Library.

72. Gardner Ackley, interview, 15 August 1979.

73. U.S., *Statutes at Large*, Public Law 87-834. This legislation also suspended accelerated depreciation.

74. Arthur M. Okun, interview transcript, Vanderbilt Institute for Public Policy Studies, p. 38.

75. Joseph Barr, Oral History Interview, tape 2, p. 20, LBJ Library. Barr served as undersecretary and (for a few weeks) secretary of the treasury during the Johnson administration.

76. Memo, Schultze to the president, 10 December 1966, BE 5-4, WHCF, LBJ Library.

77. "Annual Budget Message to the Congress, Fiscal Year 1968," *LBJ Public Papers, 1967*, I, 39–61.

78. Others were Robert B. Anderson, Rep. Frank Bow, Henry H. Fowler, Sen. Carl Hayden, Winthrop C. Lenz, Rep. George Mahon, Paul W. McCracken, Charles L. Schultze, Carl S. Shoup, Leonard S. Silk, Elmer B. Staats, Robert M. Trueblood, Robert Turner, Theodore O. Yntema, and Sen. Milton Young.

79. *Report of the President's Commission on Budget Concepts* (Washington, D.C.: Government Printing Office, 1967), p. 6.

80. *The Budget in Brief, Fiscal Year, 1969* (Washington, D.C.: Government Printing Office, 1968), p. 6.

81. Quoted in Thomas R. Wolanin, *Presidential Advisory Commission* (Madison: University of Wisconsin Press, 1975), p. 55.

82. Charles L. Schultze, interview, 28 June 1979.

83. Memo, CEA to the President's Task Force on Government Reorganization, 18 February 1967, "Economic Policy Formation" folder, Files of James Gaither, LBJ Library.

84. 1968 Outside Task Force on the Quality of Economic Data, Task Force Collection, LBJ Library.

85. President's Task Force on Government Organization, Final Report on "Government Organization for Economic Policy Formulation and Administration," 15 September 1967, LBJ Library.

86. U.S., Congress, Joint Economic Committee, Subcommittee on Economic Statistics, *The Coordination and Integration of Government Statistical Programs*, 90th Cong., 1st sess., 1967, pp. 132–133.

4. The Management of Monetary Policy

1. For a more thorough examination of the structure of the Federal Reserve System, see Michael D. Reagan, "The Political Structure of the Federal Reserve System," *American Political Science Review* 55 (March 1961): 64–76; William Poole, "The Making of Monetary Policy: Description and Analysis," *Economic Inquiry* 13 (June 1975): 253–265; and Paul Meek, *U. S. Monetary Policy and Financial Markets* (New York: New York Federal Reserve Bank, 1982).

2. See H. Parker Willis, *The Federal Reserve System* (New York: Ronald, 1923), and A. Jerome Clifford, *The Independence of the Federal Reserve System* (Philadelphia: University of Pennsylvania Press, 1965).

3. Sherman J. Maisel, *Managing the Dollar* (New York: Norton, 1973), p. 110.

4. Legal opinion supports the view that in the case of a disagreement, the board's power to "determine" discount rates overrides the authority of the individual Federal Reserve District banks to "establish" them.

5. At one time during the Johnson presidency, the FOMC established a Directive Committee charged with attempting to quantify the directive (i.e., to put it in terms of numbers as contrasted with money market jargon and to clarify the meaning of the terms being used so that use would be consistent). Interview with George W. Ellis, former president of the Federal Reserve Bank of Boston, 13 March 1979. Also, see Maisel, *Managing the Dollar*, pp. 229–231. It has been suggested that leaving the directive imprecise, focusing debate on the "facts," and adopting a goal of contracylical stabilization contributed to the submersion of value differences among the participants in the process and facilitated the forging of consensus in the FOMC. See Sanford F. Borins, "The Political Economy of 'the Fed,'" *Public Policy* 30 (Spring 1972): 175–198.

6. For example, see: Commission on Organization of the Executive Branch of the Government (Hoover Commission), *Appendix N: Task Force Report on Regulatory Commissions* (Washington, D.C.: Government Printing Office, 1949), pp. 109–112; J. Z. Rowe, *The Public-Private Character of United States Central Banking* (New Brunswick, N.J.: Rutgers University Press, 1965); Clifford, *The Independence of the Federal Reserve*; Robert Weintraub, "Congressional Supervision of Monetary Policy," *Journal of Monetary Economics* 4 (April 1978): 341–362; Ralph C. Bryant, *Money and Monetary Policy in Interdependent Nations* (Washington, D.C.: Brookings Institution, 1980), Ch. 18; Nathaniel Beck, "Presidential Influence on the Federal Reserve in the 1970s," *American Journal of Political Science* 26 (August 1982): 415–445; and Edward J. Kane, "External Pressures and the Operations of the Fed," in *Political Economy of International and Domestic Monetary Relations*, ed. Raymond E. Lombra and Willard E. Witte (Ames, Iowa: Iowa State University Press, 1982), pp. 211–232.

7. White House Press Release, 27 April 1964.

8. Letter, Rep. Patman to the president, 4 May 1964, FG 233, WHCF, LBJ Library.

9. Letter, Rep. Patman to the president, 25 May 1964, FG 233, WHCF, LBJ Library.

10. President Johnson related that he had a visit from President Eisenhower on 23 November 1963, the day after President Kennedy's assassination. Eisenhower subsequently dictated a memorandum for President Johnson in which he stated: "In accordance with your request, I present below for your consideration certain recommendations: (1) because of your known confidence in the judgment and integrity of Robert Anderson, I would suggest that in the near future you send for him to confer on general subjects, and particularly those of a fiscal and financial character." See Lyndon Baines Johnson, *The Vantage Point* (New York: Holt, Rinehart, and Winston, 1971), p. 31.

11. Memo, Anderson to Jenkins, 9 June 1964, FG 233, WHCF, LBJ Library (emphasis in the original).

12. Memo, Heller to the president, 29 November 1963, FG 11-3, WHCF, LBJ Library (emphases in original).

13. Memo, Anderson to Jenkins, 9 June 1964, FG 233, WHCF, LBJ Library.

14. Maisel, *Managing the Dollar*, p. 154.

15. John T. Woolley, *Monetary Politics* (Cambridge: Cambridge University Press, 1984), p. 11.

16. Ibid., p. 193.

17. Ibid., p. 153.

18. Maisel, *Managing the Dollar*, p. 117, and Woolley, *Monetary Politics*, pp. 127–128.

19. Memo, Heller to the president, 30 September 1964, C.F. FI 9, WHCF, LBJ Library.

20. Benjamin Haggott Beckhart, *Federal Reserve System* (Washington, D.C.: American Institute of Banking, The American Bankers Association, 1972), pp. 31–32; Willis, *The Federal Reserve System*, pp. 672–673.

21. Memo, Okun to the president, 3 January 1967, FG 233, WHCF, LBJ Library.

22. Maisel, *Managing the Dollar*, p. 147.

23. Kane, "External Pressures," pp. 211–232.

24. Woolley, *Monetary Politics*, pp. 191–192.

25. G. L. Bach, "Economics, Politics, and the Fed," *Harvard Business Review* 40 (January-February 1962): 90–91.

26. CEA, *Annual Report of the Council of Economic Advisers, 1965* (Washington, D.C.: Government Printing Office, 1965); pp. 99–100. Hereafter *CEA Annual Report*.

27. G. L. Bach, *Making Monetary and Fiscal Policy* (Washington, D.C.: The Brookings Institution, 1971), p. 88.

28. Hugh A. Norton, *The Employment Act and the Council of Economic Advisers, 1946–1976* (Columbia, S.C.: University of South Carolina Press, 1977), p. 145.

29. Ibid.

30. Bach, *Making Monetary and Fiscal Policy*, p. 101.

31. *CEA Annual Report, 1961*, p. 97.

32. Memo, Heller to the president, 29 November 1963, FG 11-3, WHCF, LBJ Library (emphasis in the original).

33. This was determined by examination of the President's Daily Diary, LBJ Library.

34. Bach, *Making Monetary and Fiscal Policy*, p. 121.

35. Walter W. Heller, *New Dimensions of Political Economy* (Cambridge: Harvard University Press, 1966), p. 36. (emphases in the original).

36. Gardner Ackley, Oral History Interview II, p. 21, LBJ Library.

37. Gardner Ackley, interview, 15 August 1979.

38. Gardner Ackley, Oral History Interview II, p. 21, LBJ Library.

39. Ibid., p. 10 (emphasis in the original).

40. Arthur Okun, Oral History Interview I, p. 22, LBJ Library.

41. Memo, Heller to the president, 29 November 1963, Documentary Supplement to the Administrative History of the CEA, Vol. II, Pt. 1, item 3, LBJ Library.

42. Memo, Heller to the president, 2 March 1964, C.F. FG 11-3, WHCF, LBJ Library.

43. Memo, Heller to the president, 14 July 1964, FG 233, WHCF, LBJ Library.

44. Memo, Ackley to the president, 1 February 1965, FG 233, WHCF, LBJ Library.

45. Memo, Ackley to the president, 8 March 1965, Documentary Supplement to the Administrative History of the CEA, Vol. II, Pt. 1, item 93, LBJ Library.

46. Administrative History of the CEA, Vol. I, Ch. 2, pp. 42–43, LBJ Library.

47. Ibid., p. 43.

48. Memo, Ackley to the president, 12 July 1965, BE 5, WHCF, LBJ Library.

49. Administrative History of the CEA, Vol. I, Ch. 2, p. 44, LBJ Library.

50. Ibid., p. 45.

51. Memo, Califano to the president, 14 May 1966, BE 5, WHCF, LBJ Library.

52. Memo, Ackley to the president, 13 July 1966, FG 11-3, WHCF, LBJ Library.

53. Maisel, *Managing the Dollar*, p. 102.

54. Administrative History of the CEA, Vol. I, Ch. 2, p. 45, LBJ Library.

55. Memo, Ackley to the president, 29 July 1966, C.F. FG 110, WHCF, LBJ Library.

56. Federal Reserve System, *Annual Report, 1966* (Washington, D.C.: Federal Reserve System, 1967).

57. Administrative History of the CEA, Vol. I, Ch. 2, p. 50, LBJ Library.

58. Ibid., p. 48.

59. Memo, Troika to the president, 11 November 1966, BE 5, WHCF, LBJ Library.

60. Memo, Ackley to the president, 23 November 1966, FG 233, WHCF, LBJ Library.

61. Memo, Ackley to the president, 23 December 1966, FG 232, WHCF, LBJ Library.

62. Memo, Ackley to the president, 27 May 1967, FG 11-3, WHCF, LBJ Library.

63. Administrative History of the CEA, Vol. 1, Ch. 2, pp. 51–52, LBJ Library.

64. Ibid., pp. 52–53.

65. Memo, Okun to the president, 12 August 1968, FI 8, WHCF, LBJ Library.

66. Arthur Okun, Oral History Interview I, p. 26, LBJ Library.

67. See for example, memo, Okun to the president, 17 July 1968, FG 233, WHCF, LBJ Library.

68. Arthur Okun, Oral History Interview I, p. 26, LBJ Library.

69. Gardner Ackley, Oral History Interview II, p. 7, LBJ Library (emphases in the original).

70. Frederick L. Deming, Oral History Interview, tape 1, p. 27, LBJ Library.

71. Bach, *Making Monetary and Fiscal Policy*, p. 163; also see Woolley, *Monetary Politics*, pp. 111–112.

72. Bach, "Economics, Politics, and the Fed," p. 88. Also, see Bach, *Making Monetary and Fiscal Policy*, pp. 163–164.

73. Woolley, *Monetary Politics*, p. 15.

74. Memo, Feldman to the president, 8 January 1964, PE 2, WHCF, LBJ Library.

75. Memo, Dungan to the president, 30 November 1963, PE 2, WHCF, LBJ Library.

76. Letter, the president to Harris, 23 January 1964, Office Files of John Macy, Seymour Harris, LBJ Library.

77. Letter, Senator Kennedy to the president, 29 January 1964, Office Files of John Macy, Seymour Harris, LBJ Library.

78. Letter, Senator Robertson to O'Brien, 10 January 1964, Office Files of John Macy, Seymour Harris, LBJ Library.

79. Letters, Senator Robertson to the president, 21 January, 23 January, 26 January, 27 January, and 29 January 1964, Office Files of John Macy, LBJ Library.

80. Letter, Fortas to Moyers, 21 January 1964, FG 233 / A, WHCF, LBJ Library.

81. Robert Roosa, Oral History Interview, tape 1, p. 40, LBJ Library.

82. Memo, Macy to the president, 22 January 1964, Office Files of John Macy, Seymour Harris, LBJ Library.

83. See memo, Dungan to the president, 13 February 1964, PE 2, WHCF, LBJ Library.

84. Memo, Heller to the president, 12 November 1964, PE 2, WHCF, LBJ Library (emphasis in the original).

85. Letter, Martin to Macy, 10 February 1965, PE 2, WHCF, LBJ Library.

86. Memo, Ackley to the president, 2 March 1966, FG 233, WHCF, LBJ Library.

87. Memo, Valenti to the president, 31 March 1965, FG 233, WHCF, LBJ Library.

88. Memo, Macy to the president, 22 February 1965, Office Files of John Macy, Sherman Maisel, LBJ Library.

89. Letter, Governor Brown to the president, 4 December 1964, Office Files of John Macy, Sherman Maisel, LBJ Library.

90. Memo, Macy to the president, 9 February 1965, Office Files of John Macy, Sherman Maisel, LBJ Library. Heller also had recommended Maisel for the Federal Home Loan Bank Board appointment. See memo, Heller to the president, 13 January 1965, Office Files of John Macy, Sherman Maisel, LBJ Library.

91. Memo, Macy to the president, 27 March 1965, Office Files of John Macy, Sherman Maisel, LBJ Library.

92. Maisel, *Managing the Dollar*, p. 13.

93. Memo, John Clinton for the Files, 29 December 1965, Office Files of John Macy, Sherman Maisel, LBJ Library.

94. Letter, Representative Patman to the president, 14 January 1966, Office Files of John Macy, Seymour Harris, LBJ Library.

95. Memo, Watson to the president, 15 January 1966, Office Files of John Macy, Seymour Harris, LBJ Library.

96. Memo, Macy to the president, 22 January 1966, Office Files of John Macy, Andrew Brimmer, LBJ Library.

97. Memo, Macy to the president, 1 February 1966, Office Files of John Macy, Andrew Brimmer, LBJ Library.

98. Memo, Heller to the president, 25 January 1966, PE 2, WHCF, LBJ Library (emphases in the original).

99. Letter, Brimmer to Macy, 27 January 1966, Office Files of John Macy, Andrew Brimmer, LBJ Library.

100. Memo, John Clinton to Macy, 29 January 1966, Office Files of John Macy, Andrew Brimmer, LBJ Library.

101. Memo, Heller to the president, 5 February 1966, PE 2, WHCF, LBJ Library (emphasis in the original).

102. Memo, Fowler to the president, 1 February 1966, Office Files of John Macy, William McChesney Martin, Jr., LBJ Library.

103. Letter, Martin to the president, 2 February 1966, Office Files of John Macy, Andrew Brimmer, LBJ Library.

104. Letter, Martin to the president, 7 February 1966, FG 233 / A, WHCF, LBJ Library.

105. Memo, Fowler to the president, 7 February 1966, FG 233 / A, WHCF, LBJ Library. The Federal Reserve Act (Section 10) states: "In selecting the members of the Board, not more than one of whom shall be selected from any one Federal Reserve district, the President shall have due regard to a fair representation of the financial, agricultural, industrial, and commercial interests, and geographical divisions of the country."

106. Memo, Heller to the president, 8 February 1966, PE 2, WHCF, LBJ Library (emphases in the original).

107. Memo, Fowler to the president, 22 February 1966, Office Files of John Macy, Andrew Brimmer, LBJ Library. Fowler had recommended Volcker for the board in November 1965. See memo, Fowler to the president, 10 November 1965, FI, WHCF, LBJ Library.

108. Memo, Macy to the president, 24 February 1966, Office Files of John Macy, Andrew Brimmer, LBJ Library.

109. Memo, Watson to the president, 28 February 1966, FG 233, WHCF, LBJ Library.

110. Woolley, *Monetary Politics*, pp. 53, 122.

111. Johnson, *The Vantage Point*, p. 179.

112. Memo, Macy to the president, 20 February 1967, Office Files of John Macy, William Sherrill, LBJ Library.

113. Memo, Heller to the president, 25 February 1967, C.F. FG 233, WHCF, LBJ Library.

114. Memo, Valenti to the president, 13 July 1965, PE 2, WHCF, LBJ Library.

115. Memo, Valenti to the president, 18 May 1965, PE 2, WHCF, LBJ Library.

116. Memo, Valenti to the president, 13 December 1965, Office Files of John Macy, William Sherrill, LBJ Library.

117. Memo, Macy to the president, 19 April 1967, FG 233 / A, WHCF, LBJ Library.

118. Memo, Macy to the president, 17 April 1967, Office Files of John Macy, William Sherrill, LBJ Library.

119. Memo, Macy to the president, 21 April 1967, Office Files of John Macy, William Sherrill, LBJ Library.

120. Letter, Martin to Macy, 24 April 1967, Office Files of John Macy, William Sherrill, LBJ Library.

121. Woolley, *Monetary Politics*, p. 54.

122. Maisel, *Managing the Dollar*, p. 115.

123. Gardner Ackley, Oral History Interview II, p. 5, LBJ Library.

124. Arthur Okun, Oral History Interview I, p. 26, LBJ Library.

125. U.S., Congress, House, Committee on Banking and Currency, Subcommittee on Domestic Finance, *The Federal Reserve System after Fifty Years*, 88th Cong., 2d sess., 21, 22, 23, 29, and 30 January and 3–6 February 1964.

126. White House Press Release, 27 April 1964, LBJ Library.

127. "Flying high—and fast," *Business Week* (2 May 1964): 21.

128. *Washington Financial Reports*, 4 May 1964.

129. Memo, Heller to the president, 5 May 1964, FG 233,WHCF, LBJ Library (emphases in the original).

130. "The Fed remodels itself," *Business Week* (16 May 1964): 65.

131. Memo, Heller to the president, 6 May 1964, BE 5-4, WHCF, LBJ Library.

132. Memo, Heller to the president, 11 May 1964, BE 5-4, WHCF, LBJ Library (emphasis in the original).

133. Memo, Heller to the president, 13 May 1964, FG 233, WHCF, LBJ Library (emphasis in the original).

134. Ibid., 17 July 1964, FG 233,WHCF, LBJ Library.

135. For example, Martin was in attendance with the other members of the Quadriad at three White House dinners given for business and financial community leaders during the summer of 1964.

136. Gardner Ackley, Oral History Interview II, p. 3, LBJ Library.

137. Memo, Macy to the president, 20 February 1967, Office Files of John Macy, William McChesney Martin, Jr., LBJ Library. It has been noted that "it was frequently said that Martin was worth a billion dollars in gold to the Treasury, at a time when the Treasury considered gold an extremely critical item." Maisel, *Managing the Dollar*, p. 148.

138. Memo, Heller to the president, 25 February 1967, C.F. FG 233, WHCF, LBJ Library.

139. Memo, Fowler to the president, 11 October 1966, FI, WHCF, LBJ Library.

140. Cross reference, memo, Ackley to the president, 20 February 1967, Confidential Alphabetic Files ("Miller"); the original is filed C.F. FG 233, WHCF, LBJ Library, but is not open to the public.

141. Maisel, *Managing the Dollar*, p. 69.

142. Memo, Ackley to the president, 15 February 1965, FG 11-3, WHCF, LBJ Library.

143. Memo, Ackley to the president, 24 March 1965, FI 9-1, WHCF, LBJ Library (emphasis in the original).

144. Memo, Fowler to the president, 25 April 1965, FG 233, WHCF, LBJ Library.

145. Maisel, *Managing the Dollar*, p. 1.

146. Memo, Ackley to the president, 17 May 1965, FI 8, WHCF, LBJ Library (emphasis in the original).

147. Memo, Ackley to the president, 2 June 1965, FG 233, WHCF, LBJ Library (emphases in the original).

148. Memo, Ackley to the president, 3 June 1965, FG 233, WHCF, LBJ Library. Representative Wright Patman expressed the same sentiments in a speech delivered on the floor of the House of Representatives on 10 June 1965 entitled "A Man Who Can't Stand Prosperity."

149. Memo, Fowler to the president, 8 June 1965, Diary Backup, (10 June 1965), LBJ Library.

150. See Press Briefing Transcript, 10 June 1965, FI, WHCF, LBJ Library.

151. Maisel, *Managing the Dollar*, p. 2.

152. Memo, Jacobson to the president, 6 July 1965, C.F. FI 8, WHCF, LBJ Library.

153. Memo, Clark to the president, 2 July 1965, attached to Memo, Jacobson to the president, 6 July 1965, C.F. FI 8, WHCF, LBJ Library.

154. Memo, Clark to the president, 2 July 1965, attached to Memo, Jacobson to the president, 6 July 1965, C.F. FI 8, WHCF, LBJ Library.

155. Ibid.

156. Memo, Ackley to the president, 30 July 1965, Documentary Supplement to the Administrative History of the CEA, Vol. II, Pt. 1, item 88, LBJ Library (emphasis in the original).

157. CEA, Administrative History of the CEA, Vol. I, Ch. 2, p. 44, LBJ Library.

158. Walter Heller, interview transcript, Vanderbilt Institute for Public Policy Studies, p. 122. This story is corroborated by Dewey Daane, who was then a member of the Federal Reserve Board, as well as by a number of individuals who were members of the board's staff during this period. George W. Ellis, president of the Federal Reserve Bank of Boston during the Johnson presidency, suggests that the board had better information on defense spending than the administration because the board's staff relied on well-developed lines of communication with the key congressional committees which were overseeing defense spending. Interview, 13 March 1979.

159. Memo, Fowler to the president, 27 August 1965, FI 8, WHCF, LBJ Library.

160. Memo, Ackley to the president, 10 September 1965, FI 8, WHCF, LBJ Library.

161. Memo, Ackley to the president, 16 September 1965, filed with memo, Ackley to the president, 1 October 1965, FI 8, WHCF, LBJ Library (emphasis in the original).

162. Memo, Ackley to the president, 29 September 1965, filed with memo, Ackley to the president, 1 October 1965, FI 8, WHCF, LBJ Library (emphasis in the original).

163. Memo, Ackley to the president, 1 October 1965, FI 8, WHCF, LBJ Library (emphases in the original).

164. Memo, Schultze to the president, 4 October 1965, FI 9, WHCF, LBJ Library (emphasis in the original).

165. Memo, Ackley to the president, 5 October 1965, FI, WHCF, LBJ Library (emphasis in the original).

166. Memo, Martin to the president, 6 October 1965, President's Appointment File (Diary Backup), (8 October 1965), LBJ Library.

167. Memo, Ackley to the president, 17 October 1965, FI 8, WHCF, LBJ Library.

168. Maisel, *Managing the Dollar*, p. 75.

169. Arthur Okun, Oral History Interview I, p. 23, LBJ Library.

170. Memo, Volcker, Zwick, Brill and Okun to Fowler, Schultze, Martin, and Ackley, 6 November 1965, Documentary Supplement to the Administrative History of the CEA, Vol. II, Pt. 1, item 84, LBJ Library.

171. Charles J. Zwick, Oral History Interview, tape 1, p. 26, LBJ Library.

172. Arthur Okun, Oral History Interview I, pp. 24–25, LBJ Library.

173. Memo, Ackley to the president, 13 November 1965, FI, WHCF, LBJ Library.

174. Memo, Wallace, Zwick, and Okun to Fowler, Schultze, and Ackley, 1 November 1965, Documentary Supplement to the CEA Administrative History, Vol. II, Pt. 1, item 85, LBJ Library.

175. Joseph Barr, Oral History Interview, tape 1, p. 25, LBJ Library.

176. Memo, Ackley to the president, 25 November 1965, Documentary Supplement to the Administrative History of the CEA, Vol. II, Pt. 1, item 82, LBJ Library.

177. Memo, Ackley to the president, 29 November 1965, FI 8, WHCF, LBJ Library.

178. Letter, Jacobson to the president, 30 November 1965, FG 233, WHCF, LBJ Library.

179. Memo, Maisel to the president, 30 November 1965, FI 8, WHCF, LBJ Library.

180. Memo, Fowler, Schultze, and Ackley to the president, 1 December 1965, FI 9, WHCF, LBJ Library.

181. Ibid. The reference to the Treasury financing constraint stems from a convention followed by the Federal Reserve that it refrains from making a major change in monetary policy while the Treasury is selling securities to finance the federal debt. Such action was thought to result in market instability and to be capable of threatening the success of the Treasury financing (i.e., preventing the Treasury from selling its securities at the market rate).

182. Maisel, *Managing the Dollar*, p. 69.

183. Ibid., p. 73.

184. Ibid., pp. 74–75.

185. Arthur Okun, Oral History Interview I, p. 25, LBJ Library.

186. "Statement by the President on the Raising of the Discount Rate by the Federal Reserve Board, December 5, 1965," *Public Papers of the Presidents of the United States: Lyndon B. Johnson, 1965*, Vol. II (Washington, D.C.: Government Printing Office, 1966), pp. 1137–1138.

187. Johnson, *The Vantage Point*, p. 445.

188. Memo, Fowler, Schultze, and Ackley to the president, 4 December 1965, Documentary Supplement to the Administrative History of the CEA, Vol. II, Pt. 1, item 81, LBJ Library.

189. Gardner Ackley, Oral History Interview II, p. 3, LBJ Library.

190. Arthur Okun, *The Political Economy of Prosperity* (Washington, D.C.: The Brookings Institution, 1970), p. 69.

191. Gardner Ackley, Oral History Interview II, p. 4, LBJ Library.

192. Okun, *The Political Economy of Prosperity*, pp. 69–70.

193. Memo, Maisel and Robertson to the president, 18 January 1966, FI 8, WHCF, LBJ Library.

194. Memo, Ackley to the president, 18 January 1965, FI 8, WHCF, LBJ Library.

195. Okun, *The Political Economy of Prosperity*, p. 81.

196. Commission on Money and Credit, *Money and Credit: Their Influence on Jobs, Prices, and Growth* (Englewood Cliffs, N.J.: Prentice-Hall, 1961).

197. Bach, *Making Monetary and Fiscal Policy*, p. 247.

198. Memo, Dillon to the president, 31 March 1965, FI 8, WHCF, LBJ Library.

199. Memo, Ackley to the president, 31 January 1966, FG 233, WHCF, LBJ Library. The president's brief response is attached.

200. Ben W. Heineman was chairman and president of the Chicago and North Western Railway Company. The other members of the task force were: McGeorge Bundy, William Capron, Hale Champion, Kermit Gordon, Herbert Kaufman, Richard C. Lee, Bayless Manning, Robert S. McNamara, Harry Ransom, and Charles L. Schultze.

201. "Final Report of the Task Force on Government Organization: Government Organization for Economic Policy Formulation and Administration," 11, Task Forces (1966 Outside), LBJ Library (emphasis in the original.)

202. Ibid., 12–13 (emphasis in the original).

203. Memo, Okun to the president, 3 September 1968, C.F. SP 2-4 / 1969, WHCF, LBJ Library.

204. Memo, Okun to Califano, 3 September 1968, C.F. SP 2-4 / 1969, WHCF, LBJ Library.

5. The Management of Wage-Price Policy

1. *Economic Report of the President, 1964* (Washington, D.C.: Government Printing Office, 1964).

2. See John Sheahan, *The Wage-Price Guideposts* (Washington, D.C.: The Brookings Institution, 1967), Chs. 4–6.

3. For a more, but not exclusively, chronological treatment, see James L. Cochrane, "The Johnson Administration: Moral Suasion Goes to War," in *Exhortation and Controls: The Search for a Wage-Price Policy, 1945–1971*, ed. Crawford D. Goodwin (Washington, D.C.: The Brookings Institution, 1975), pp. 193–293.

4. CEA, *Annual Report of the Council of Economic Advisers, 1962* (Washington, D.C.: Government Printing Office, 1962), p. 189. Hereafter *CEA Annual Report* (emphasis in the original).

5. Memo, Ackley to Heller, 11 December 1963, Documentary Supple-

ment to the Administrative History of the CEA, Vol. II, Pt. 2, item A.3, LBJ Library (emphasis in the original).

6. Gardner Ackley, Oral History Interview I, p. 30, LBJ Library.

7. Memo, Ackley to the president, 28 December 1965, FG 11-3, WHCF, LBJ Library. Handwritten on the memorandum is the phrase "an historic document." For a rationalization of this action, see the *CEA Annual Report, 1966*, pp. 92–93.

8. Memo, Wirtz to the president, 24 August 1966, LA 6, WHCF, LBJ Library.

9. Memo, Ackley to the president, 10 December 1966, BE 5-2, WHCF, LBJ Library.

10. Memo, Ackley to the president, 19 January 1967, FG 11-3, WHCF, LBJ Library.

11. *CEA Annual Report, 1967*, p. 129.

12. Memo, Duesenberry to Califano, 9 August 1967, Robson-Ross Office Files, Box 18, "Prices, July–August 1967," LBJ Library.

13. Memo, Ackley to Califano, 21 December 1967, C.F. BE 5-2, WHCF, LBJ Library.

14. Memo, Ackley to the president, 23 January 1968, SPZ-2 / 1968, WHCF, LBJ Library.

15. *CEA Annual Report, 1968*, p. 126.

16. For example, "Meeting with General Motors Executives," memo, Okun to the president, 26 August 1968, C.F. BE 5-2, WHCF, LBJ Library.

17. Memo, Ackley to the president, 13 November 1965, BE 5, WHCF, LBJ Library (emphases in original).

18. Otto Eckstein, Speech to the American Economic Association, 28 December 1966, CEA Microfilm, roll 64, LBJ Library.

19. Memo, Ackley to Califano, 9 December 1967, CEA Microfilm, roll 69, LBJ Library.

20. Arthur M. Okun, interview, 29 June 1979.

21. Memo, Ross to Califano, 1 February 1968, Califano Papers, LBJ Library. Califano sent this memorandum on to the president a couple of days later. See also memo, Califano to the president, 1 February 1968, C.F. BE 3, WHCF, LBJ Library.

22. Joseph A. Califano, interview, 17 May 1980.

23. Memo, Okun to the president, 20 May 1968, C.F. BE 5-2, WHCF, LBJ Library.

24. Gardner Ackley, interview, 15 August 1979.

25. In addition to the other sources cited, the following account draws upon Cochrane, "The Johnson Administration." This is a very useful and insightful account.

26. Memo, Heller to the president, 3 February 1964, BE 5, WHCF, LBJ Library.

27. Ibid.

28. Memo, Califano to the president, 16 November 1965, BE 4 / Aluminum, WHCF, LBJ Library. Lawson Knott headed the General Services Administration, which handled stockpile disposals, while Buford Ellington

was director of the Office of Emergency Planning, which was in charge of stockpile storage.

29. Memo, Eckstein to the CEA, 9 September 1965, Administrative History of the CEA, Vol. 2, pt. 2, LBJ Library.

30. Memo, Ackley to the president, 13 November 1968, BE 5, WHCF, LBJ Library.

31. Ibid.

32. Memo, Connor to the president, 3 November 1965, C.F. BE 5, WHCF, LBJ Library (emphasis in the original).

33. Memo, Fowler to the president, 27 December 1965, BE 5-2, WHCF, LBJ Library.

34. Memo, Califano to the president, 28 December 1965, BE 5-2, WHCF, LBJ Library (emphasis in the original).

35. Memo, Fowler to the president, 7 January 1966, C.F. BE 5, WHCF, LBJ Library.

36. Memo, Ackley to Califano, 5 January 1966, FG 11-3, WHCF, LBJ Library.

37. Memo, Eckstein to Ackley, 31 January 1966, CEA Microfilm, roll 55, LBJ Library.

38. Memo, Califano to the president, 11 February 1966, BE 5-2, WHCF, LBJ Library.

39. Memo, Ackley to Califano, 5 February 1966, C.F. FG 11-3, WHCF, LBJ Library.

40. Memo, Robson to Califano, 12 October 1966, Califano Papers, Pricing Folder, LBJ Library.

41. Draft statement by Gardner Ackley, 4 August 1966, Robson-Ross Office Files, "Pricing Files: Guideposts," LBJ Library.

42. Memo, Califano to the president, 4 August 1966, BE 5-2, WHCF, LBJ Library. It is accompanied by a memorandum to Joe Califano from John Robson, from which the quoted material is taken.

43. Memo, Ackley to Califano, 8 August 1966, FG 999, WHCF, LBJ Library.

44. "Processes and Problems in the Area of Economic Policy Formulation and Administration," James C. Gaither Papers, Box 246, "Economic Policy Formation," LBJ Library.

45. For example, memo, Trowbridge to the president, 2 August 1967, BE 4 / Chemicals, WHCF, LBJ Library.

46. Memo, Ross to Califano, 29 June 1967, Robson-Ross Office Files, "Pricing Files: Guidelines," LBJ Library (emphasis in original).

47. Ibid. In August, Duesenberry sent Califano an eight-page memorandum on the "Price Stabilization Program" that said almost nothing about how a new or strengthened program would be administered. Memo, Duesenberry to Califano, 9 August 1967, Robson-Ross Office Files, "Prices, July–Aug. 1967," LBJ Library.

48. Gardner Ackley, "Outline of an Income Policy," 15 June 1967, CEA Microfilm, roll 70, LBJ Library.

49. Memo, Ross to Ackley, 7 July 1967, Robson-Ross Office Files, "Pricing Files: Guidelines," LBJ Library.

50. Memo, Califano to the president, 3 October 1967, FG 11-3, WHCF, LBJ Library.

51. Memo, Ackley to Califano, 11 October 1967, Robson-Ross Office Files, "Pricing Files: Prices, Sept.–Oct. 1967," LBJ Library.

52. The task force statement accompanies a memo by Stan Ross to Joe Califano, 14 December 1967, Robson-Ross Office Files, "Pricing Files: Prices, December 1967," LBJ Library.

53. This categorization borrows from Alan Altshuler, "The Politics of Managing a Full Employment Economy," paper presented at the 63d annual meeting of the American Political Science Association, Chicago, 5–9 September 1967, pp. 16–19.

54. Telegram, Johnson to Martin, 2 January 1966, BE 4 / Steel, WHCF, LBJ Library.

55. Memo, Dorsey to Joe Califano, 26 April 1966, BE 5, WHCF, LBJ Library.

56. John D. Pomfret, "Johnson Striving to Cool Off Boom," *New York Times*, 4 April 1966, p. 27.

57. Ibid.

58. *CEA Annual Report, 1967*, pp. 125–126.

59. Joseph A. Califano, Jr., *A Presidential Nation* (New York: W. W. Norton and Co., 1975), p. 264.

60. Stanford Ross, interview, 25 June 1979.

61. Memo, Okun to the president, 18 February 1966, BE 5-2, WHCF, LBJ Library.

62. Memo, Ignatius to Califano, 26 April 1967, CM / Butter, WHCF, LBJ Library.

63. Memo, Robson to Califano, 12 October 1966, Califano Papers, Pricing Folder, LBJ Library.

64. Memo, Ackley to Califano, 9 March 1966, BE 5-2, WHCF, LBJ Library.

65. Memo, Califano to the president, 17 December 1965, BE 5-2, WHCF, LBJ Library.

66. Memo, Ackley to the president, 6 March 1966, FG 11-3, WHCF, LBJ Library.

67. Memo, Levinson to Califano, 13 October 1966, C.F. BE 5-2, WHCF, LBJ Library.

68. Memo, Ackley to the president, 24 June 1967, BE 5-2, WHCF, LBJ Library.

69. Memo, Ackley to Califano, 27 December 1965, BE 5-2, WHCF, LBJ Library.

70. Harry McPherson, interview, 27 June 1979.

71. Memo, McPherson to the president, 28 February 1966, CM / Milk, WHCF, LBJ Library.

72. Memo, Ackley to the president, 16 November 1965, BE 5-2, WHCF, LBJ Library.

73. Memo, Udall to the president, 24 May 1966, BE 5-2, WHCF, LBJ Library.

74. Memo, Heller to the president, 6 August 1964, BE 5-2, WHCF, LBJ Library (emphasis in original).

75. Memo, Ackley to the president, 17 October 1965, LE / PE 11, WHCF, LBJ Library (emphasis in original).

76. Memo, Okun to the president, 25 May 1966, CEA Microfilm, roll 69, LBJ Library.

77. *Public Papers of the Presidents of the United States: Lyndon B. Johnson, 1966*, Vol. II (Washington, D.C.: Government Printing Office, 1967), p. 735.

78. See memorandums by Charles L. Schultze to Mr. Califano, 3 June 1966, and by Gardner Ackley to James Duesenberry and Martin Segal, 23 July 1966. Both are in CEA Microfilm, roll 64, LBJ Library.

79. Memo, Ackley to the president, 11 July 1966, LA 8, WHCF, LBJ Library.

80. Joseph A. Califano, Jr., interview, 17 May 1980.

81. Cochrane, "The Johnson Administration," p. 247.

82. Meeting of Gardner Ackley and James Duesenberry with officials from American Metal Climax, 11 July 1966, CEA Microfilm, roll 53, LBJ Library.

83. *Wall Street Journal*, 14 July 1966, p. 4.

84. Administrative History of the Council of Economic Advisers (hereafter CEA), Vol. I, Ch. 3, p. 27, LBJ Library; memo, Nelson to CEA, 6 October 1966, ibid., Vol. II, part II, item 8.30.

85. *Economic Report of the President, 1968* (Washington, D.C.: Government Printing Office, 1968), pp. 19–21.

86. Memo, Johnson to the secretary of treasury, secretary of commerce, secretary of labor, director of the Bureau of the Budget, and chairman of the CEA, 23 February 1968, FG 631, WHCF, LBJ Library.

87. Memo, Johnson to all departments and agencies, 23 February 1968, FG 631, WHCF, LBJ Library.

88. Memo, Okun to the president, 29 April 1968, FG 631, WHCF, LBJ Library.

89. Memo, Okun to Califano, 15 July 1968, LA 8, WHCF, LBJ Library.

90. Memo, Okun to Califano, 27 April 1968, BE 5-2, WHCF, LBJ Library.

91. Memo, Okun to the president, 18 December 1968, FG 631, WHCF, LBJ Library. The CCPS report accompanies this memorandum.

92. Letter, Mueller to Cochrane in Cochrane, "The Johnson Administration," pp. 287–288.

93. Stanford Ross, interview, 25 June 1979.

94. U.S., Congress, Joint Economic Committee, *Hearings on the President's New Economic Program*, 92d Cong., 2d sess., 1971, pp. 245–246.

95. Memo, Califano to the president, 18 July 1966, FG 730, WHCF, LBJ Library.

96. Memo, Gardner Ackley to Califano, 18 June 1966, Robson-Ross Office Files, Box 9, "Pricing Files: Guideposts," LBJ Library.

97. Administrative History of the Department of Commerce, Vol. I, Pt. 3, p. 49.

98. John Robson, interview, 14 August 1979.

99. Myron L. Joseph, "Wage-Price Guideposts in the U.S.A.," *British Journal of Industrial Relations* 5 (November 1967): 318–319.

100. Note "Wage-Price Guidelines: Informal Government Regulation of Labor and Industry," *Harvard Law Review* 80 (January 1967): 623–647.

101. Joseph A. Califano, Jr., interview, 17 May 1980.

102. Quoted in Gilbert Burck, "Aluminum: The Classic Rollback," *Fortune* 73 (February 1966): 224.

103. J. T. Romans, "Moral Suasion as an Instrument of Economic Policy," *American Economic Review* 56 (December 1966): 1221.

104. Memo, Reedy to the president, 3 January 1966, BE 4 / Steel, WHCF, LBJ Library.

105. Arthur J. Alexander, "Prices and the Guideposts: The Effects of Government Persuasion on Individual Prices," *Review of Economics and Statistics* 53 (February 1971): 67–75. Cf. Sheahan, *The Wage-Price Guideposts*, Chs. 7, 14.

6. The Management of Foreign Economic Policy

1. *Economic Report of the President, 1966* (Washington, D.C.: Government Printing Office, 1966), p. 13.

2. I. M. Destler, *Making Foreign Economic Policy* (Washington, D.C.: The Brookings Institution, 1980), p. 1. Stephen D. Cohen contends that the term "international economic policy" is preferable to "foreign economic policy" because it more accurately reflects the mixture of foreign and domestic economic and political concerns. See *The Making of United States International Economic Policy* (New York: Praeger Publishers, 1977), p. vii.

3. Harold B. Malmgren, "Managing Foreign Economic Policy," *Foreign Policy* 6 (Spring 1972): 43.

4. Destler, *Making Foreign Economic Policy*, p. 6.

5. Cohen, *International Economic Policy*, pp. 63–64.

6. Graham Allison and Peter Szanton, *Remaking Foreign Policy: The Organizational Connection* (New York: Basic Books, 1976), p. 155.

7. Quoted in *Life*, 17 January 1969, p. 62B, as cited in I. M. Destler, *Presidents, Bureaucrats, and Foreign Policy* (Princeton, N.J.: Princeton University Press, 1972), p. 90.

8. Destler, *Making Foreign Economic Policy*, p. 11.

9. Cohen, *International Economic Policy*, pp. 27–28.

10. Destler, *Presidents, Bureaucrats, and Foreign Policy*, p. 14.

11. For a detailed account of the organization and operation of the Office of the STR in the Johnson years, see Anne H. Rightor-Thornton, "An Analysis of the Office of the Special Representative for Trade Negotiations: The Evolving Role, 1962–1974," in (Report of the) *Commission on the Organization of the Government for the Conduct of Foreign Policy* (Murphy Com-

mission), Vol. III, App. H, (Washington D.C.: Government Printing Office, 1975), pp. 88–104. (Hereafter *Murphy Commission Report.*)

12. Destler, *Presidents, Bureaucrats, and Foreign Policy*, p. 106. Walt W. Rostow, special assistant to the president for national security affairs in the Johnson White House, states that President Johnson took an active role in allocating food aid, particularly to countries like India, where he sought to couple food provisions with efforts by the Indian government to improve the internal distribution of food supplies, increase food production, and restrain population growth. Rostow notes that Johnson "followed the rain figures in India in the same way he did on his own Texas ranch." Personal communication with the author. Also see Joseph A. Califano, Jr., *A Presidential Nation* (New York: W. W. Norton Co., 1975), p. 206; and Destler, *Making Foreign Economic Policy*, p. 84.

13. Harold Seidman, *Politics, Position, and Power* (New York: Oxford University Press, 1970), p. 71.

14. For a description of the foreign economic policy – coordinating mechanisms under President Eisenhower, see the testimony of Douglas Dillon, *U.S. Foreign Economic Policy: Implications for the Organization of the Executive Branch*, Hearings before the Committee on Foreign Affairs and the Subcommittee on Foreign Economic Policy, U.S. House of Representatives, 92d Cong., 2d sess., 1972, pp. 92–107.

15. Rostow reports that he did not want a deputy, but he "honored a commitment made by McGeorge Bundy to Francis Bator." When Fried replaced Bator, he was not given the title of deputy, but retained his title as deputy assistant secretary of state for international resources. Personal communication with the author.

16. Edward Fried, Oral History Interview, tape 1, pp. 10–11, LBJ Library.

17. DeVier Pierson, Oral History Interview, tape 1, p. 12, LBJ Library.

18. Ibid., p. 14.

19. Memo, Ernest Goldstein to the president, 23 May 1968, EXTRA 4, WHCF, LBJ Library.

20. Presidential Task Force on Government Reorganization, Appendix A, "The Coordination of Foreign Economic Policy," LBJ Library.

21. In more technical terms, the balance of payments for a country is a summary of all economic transactions with the rest of the world for a given period of time. The balance of payments reflects all payments due and made to the country as well as all liabilities accrued and paid to other countries. All transactions are recorded as debits or credits. The balance of payments may be divided into a "real" and a "financial" component. The "real" component is the current account comprising all transactions in goods and services. Exports are recorded as credits and imports as debits. The "financial" component consists of transfers (payments made not in exchange for goods and services), capital movements, and movements of reserve assets (primarily gold). Transfers abroad, capital outflows, and reserve-asset outflows are recorded as debits, while transfers received from abroad, capital inflows, and reserve-asset inflows are recorded as credits. The capital account is fur-

ther divided into short-term and long-term flows, and each is identified as being private or public (i.e., governmental). Under the "official settlements" basis of accounting used in this chapter, balance-of-payments equilibrium means that the sum of the credits from current-account exports of goods and services plus transfers received from abroad plus private capital imports equals the sum of the debits from current-account imports of goods and services plus transfers made abroad plus public and private capital exports. If total debits exceed total credits, then the balance of payments is said to be in deficit. The deficit is "paid for," that is, the accounts are made to balance, by gold or other reserve-asset exports or by short- or long-term capital imports from foreign official agencies.

22. Agreements reached by representatives of the major trading countries at the Smithsonian Institution in Washington, D.C. on 18 December 1971 resulted in a multilateral realignment of exchange rates entailing a 7.8 percent devaluation of the dollar in favor of gold and a simultaneous appreciation of many other currencies.

23. International Monetary Fund, *Annual Report* (1960), p. 62.

24. "Special Message to the Congress on Gold and the Balance of Payments Deficit, 6 February 1961," *Public Papers of the Presidents of the United States: John F. Kennedy, 1961* (Washington, D.C.: Government Printing Office, 1962), pp. 57–66. Hereafter *JFK Public Papers.*

25. "Special Message to the Congress on Balance of Payments, 18 July 1963," *JFK Public Papers, 1963*, pp. 574–584. The tax was not applied to borrowings of less-developed countries (LDCs).

26. Memo, Dillon to the president, 2 December 1963, C.F. FO 4-1, WHCF, LBJ Library.

27. Letter, President Johnson to heads of departments and agencies, 14 May 1964, FO 4-1, WHCF, LBJ Library.

28. "Special Message to the Congress on International Balance of Payments February 1965," *Public Papers of the Presidents of the United States: Lyndon B. Johnson, 1965*, Vol. I (Washington, D.C.: Government Printing Office, 1966), pp. 170–177. (Hereafter *LBJ Public Papers.*)

29. Memo, Cabinet Committee on Balance of Payments to the president, 6 December 1966, filed with memo, Bator to the president, 7 December 1966, C.F. FO 4-1, WHCF, LBJ Library.

30. "Annual Message to the Congress: The Economic Report of the President, 26 January 1967," *LBJ Public Papers, 1967*, I, pp. 80–81.

31. "Message to the Nation on Balance of Payments," 31 December 1967, C.F. FO 4-1, WHCF, LBJ Library.

32. CEA, *Annual Report of the Council of Economic Advisers, 1969* (Washington, D.C.: Government Printing Office, 1969), pp. 324–325. Hereafter *CEA Annual Report.*

33. C. Douglas Dillon, Oral History Interview, tape, 1, p. 7, LBJ Library.

34. Gardner Ackley, Oral History Interview II, p. 45, LBJ Library.

35. Lawrence McQuade, Oral History Interview, p. 15, LBJ Library.

36. Memo, Heller to the president, 16 February 1965, FO 4-1, WHCF, LBJ Library.

37. Memo, Ackley to the president, 5 March 1965, FO 4-1, WHCF, LBJ Library (emphasis in the original).

38. See "Voice for Business in U.S. Policy," *Business Week*, 13 March 1965, pp. 96–98, 100, 102. The members of the committee included: Albert L. Nickerson (chairman), chairman of the board of Socony Mobil Oil Company; Carter L. Burgess (vice chairman), chairman of the board of American Machine & Foundry Company; Fred J. Borch, president of General Electric Company; Carl L. Gilbert, chairman of the board of the Gillette Company; Elisha Gray, II, chairman of the board of the Whirlpool Corporation; J. Ward Keener, president of the B. F. Goodrich Company; George S. Moore, president of the First City National Bank of New York; Stuart T. Saunders, chairman of the board of the Pennsylvania Railroad Company; and Sidney J. Weinberg, general partner in Goldman Sachs & Company (New York investment bankers).

39. Memo, Ackley to the president, 8 March 1965, FO 4-1, WHCF, LBJ Library.

40. Letter, Secretary Connor to the chief executive officers of selected companies, 12 March 1965, filed with memo, Moyers to Connor, 17 March 1965, FO 4-1, WHCF, LBJ Library.

41. Memo, Ackley to the president, 21 May 1965, filed with memo, Busby to Fowler, 13 May 1965, FO 4-1, WHCF, LBJ Library.

42. Memo, Dillon to the president, 2 December 1963, FG 267, WHCF, LBJ Library.

43. See memo, Califano to the president, 20 September 1965, C.F. FO 4-1, WHCF, LBJ Library, and memo, Fowler to the president, 16 November 1965, filed with memo, Bator to the president, 18 November 1965, C.F. FO 4-1, WHCF, LBJ Library.

44. Memo, Fowler to the president, 16 November 1965, filed with memo, Bator to the president, 18 November 1965, C.F. FO 4-1, WHCF, LBJ Library.

45. Memo, Bator to the President, 29 November 1965, C.F. FO 4-1, WHCF, LBJ Library (emphasis in original).

46. Memo, Fowler to the president, 30 March 1966, cited in Administrative History of the Treasury Department, Vol. IX, p. 21, LBJ Library.

47. Memo, Fowler to the president, 10 May 1966, C.F. FO 4-1, WHCF, LBJ Library.

48. Memo, Fowler to the president, 9 November 1966, C.F. FO 4-1, WHCF, LBJ Library.

49. Memo, Robson to Califano, 20 September 1966, FO 4-1, WHCF, LBJ Library.

50. Letter, Wozencraft to the president, 27 September 1966, filed with memo, Califano to the president, 28 September 1966, FO 4-1, WHCF, LBJ Library.

51. Califano to the president, 28 September 1966, FO 4-1, WHCF, LBJ Library.

52. Memo, Cabinet Committee on Balance of Payments to the president, 6 December 1966, filed with memo, Bator to the president, 7 December 1966, C.F. FO 4-1, WHCF, LBJ Library.

53. Memo, Fowler to the president, 6 December 1966, filed with Bator to the president, 7 December 1966, C.F. FO 4-1, WHCF, LBJ Library.

54. Telegram, Califano to the president, 29 November 1966, C.F. FG 11-3, WHCF, LBJ Library.

55. Memo, Ackley to the president, 1 December 1966, FO 4-1, WHCF, LBJ Library (emphasis in the original).

56. Bator to the president, 7 December 1966, C.F. FO 4-1, WHCF, LBJ Library.

57. Memo, Califano to the president, 7 December 1966, FG 627, WHCF, LBJ Library.

58. Memo, Bator to the president, 9 December 1966, C.F. FO 4-1, WHCF, LBJ Library.

59. Memo, Califano to the president, 12 December 1966, filed with memo, the president to Fowler, 12 December 1966, C.F. FO 4-1, WHCF, LBJ Library.

60. Memo, Ackley to the president, 27 January 1967, FO 4-1, WHCF, LBJ Library.

61. Ibid.

62. Administrative History of the Treasury Department, Vol. IX, p. 27, LBJ Library.

63. Edward Fried, Oral History Interview, tape 1, pp. 38–39, LBJ Library.

64. Federal Reserve and Commerce Department press release, 16 November 1967, as cited in the Administrative History of the Treasury Department, Vol. IX, p. 33, LBJ Library.

65. Edward Fried, Oral History Interview, tape 1, p. 39, LBJ Library.

66. Ibid., tape 2, p. 1.

67. Memo, the president to Fowler, 16 June 1965, C.F. FI 9, WHCF, LBJ Library.

68. Edward Fried, Oral History Interview, tape 2, p. 1, LBJ Library.

69. E. Ernest Goldstein, Oral History Interview, tape 3, p. 1, LBJ Library.

70. Alexander Trowbridge, Oral History Interview, tape 2, p. 8, LBJ Library.

71. Ibid., tape 1, p. 21.

72. Lawrence McQuade, Oral History Interview, p. 17, LBJ Library.

73. Califano to the president, 28 September 1966, FO 4-1, WHCF, LBJ Library.

74. Lawrence McQuade, Oral History Interview, p. 17, LBJ Library.

75. E. Ernest Goldstein, Oral History Interview, tape 3, p. 3, LBJ Library.

76. Ibid., p. 4.

77. Lawrence McQuade, Oral History Interview, p. 21, LBJ Library.

78. Alexander Trowbridge, Oral History Interview, tape 2, p. 9, LBJ Library.

79. Ibid., pp. 9–10. The same reasoning for Trowbridge's decision is reported by Fried, Solomon, McQuade, and Goldstein.

80. Edward Fried, Oral History Interview, tape 2, p. 4, LBJ Library.

81. Administrative History of the Treasury Department, Vol. IX, p. 34, LBJ Library. Since the completion of the Kennedy Round negotiations in the

summer of 1967, a small subgroup of the Executive Committee of the Cabinet Committee on Balance of Payments had focused on the provisions of the General Agreement on Tariffs and Trade (GATT) dealing with border-tax adjustments. The border-tax provisions of the GATT were felt to be prejudicial to U.S. trade interests, particularly in view of the increasingly frequent resort by European countries to indirect taxes and the value-added system of taxation. The work of the subgroup led the Cabinet Committee in early November 1967 to agree to recommend to the president a renegotiation of the border-tax provisions of the GATT.

82. Administrative History of the Treasury Department, Vol. IX, p. 31, LBJ Library.

83. Memo, Califano to the president, 16 November 1967, FO 4-1, WHCF, LBJ Library.

84. Administrative History of the Treasury Department, Vol. IX, p. 31, LBJ Library.

85. Edward Fried, Oral History Interview, tape 2, p. 7, LBJ Library.

86. Ibid., p. 9.

87. Ibid., pp. 7–9.

88. Memo, Califano to the president, 26 December 1967, FO 4-1, LBJ Library. Manatos and Sprague were administrative assistants to the president with responsibility for congressional liaison with the Senate and House, respectively. Lawrence O'Brien served as special assistant to the president for congressional relations from 1961 to 1965 and as postmaster general from 1965 to 1968, while Harold Barefoot Sanders, Jr. was an assistant attorney general.

89. E. Ernest Goldstein, Oral History Interview, tape 3, pp. 6–7, LBJ Library.

90. Alexander Trowbridge, Oral History Interview, tape 2, p. 12, LBJ Library.

91. Edward Fried, Oral History Interview, tape 2, p. 10, LBJ Library.

92. Joseph Califano, interview, 17 May 1980.

93. Memo, Larry Levinson and Joseph Barr to the president, 1 January 1968, FO 4-1, WHCF, LBJ Library.

94. Memo, Califano to the president, 9 January 1968, FO 4-1, WHCF, LBJ Library.

95. Memo, the president to secretary of state and director, Bureau of the Budget, 18 January 1968, filed with memo, the president to the heads of executive departments and establishments, 18 January 1968, FO 4-1, WHCF, LBJ Library.

96. Ibid.

97. Memo, William J. Hopkins for the record, 29 January 1968, FO 4-1, WHCF, LBJ Library.

98. Memo, John M. Steadman to Hopkins, 1 February 1968, FO 4-1, WHCF, LBJ Library.

99. Memo, Hopkins to Marvin Watson, 2 February 1968, FO 4-1, LBJ Library (emphasis in the original).

100. Bulletin No. 68-8, Charles J. Zwick to the heads of executive depart-

ments and establishments, 14 February 1968, FO 4-1, WHCF, LBJ Library.

101. Memo, Zwick to the president, 25 October 1968, FO 4-1, WHCF, LBJ Library.

102. Opposition came from McNamara, Fowler, Martin, Rusk, and others. See memo, Califano to the president, 9 January 1968, FO 4-1, WHCF, LBJ Library. Also see memo, Goldstein to the president, 30 January 1968, C.F. FO 4-1, WHCF, LBJ Library; memo, Ackley to the president, 11 January 1968, C.F. FO 4-1, WHCF, LBJ Library; memo, Fowler to the president, 12 January 1968, filed with memo, Califano to the president, 12 January 1968, C.F. FO 4-1, WHCF, LBJ Library; memo, vice president to Califano, 12 January 1968, FO 4-1, WHCF, LBJ Library; and memo, vice president to Marvin Watson, 16 February 1968, FO 4-1, WHCF, LBJ Library.

103. See memo, Goldstein to Califano, 12 February 1968, FO 4-1, WHCF, LBJ Library; memo, Okun to the president, 17 February 1968, C.F. FO 4-1, WHCF, LBJ Library; memo, Jones to Sanders, 12 March 1968, FO 4-1, WHCF, LBJ Library; and memo, Goldstein to the president, 27 March 1968, FO 4-1, WHCF, LBJ Library.

104. Memo, Goldstein to the president, 23 April 1968, FO 4-1, WHCF, LBJ Library.

105. For example, see memo, Goldstein to the president, 8 January 1968, FO 4-1, WHCF, LBJ Library; memo, Goldstein to the president, 10 January 1968, C.F. FO 4-1, WHCF, LBJ Library; memo, Goldstein to the president, 19 January 1968, FO 4-1, WHCF, LBJ Library; memo, Goldstein to the president, 29 January 1968, FO 4-1, WHCF, LBJ Library; and memo, Goldstein to the president, 16 March 1968, FO 4-1, WHCF, LBJ Library.

106. Memo, Califano to the president, 10 January 1968, FO 4-1, WHCF, LBJ Library, and memo, Goldstein to Califano, 15 January 1968, FO 4-1, WHCF, LBJ Library.

107. Memo, Goldstein to the president, 4 January 1968, FO 4-1, WHCF, LBJ Library.

108. E. Ernest Goldstein, Oral History Interview, tape 3, p. 8, LBJ Library.

109. Memo, Goldstein to the president, 12 March 1968, FO 4-1, WHCF, LBJ Library.

110. Memo, Goldstein to the president, 25 April 1968, FO 4-1, WHCF, LBJ Library.

111. Memo, Goldstein to the president, 12 June 1968, FO 4-1, WHCF, LBJ Library.

112. Memo, Smith to the president, 11 June 1968, filed with Goldstein to the president, 12 June 1968, FO 4-1, WHCF, LBJ Library (emphasis in the original).

113. Memo, Smith to the president, 5 August 1968, FO 4-3, WHCF, LBJ Library.

114. Memo, Goldstein to the president, 4 September 1968, C.F. FG 155-24, WHCF, LBJ Library.

115. Letter, Smith to the president, 2 October 1968, FO 4-1, WHCF, LBJ Library.

116. Memo, Goldstein to the president, 12 November 1968, C.F. FO 4-1, WHCF, LBJ Library.

117. Memo, Fowler to the president, 28 November 1968, filed with Goldstein to the president, 12 November 1968, C.F. FO 4-1, WHCF, LBJ Library.

118. Memo, Goldstein to the president, 18 December 1968, FO 4-1, WHCF, LBJ Library; and letter, Smith to the president, 24 December 1968, FO 4-1, WHCF, LBJ Library.

119. Gardner Ackley, Oral History Interview II, p. 47, LBJ Library.

120. Memo, Heller to the president, 5 June 1964, FO 4, WHCF, LBJ Library.

121. Memo, Heller to the president, 22 July 1964, C.F. FI 9 WHCF, LBJ Library.

122. U.S. deficits in effect supplied the liquidity to finance a growth in world trade that was much more rapid than the expansion in gold available for central bank reserves. Walt Rostow states that he used to put the matter this way: " . . . for four days a week the Europeans welcome our contribution to financial liquidity; but on Friday before going away for a long country weekend, they read us a lecture on excessive U.S. deficits, imposed inflation, etc." Personal communication with the author.

123. Memo, Heller to the president, 5 August 1964, FO 4, WHCF, LBJ Library.

124. *Ministerial Statement of the Group of Ten and Annex Prepared by Deputies* (August 1964).

125. Memo, Dillon to the president, 30 July 1964, filed with memo, Bator and Bundy to the president, 10 August 1964, C.F. FO 4, WHCF, LBJ Library.

126. Bator and Bundy to the president, 10 August 1964, C.F. FO 4, WHCF, LBJ Library.

127. "Special Message to the Congress on International Balance of Payments, February 1965," *LBJ Public Papers, 1965*, I, pp. 170–177.

128. W. H. Bruce Brittain, "Two International Monetary Decisions," in *Murphy Commission Report*, Vol. III, App. H. p. 129.

129. See, for example, memo, Dillon to the president, 27 March 1965, C.F. FO 4-1, WHCF, LBJ Library, and memo, Heller to the president, 30 March 1965, C.F. F 19, WHCF, LBJ Library.

130. Memo, Ackley to the president, 17 April 1965, C.F. F 19, WHCF, LBJ Library.

131. Memo, Ackley to the president, 5 May 1966, Documentary Supplement to the Administrative History of the CEA, Vol. II, pt. 3, item B.9, LBJ Library.

132. Administrative History of the Treasury Department, Vol. XII, pp. 43–44, LBJ Library.

133. Administrative History of the Treasury Department, Vol. X, Annex A, LBJ Library.

134. Arthur M. Okun, Oral History Interview II, tape 1, p. 22, LBJ Library.

135. Brittain, "Two International Monetary Decisions," p. 130.

136. Memo, the president to Fowler, 16 June 1965, C.F. F 19, WHCF, LBJ Library.

137. Administrative History of the Treasury Department, Vol. X, Annex B, LBJ Library.

138. Arthur M. Okun, Oral History Interview II, tape 1, p. 22, LBJ Library.

139. Anthony Solomon, Oral History Interview, p. 16, LBJ Library.

140. Frederick L. Deming, Oral History Interview, tape 1, p. 16, LBJ Library.

141. Anthony Solomon, Oral History Interview, p. 17, LBJ Library.

142. In addition to Dillon, Roosa, and Gordon, the committee included Edward Bernstein, an economic consultant specializing in international monetary policy; Andre Meyer, of the investment banking firm of Lazard Freres; David Rockefeller, president of the Chase Manhattan Bank of New York City; Charles Kindleberger, professor of economics at the Massachusetts Institute of Technology; and Francis Bator, who became a member of the committee after leaving the White House to return to the Massachusetts Institute of Technology in September 1967. See Administrative History of the Treasury Department, Vol. XII, pp. 47–48, LBJ Library.

143. Robert V. Roosa, Oral History Interview, tape 2, p. 48, LBJ Library.

144. Henry H. Fowler, Oral History Interview, tape 3, pp. 27–28, LBJ Library.

145. *Remarks by the Honorable Henry H. Fowler, Secretary of the Treasury before the Virginia State Bar Association at the Homestead, Hot Springs, Virginia* (10 July 1965).

146. U.S., Congress, Joint Economic Committee, *Guidelines for Improving the International Monetary System*, Committee Print, 89th Cong. (Washington, D.C.: Government Printing Office, 1965).

147. Henry H. Fowler, Oral History Interview, tape 3, p. 28, LBJ Library.

148. Administrative History of the Treasury Department, Vol. XII, p. 31, LBJ Library. Also see William B. Dale, Oral History Interview, pp. 26–28, LBJ Library.

149. Administrative History of the Treasury Department, Vol. XII, pp. 33–38, LBJ Library.

150. William B. Dale has described the passage of this legislation by Congress as "almost embarrassingly unanimous." See William B. Dale, Oral History Interview, p. 36, LBJ Library.

151. Edward Fried, Oral History Interview, tape 1, p. 32, LBJ Library.

152. Frederick L. Deming, Oral History Interview, tape 2, p. 45, LBJ Library.

153. Cohen, *International Economic Policy*, p. 63.

154. Francis Bator, testimony before the Committee on Foreign Affairs and the Subcommittee on Foreign Economic Policy, U.S. House of Representatives, 92d Cong., 2d sess., 1972, pp. 113–114.

155. Ibid., p. 115.

156. Ibid., pp. 116–117.

157. Destler, *Presidents, Bureaucrats, and Foreign Policy*, p. 105.

158. Walt W. Rostow, *The Diffusion of Power* (New York: The Macmillian Company, 1972), pp. 398–399.

159. Edward Fried, Oral History Interview, tape 2, p. 24, LBJ Library.

160. Alexander Trowbridge, Oral History Interview, tape 2, p. 21, LBJ Library.

161. Destler, *Presidents, Bureaucrats, and Foreign Policy,* p. 207. Also see Cohen, *International Economic Policy,* p. 76, for similar judgment.

162. C. Fred Bergsten, in foreword, to Cohen, *International Economic Policy,* p. vii.

163. See *Murphy Commission Report,* Allison and Szanton, *Remaking Foreign Policy;* Cohen, *International Economic Policy;* and Destler, *Making Foreign Economic Policy.*

164. Bator, testimony before the Committee on Foreign Affairs and the Subcommittee on Foreign Economic Policy, p. 112.

7. Conclusions

1. See Rudiger Dornbusch and Stanley Fisher, *Macroeconomics,* 2d ed. (New York: McGraw-Hill, 1980), Chs. 10 and 16, and George L. Perry, "Stabilization Policy and Inflation" in *Setting National Priorities: The Next Ten Years,* ed. Henry Owen and Charles L. Schultze (Washington, D.C.: The Brookings Institution, 1976), Ch. 7.

2. See Richard Schott and Dagmar Hamilton, *People, Positions, and Power: The Political Appointments of Lyndon B. Johnson,* (Chicago: University of Chicago Press, 1984).

3. Roger B. Porter, *Presidential Decision Making: The Economic Policy Board* (New York: Cambridge University Press, 1980).

4. Roger B. Porter, "The President and Economic Policy: Problems, Patterns and Alternatives," in *The Illusion of Presidential Government,* ed. Hugh Heclo and Lester M. Salamon (Boulder, Colo.: Westview Press, 1981), Ch. 7.

5. An opposing viewpoint is contained in Larry Berman, *The Office of Management and Budget and the Presidency, 1921–1979* (Princeton, N.J.: Princeton University Press, 1979), Ch. 4.

6. Based on a letter to one of the authors from Stanford G. Ross, 31 March 1981.

Index